SPACE AND PLACE
IN JEWISH STUDIES

Key Words in Jewish Studies

Series Editors
Deborah Dash Moore, University of Michigan
MacDonald Moore, University of Michigan
Andrew Bush, Vassar College

SPACE AND PLACE IN JEWISH STUDIES

BARBARA E. MANN

RUTGERS UNIVERSITY PRESS

New Brunswick, New Jersey and London

Library of Congress Cataloging-in-Publication Data

Mann, Barbara E.

Space and place in Jewish studies / Barbara E. Mann.

p. cm. — (Key words in Jewish studies)

Includes bibliographical references and index.

ISBN 978-0-8135-5181-4 (hardcover : alk. paper) — ISBN 978-0-8135-5182-1
(pbk. : alk. paper)

1. Space—Religious aspects—Judaism. 2. Geographical perception. 3. Geographical
perception in literature. 4. Place (Philosophy) I. Title.

BM729.S76M36 2011

296.4'8—dc22

2011012798

A British Cataloging-in-Publication record for this book is available from the British Library.

Visit our Web site: http://rutgerspress.rutgers.edu

Manufactured in the United States of America

To Israeli environmentalists, who struggle to make the world a safer and cleaner place

Contents

Foreword

The Rutgers book series Key Words in Jewish Studies seeks to introduce students and scholars alike to vigorous developments in the field by exploring its terms. These words and phrases reference important concepts, issues, practices, events, and circumstances. But terms also refer to standards, even to preconditions; they patrol the boundaries of the field of Jewish studies. This series aims to transform outsiders into insiders and let insiders gain new perspectives on usages, some of which shift even as we apply them.

Key words mutate through repetition, suppression, amplification, and competitive sharing. Jewish studies finds itself attending to such processes in the context of an academic milieu where terms are frequently repurposed. Diaspora offers an example of an ancient word, one with a specific Jewish resonance, which has traveled into new regions and usage. Such terms migrate from the religious milieu of Jewish learning to the secular environment of universities, from Jewish community discussion to arenas of academic discourse, from political debates to intellectual arguments and back again. As these key words travel, they acquire additional meanings even as they occasionally shed long-established connotations. On occasion, key words can become so politicized that they serve as accusations. The sociopolitical concept of assimilation, for example, when turned into a term—assimilationist—describing an advocate of the process among Jews, became an epithet hurled by political opponents struggling for the mantle of authority in Jewish communities.

When approached dispassionately, key words provide analytical leverage to expand debate in Jewish studies. Some key words will be familiar from long use, and yet they may have gained new valences, attracting or repelling other terms in contemporary discussion. But there are prominent terms in Jewish culture whose keys lie in a particular understanding of prior usage. Terms of the past may bolster claims to continuity in the present while newly minted language sometimes disguises deep connections reaching back into history. Attention must be paid as well to the transmigration of key words among Jewish languages—especially Hebrew, Yiddish, and Ladino—and among languages used by Jews, knitting connections even while highlighting distinctions.

An exploration of the current state of Jewish studies through its key words highlights some interconnections often only glimpsed and holds out the prospect of a reorganization of Jewish knowledge. Key words act as magnets and attract a nexus of ideas and arguments as well as related terms into their orbits. This series plunges into several of these intersecting constellations, providing a path from past to present.

The volumes in the series share a common organization. They open with a first section, Terms of Debate, which defines the key word as it has developed over the course of Jewish history. Allied concepts and traditional terms appear here as well. The second section, State of the Question, analyzes contemporary debates in scholarship and popular venues, especially for those key words that have crossed over into popular culture. The final section, In a New Key, explicitly addresses contemporary culture and future possibilities for understanding the key word.

To decipher key words is to learn the varied languages of Jewish studies at points of intersection between academic disciplines and wider spheres of culture. The series, then, does not seek to consolidate and narrow a particular critical lexicon. Its purpose is to question, not to canonize, and to invite readers to sample the debate and ferment of an exciting field of study.

Andrew Bush
Deborah Dash Moore
MacDonald Moore
Series Editors

Acknowledgments

I acknowledge the friends and colleagues who have nurtured this project, even as they continued to ask the most difficult questions, and I am grateful to those settings that have hosted and supported my work. These include my institutional home at the Jewish Theological Seminary, especially Provost Alan Cooper for his steady support, and Richard Kalmin, Seth Schwartz, Stefanie Sigmund, and Ben Sommers for *sichot prozdor* about sources. I was fortunate to spend a year conceptualizing the shape and arguments of this book at the Frankel Institute of Judaic Studies at the University of Michigan, where I enjoyed the stimulating feedback of our interdisciplinary group. I thank Murray Baumgarten, Sara Blair, Lila Corwin Berman, Deborah Dash Moore, Gil Klein, Scott Lerner, Julian Levinson, Alona Nitzan-Shiftan, Anita Norich, Shachar Pinsker, Catherine Rottenberg, Yael Shenker, Verle Vanden Daelen, and Deborah Yalen for their humor and intellectual camaraderie, inside and outside the seminar room.

This book would not have seen the light of day without the intellectual integrity and tough love of the editorial committee of the Key Words series—Andrew Bush, Deborah Dash Moore, and MacDonald Moore. They shepherded the project from its inception, copiously and critically commented on several drafts, and pushed me to develop the manuscript in challenging and unanticipated directions. I am indebted to them for their candor and collegiality, their faith in me and in this book.

The generous feedback of friends who read portions of the manuscript-in-progress—Jeremy Benstein, Beth Berkowitz, Todd Hasak-Lowy, and Rebecca Kobrin—is much appreciated. I am also grateful to Marlie Wasserman of Rutgers University Press for her support and guidance, and to the press's anonymous reader for supplying helpful comments and queries.

Finally, I thank my family for providing the emotional stability that sustains my intellectual passions. And a special thanks to Maya for her patience and giggles, and for bringing home that book on the planets because "Mommy is writing a book about space."

Permissions

Excerpt from "Jerusalem 1967," by Yehuda Amichai, from *Poems of Jerusalem and Love Poems* (The Sheep Meadow Press, 1992). Reprinted by permission of the Amichai Estate.

"An Old Bus Stop," by Yehuda Amichai, from *Yehuda Amichai: A Life of Poetry 1948–1994*. Translated by Benjamin and Barbara Harshav. Copyright © 1994 by HarperCollins Publishers Inc. Hebrew-language version copyright © by Yehuda Amichai. Reprinted by permission of HarperCollins Publishers.

Excerpt from *Open Closed Open*, by Yehuda Amichai, copyright © 2000 by Yehuda Amichai, English translation copyright © 2000 by Chana Bloch and Chana Kronfeld, reprinted by permission of Houghton Mifflin Harcourt Publishing Company.

Excerpt from poem by Yehuda Halevi, from *Song of the Distant Dove*, by Raymond Scheindlin, 168–169 (2007), © 2006 by Oxford University Press, Inc. Reprinted by permission of Oxford University Press, Inc.

Excerpt from Moshe Leyb Halpern from *In New York: A Selection*, © 1982, translated by Kathryn Hellerstein, reprinted by permission of the Jewish Publication Society.

Excerpt from *Selected Poems of Moses Ibn Ezra*, © 1945 by Heinrich Brody, reprinted by permission of the Jewish Publication Society.

"In My Hand Two Feathers from a Pheasant," by Kadya Molodowsky, from *Paper Bridges: Selected Poems of Kadya Molodowsky*, edited by Kathryn Hellerstein. Copyright © 1999 Wayne State University Press, reprinted by permission of Wayne State University Press.

Excerpts from *The Dream of the Poem: Hebrew Poetry from Muslim and Christian Spain, 950–1492*, © 2007 by Peter Cole, reprinted by permission of Princeton University Press.

Excerpts from *JPS Hebrew-English Tanakh*, © 2000, reprinted by permission of the Jewish Publication Society.

Excerpts from *The Penguin Book of Hebrew Verse*, edited by T. Carmi, 280, 323, 360–61, 407 (Allen Lane, 1981). Copyright 1981 © by T. Carmi. Reprinted by permission of Penguin Books, Ltd.

Excerpt from *Unveiling Eve: Reading Gender in Medieval Hebrew Literature*, 9, © 2003 by Tova Rosen, reprinted by permission of the University of Pennsylvania Press.

Excerpts from *Wine, Women, and Death: Medieval Hebrew Poems on the Good Life*, © 1986 by Raymond Scheindlin, reprinted by permission of the Jewish Publication Society.

SPACE AND PLACE
IN JEWISH STUDIES

Introduction

THE SHAPE OF THE BOOK

People tend to have a very personal relationship to space, so I begin with a story about my neighborhood in the Bronx. On a recent Friday afternoon, as daylight dwindled into evening, I watched my daughter play a pick-up soccer game in a local park. The teams were boys against girls, ages roughly seven through twelve. The core of my daughter's team consisted of three sisters, the oldest of whom, dressed in cleats and shin guards, was practicing for another game the next day. The girls' coach was their Spanish-speaking father, who stood next to me on the sidelines. According to their T-shirts, the boys were students at a nearby Jewish day school. As they moved the ball downfield, they began speaking to each other in rudimentary Hebrew, mostly for fun, but also as a strategy to prevent the girls' team from figuring out how they planned to score. At one point, I gently corrected them: "You don't give [*noten*] the ball," I said, "you pass [*moser*] it." They seemed grateful but confused: why was the mother of a girl on the Spanish-speaking team correcting their Hebrew? For her part, my daughter's Hebrew knowledge effectively spoiled their linguistic subterfuge; as darkness fell and we left the field, she yelled out, "*Shabbat shalom*" [wishing them a "peaceful Sabbath," or, more colloquially, a "good weekend"], putting the final touch on a perfect allegory of how space is produced.

I began to consider the fact that residents of my neighborhood all share the same playing fields, just as we share the same streets and sidewalks. And though we may not all go to the same schools, we shop mostly in the same stores and probably all complain about the unfairness of parking rules and the limits of the Number 1 train. Yet through our daily perambulations—to and from church or synagogue, to and from parochial and public schools—we create different, overlapping spaces, speaking about them in different languages, even calling the very same sites by different names. For example, adjacent to that field where my daughter played soccer is a park called by some "the *shabbes* park," because it is frequented by Orthodox Jewish families on the Sabbath, especially in the late afternoon hours. And while it may be known as such to the large Jewish population in the neighborhood, not everyone feels comfortable there on a Saturday afternoon, especially if they are not dressed in exactly the right kind of Sabbath finery.

Some people think of my neighborhood as a white Jewish suburb; others see it as the last, great diverse middle-class neighborhood in New York City. In fact, it's both. Thinking about the ways in which this same set of blocks constitutes radically different spaces for diverse groups of people has spurred me to consider how Jews have historically regarded and produced space in a variety of geographic settings. As a literary scholar, I am a devoted close reader of texts, and it could be that almost any text written by a Jewish author in some way relates to space. Be that as it may, the volume you hold attempts to make sense of the various ways space and place have mattered, and continue to matter, in Jewish communities here and elsewhere, as recorded largely in their literary and cultural production. Many of the texts and sites that I have selected for discussion are paradigmatic; in other words, they display some qualities or traits that have rendered them central to Jewish history and experience, and the subject of intensive study, debate, or controversy. Their inclusion within what we might call a provisional "canon"[1] of Jewish spaces emerges from this prominence in Jewish life and also from their tendency to point toward the ever-evolving and often fraught relation between Jewish and non-Jewish cultures. Therefore, my principles of selection have led me to choose spaces that often mark, or are marked by, Jewishness in relation to difference—difference that may itself be construed in religious, ethnic, linguistic, or gendered terms. I focus on literary texts (though not exclusively) first and foremost because of my own training and field of expertise but also because of the centrality of textuality in Jewish cultures. However, it has been suggested that the abiding attention to text within the study of Jewish life has actually led to an overreliance on historical models (see discussion in chapter 1).[2] My own intervention here—thinking about space through the lens of text—is offered as a part of this general corrective, in the hopes that the introduction of these new interdisciplinary paradigms will provoke further discussion and debate.

This is an unusual book. First, though there has been a significant amount of space-related research in Jewish studies in recent years, this is the first volume to treat this theme in a sustained fashion. Second, this book is not organized thematically or chronologically as are many other studies of Jewish culture. Rather, the book is organized by specific places, some well known, others less so. Some are referred to with a Hebrew term, others with a proper place name. These place-centered chapters are all related to each other and linked by a set of common themes. These themes and questions are threaded throughout the book: What makes a place Jewish? What makes a space a home? How has the tension between homeland and diaspora informed Jewish experience? What kinds of symbolic and material networks have Jewish communities invented to create a sense of place and rootedness? What makes a place sacred? Can a place be Jewish but not sacred? How has Israel's political sovereignty altered the relationship between Jews and space? How have Jews begun to reconceptualize space in the postmodern world of virtual communities? And so on.

Finally, all these place-centered chapters are gathered under the template that is the hallmark of this series, three broad sections that here provide a sense of the evolving meaning of space and place in Jewish cultures. However, this book need not be read from start to finish, beginning with the introductory chapter and ending with the conclusion. Rather, one may begin with a particular chapter of interest and then circle back or forward to another chapter, making use of the linkages suggested in the notes. More ambitious readers will begin with the chapter on *makom* and then consider the ways in which its theoretical constructs frame the book as a whole.

Working against the old ping-pong of here and there, the to-ing and fro-ing of exile and homeland, this book thus pursues a spatial practice of widening circles of engagement. There *is* a center, of sorts, though it has not held. And the varieties of Jewish experience that radiate from this fragmented center have produced unpredictable and irregular shapes, irreducible trajectories of their own that emanate far beyond any notion of an original center. A *mikveh*. A tour bus in Auschwitz. The Sinai Desert. The kitchen. The *geniza* in Cairo. Two Jews talking on a street corner. Jewish summer camp. The Lower East Side. A mezuzah. The address 770 Eastern Parkway. A falafel restaurant in Kathmandu. What makes each of these spaces potentially "Jewish" is also what constitutes them as places— memory, history, and ritual. They may be considered Jewish by virtue of singular events or the ongoing, everyday business of life, both privately and publicly conducted. And of course these same sites may be conceived as other kinds of spaces as well, experienced quite differently by different people, and even by the same people across time. For example, many Eastern European landscapes were once home to large Jewish communities. While these places may still be remembered as home for those who once lived there, they have also become sites of mourning and memorial. And for those who currently live there, a former synagogue has now become a youth center, and the place's Jewishness is a thing of the past. The performance of ritual behaviors, whether drawn from the sacred domain or simply an instance of local or personal custom, may also constitute a space, a space that can be thought of in Jewish terms. Does the playing of klezmer music in a club in Krakow constitute a Jewish place? How does the choice of language influence or shape our notion of Jewish space? And how might attitudes toward space evolve over time and from place to place?

Take the journey alluded to in Yehuda Amichai's "An Old Bus Stop,"
a Hebrew poem that may or may not be written about Jerusalem:

An Old Bus Stop
I passed by an old bus stop where I stood
Many years ago, waiting for a vehicle to take me
Someplace else.

There I stood, consoled before loss
And healed before pain, resurrected
Before death and full of love before separation.

There I stood. The groggy fragrance
Of orange groves in blossom anesthetized me
For all the years to come, to this very day.

The stop is still there. God is still
Called "Place," and I, sometimes,
Call Him "Time."[3]

Amichai's short poem evocatively renders the confounding dilemma of
space and place in contemporary Israeli society. The poem capitalizes on
the mundanities of an unidentified urban landscape—perhaps the "heavenly" and "earthly" Jerusalems—*Yerushalayim shel mala, Yerushalayim shel
mata*—that appear throughout Amichai's work. However, the orange
blossoms belong not to Jerusalem, but to Israel's wide middle, a landscape
often traveled *through* on the way to somewhere else. The speaker recalls
being retrieved—at that early morning hour when the blossoms' fragrance
is most intoxicating, the body still half-asleep and most susceptible—
not by a bus but by a *rechev*, a vehicle; and after this comes pain, loss,
death. In the poem's imaginative world, all these ruptures are somehow,
fantastically, preemptively "fixed" or "cured," an allusion to the desire
to turn time back to a moment before those losses—to get on the bus, so to
speak, at a different stop. Perhaps the speaker remembers his past as a soldier and grieves over lost friends, a memory lurking in many of Amichai's
poems. Despite this recollection of grief, the speaker remains "anesthetized," unconscious or oblivious to some potentially painful, and still
ongoing, condition. Some piece of these events is still buried, forgotten
and lost to the speaker. The bus stop itself marks the spot where movement pauses; it has been made holy, marked by a divinity that appears in
both time and space, as well as by the speaker's memory of the bus stop
as it appeared, even fleetingly, in an important sequence of events in his

life. "Place" (*makom*) is capitalized in the English translation because, as we see in the following chapter, the term may also be used as a synonym for God. Though Judaism's God was normatively revealed in history, the modern encounter with the space of the Land, especially in Jerusalem, could lead to a potentially new relationship with God and new conceptions of sacred space. Zionism clearly had an ideological investment in this insistence on God's presence in both territory and history. In a newly imagined theological landscape, God's presence may be felt, and recalled, in the humble structure of the bus stop.

Yi-Fu Tuan's seminal work of human geography, *Space and Place: The Perspective of Experience*, parses the difference between space and place in terms of their relation to time: "If we think of space as that which allows movement, then place is pause."[4] The bus stop represents precisely this pause, a caesura in theological experience wherein the God of History is encountered in intimate terms, through a simple address in a particular location. The poem addresses a foundational question in Jewish theology: Is God revealed in time, in history, or in space, in "the Land"? In imagining the bus stop as a sacred space, the poem traces the distance between history and place, between text and artifact, between what Israeli anthropologist Zali Gurevitch has called "the Story about the Place" and "the Place Itself."[5]

Indeed, Hebrew has other terms that roughly approximate either space (*merkhav*) or place (*atar*). *Makom*, however, may mean both, or—rather—contains some sense of both the transcendent and the vernacular. The potential tension between space and place, and its relation to larger questions of cultural and national identity, has emerged as an important topic of academic discourse in recent years. What has been called the "spatial turn" of the humanities and social sciences in recent decades has had a profound impact on Jewish studies, the dimensions of which have only recently begun to emerge.[6] If, historically, Judaic studies in the American academy had been devoted to the study of texts per se, Jewish studies has expanded both object and method; it has widened the definition of "what is a text" to include a broad array of material culture and complicated the methodological frame by introducing a poststructuralist critique of language and subject-object relations. The growing importance of space as a critical category has figured in history, geography, ethnography/anthropology, and literary studies, to name just a few prominent examples. In newly formed area studies such as diaspora and postcolonial studies, where theorization of space is paramount, the presence of a specifically Jewish studies seems, in some sense, almost redundant, given the historical bond between Jewish communal life and a diasporic condition. At the same time, the fierce divide between notions of homeland and exile that normatively characterized scholarly treatment of Jewish space has diminished in recent years; instead, alternative approaches now conceptualize Jewish identity along more multiple, fragmented lines. Within the academy, the emergent field of cultural studies has provided a network of institutional and theoretical relations that facilitate interdisciplinary discussion of space and its attributes. Jewish studies' growing preoccupation with space is both consonant with and distinct from this broader trend. This volume offers an overview of what space and place has meant within Jewish cultures, and how it continues to figure in contemporary discourse.

As in other volumes in this series, this book is divided into three sections: "Terms of Debate," "State of the Question," and "In a New Key." The first section begins with a discussion of the term *makom* and its origins, in relation to wider, often conflicting meanings of space and place in critical discourse. The remaining chapters of the first section treat those kinds of spaces that have largely been conceptualized in relation to the idea of *makom*—to both its theological dimension and its connection to the ancient setting of Jews in the Land of Israel. The second section, "State of the Question," examines how this ostensibly privileged relation to a center has been challenged, or ignored altogether, through the creation of a wide and imaginative network of alternative places and alternate means of conceptualizing home. The difference between roots and routes is one helpful way to conceptualize the distinctive qualities of these two broad sections. The book's final section, "In a New Key," offers meditations on two spaces that have become contested sites of contemporary Jewish experience—the *eruv* and the environment. Each chapter moves among a broad array of texts from ancient to contemporary settings. From postmodern iterations of a rabbinic practice to a global engagement with climate change, travel, and diaspora, space and place continue to provide a framework in which to explore questions of Jewish community and Jewish identity.

As mentioned, this study reads space largely through the lens of text. The relation between substance and method is key here: the very idea of *makom*, with its physical and metaphysical dimensions, may be particularly suitable to a literary approach, given the play of surface and depth that distinguishes textual discourse. And while this study recognizes, and respects, the discursive, social force of space, its primary realm of inquiry is . . . the text. Indeed, a study of space in Jewish cultures that takes the idea of *makom* as its organizing premise produces a particular set of observations, conclusions that may necessarily derive from *makom*'s theological, collective underpinnings—its grounding in a specific territory and the use of a particular language—Hebrew—itself also conceived as sacred.

There are, of course, other possible starting points. For example, the idea that Jews have historically been an urban people might lead to a study exploring the ways that Jews have lived with different kinds of people in close proximity, and the spatial and social forms that developed either to preserve their own Jewishness and/or interact with these other groups. Likewise, a study whose initial premise was a substantively different notion of how space is constituted—for example, one that was not tied to territory or to physical places but something like the space created by music—might produce a different set of meditations, a different set of observations. It is hoped that this book will generate more questions than answers and provide a conceptual template for thinking about these important critical and cultural issues.

The sources used in this book draw on examples from a wide variety of genres and historical periods. Though the book proceeds from an introduction of some historically normative uses of space and place in Jewish cultures and moves through an exploration of their appearance in more contemporary critical works, there is no attempt to present here a "history" of Jewish space, if by history we might mean some sort of sequential rendering of discrete facts that bear some relation to the reality of lived experience. Instead, I offer a series of meditations on what seem to me the formative characteristics of space in Jewish experience. Space within Jewish culture has always described relation to Others; spatial configurations—whether rendered through the intricate prohibitions of the talmudic *eruv* or the globally inspired architecture of postmodern Jerusalem—have been methods of signaling both difference and community, both power and powerlessness. And while Jewish attitudes toward space may have historically been shaped by the monumental memory of what was—be it the Temple or a simple bus stop—this condition of absence has nurtured a diasporic existence that has itself produced its own paradigms of absence and loss. We follow these trajectories across a series of spaces both imagined and real, paying attention to how their significance has evolved in disparate historical, cultural, and geographic settings.

PART I

TERMS OF DEBATE

The discussion of the Hebrew term for place (*makom*) in chapter 1 sets the stage for the three chapters that follow it in this section. As indicated in the introduction, *makom* is initially and for a very long time a key to Jewish cultures precisely because its meaning was consistently mapped onto a single space—the Land of Israel—and linked to some notion of transcendence or sacredness. The chapter on *makom* discusses these particular qualities of space in Jewish cultures in relation to contemporary critical theory about space, place, history, and memory. While the holiness of *makom* may be accessed in different ways, the abiding presence of a lost center—variously figured as the Garden, Jerusalem, and the Land—was often experienced from some marginal site. The tension between these peripheries and their imagined center creates the Terms of Debate of chapters 2, 3, and 4, which explore this tension between center and margins through a variety of texts produced in widely ranging historical and cultural contexts. While these three chapters rely on material depicting an imagined sense of space, the chapters on Jerusalem and the Land will also consider the "collision" of these fictional materials with the reality of contemporary Israel.

1 *Makom*

The term *makom* in Hebrew may be translated, in deceptively simple fashion, as "place." As in English, the word has both concrete and abstract significance, and may also be used metaphorically, as in "to know one's place," in a social, relational sense. Yet Hebrew usages of *makom* potentially bear another, more hidden burden, due to a special meaning of the term in Jewish tradition, where *makom* is also used as a synonym for God. This usage originates in a midrashic gloss on the book of Genesis: "Why is the Holy One, blessed be he, called *Makom*? Because he is the place of the world."[1] Perhaps the rabbis who produced this text felt themselves to be in some sort of exile, and therefore invested space with transcendence, and God with the materiality of place.[2] This midrash refers specifically to the use of the term *makom* in the Jacob story, itself a classic tale of wandering. Jacob's journey from place to place, from Paddan Aram (28:5) through Beer Sheva and Haran (28:10), into the land of *bnei kedem* [literally, sons of the East] (29:1) and eventually back home through Machanayim (32:3), is itself an attempt to find his own place, in social and familiar terms. His journey, of course, echoes that of his grandfather Abraham, who inaugurated the national drama with God's command to "go forth from your land, from your birthplace, and from your father's house to the land that I will show you" (12:1). This process of identity formation occurs in relation to movement toward and from particular locations. At the beginning of his travels, Jacob "came upon a certain place and stopped there for the night. . . . Taking one of the stones of that place, he put it under his head and lay down in that place" (28:11). The dense, repetitive patterning of the word *makom* (three times in a short, fifteen-word verse) alerts the reader that a moment of divine revelation approaches. In the very next verse, Jacob dreams of a ladder reaching to heaven, and of God "standing beside him," announcing the terms of the covenantal promise with Jacob, his ancestors, and his descendants. When Jacob awakes, he again notes the sacred quality of *makom*: "Surely the Lord is present in this place, and I did not know it! Shaken, he said, 'How awesome is this place! This is none other than the abode of God'" (28:16–17). And so Jacob names the place "Bethel" (*Bet-El*), literally, "house of God," the place where God is housed.

Another well-known example of *makom* marking an important moment of interaction, even relative intimacy, with God is found in

Genesis 22, the *akeda* or Binding of Isaac, where Abraham is called upon to sacrifice his son Isaac as a sign of loyalty to God. The term *makom* appears twice near the beginning of this tersely told narrative, as Abraham approaches Mount Moriah and in both instances refers to the particular "place of which God has told him" (verses 3 and 9). *Makom* here signifies the proximity of God to man, unlike the term *shamayim* [heavens], which indicates God's remoteness or remove.[3] *Makom* indicates both the biblical topography—in this case, the heights—as well the presence (or absence) of the divinity. The idea of *makom* in these foundational biblical passages suggests an intermediary location between heaven and earth, between transcendence and the earthly profane, one in which God potentially "stands beside" human beings. Those events connected with *makom* are crucial moments of discovery, both for the biblical protagonist and the larger, national drama they represent.[4]

The potential difficulty of limiting God's presence to a single place is also addressed within biblical sources. Thus, for example, in 1 Kings, we find an express articulation of the problem of God "dwelling on earth" in relation to the placement of the Ark of the Covenant within Solomon's Temple in Jerusalem: "Even the heavens to their uttermost reaches cannot contain You, how much less this House that I have built. . . . May Your eyes be open day and night toward this House, toward the place [*makom*] of which You have said, 'My name shall abide there'; May You heed the prayers which Your servant will offer toward this place [*makom*]" (8:27–29). Within later texts such as Deuteronomy and Leviticus we find an essential connection between sacred space and certain acts and rituals. Thus, "while God may be found in the whole world, the Lord may make the divine presence more acutely felt in certain places. God may therefore be in a specified locale but need not be limited to it."[5] Just as God's presence will at all times and in all places "dwell" with the people, so certain forms of ethical behavior are also always expected, so that the people will retain their "purity" in God's presence.

These interpretations of *makom* as it appeared in biblical texts—a place that is potentially holy—developed in relation to the rise of Jerusalem and the construction of the Second Temple as political and cultic centers of Judaism. They are part of a worldview that evolved during and after the Second Temple period, and especially in the post-exilic world of rabbinic culture, within and without the borders of the land. Thus it is important to stress that the idea of *makom* discussed so far does not necessarily inhere in the biblical texts, but is itself a reflection of a postbiblical world, of a world located at a distance from the originary landscape of the Bible. One way of understanding this is to suggest that as the foundational, even mythological events of the Bible receded further in time, and in place, the desire to find holiness in some abstract or substitute space increased, especially in what was perceived as an exilic or diasporic condition. Indeed, as rabbinic literature developed, from roughly the third through the ninth centuries, the relation to the land became more symbolic, farther from "the source." Here is one example of how we might think about this process appearing in a rabbinic text, in this case a mishnaic tractate from about the third century C.E., describing various degrees of holiness in reference to particular elements of the Temple that no longer exists:

There are ten (degrees of) holiness:

1) The land of Israel is holier than all lands . . .
2) The cities surrounded by a wall are holier than it [the land]. . . .
3) Within the wall [Jerusalem] is holier than they [other walled cities]. . . .
4) The Temple mount is holier than it. . . .
5) The rampart is holier than it [the Temple Mount] . . .
6) The court of women is holier than it [the rampart] . . .
7) The court of Israel is holier than it [the court of women].
8) The court of the priest is holier than it [the court of Israel].
9) [The area] between the porch and the altar is holier than it [the court of the priest].
10) The sanctuary is holier than it [the area between porch and altar].
11) The house of the holy of holies is holier than they . . .

Some of the specific reasoning explaining the attribution of holiness has been edited out of this lengthy passage; note, however, that the progress of physical detail, from largest (the Land of Israel) to smallest and most insular—a kind of spatial telescoping—may be read as an allusion to the growing temporal remove from the Temple, an awareness of the Temple's increasing historicity. This focus on detail makes of the Temple almost "a memory palace,"[6] as the rabbinic imagination moves in and out of its interior spaces, remembering its contours in a way that mimics the much more elaborate visions of the Temple contained in Ezekiel. In relation to this particular passage, one scholar notes, "since the Mishnah speaks as if such regulations were still in effect, it is not just recording 'ancient' practices but is making an ahistorical assertion that the lines of holiness continue: despite the fall of Jerusalem and the destruction of the Temple in 70 C.E. and the expulsion of Jews from Jerusalem in 135, the sacred is still found in the world."[7]

This ability to imagine that "the sacred is still found in the world," at a remove from—or even following the destruction of—a holy center, characterizes what Jonathan Z. Smith, in his influential work on ancient religious practices, has called a "locative" view of the sacred. In a sense,

Judaism is paradigmatic of a certain stage in the development of ancient religions, as they evolved away from viewing the sacred as necessarily immanent to a particular place to conceptualizing sacredness as mobile and portable.[8] This concept of sacredness as something that may be recovered and engaged through human activity, both individual and collective, and as a condition that may have originally derived from a particular place but is no longer dependent upon it, became increasingly important as Jewish communities continue to exist at a remove from ancient, biblical landscapes. Jewish culture's engagement with *makom*—understood as both transcendent and earthbound, sacred and profane—has generated a wealth of fascinating rituals, texts, and artifacts. For example, the tension between text and artifact at the heart of rabbinic culture, between textual depiction and material remains, may be related to the authors' sense of some gap—geographic, spiritual, practical—between their own place of domicile and the symbolic space of the homeland. Modern Zionism may also be understood as a collision of space's material and abstract faces, between the physical reality of the modern Middle East and biblical stories about the ancient Land of Israel.

One further illustration of this general property of *makom* as reflected in a Jewish ritual practice will suffice. After the death of a loved one, the mourner is traditionally comforted with the words "Ha-makom yinachem etkhem b'tokh she'ar avelei tsiyon ve-rushalayim"—"May God [*makom*] console you among the other mourners of Zion and Jerusalem." Jews are encouraged to repeat this formulaic expression in Hebrew to the mourner, even in lieu of a direct greeting or salutation. Within this phrase the mourner is connected not only to other mourners, whose shared experience may possibly provide comfort, but also to a wider, historical situation—the exile from Zion and destruction of Jerusalem, a paradigmatic event of expulsion and wandering. Grief has a social and, in this case, geographical context. Even the most private moments of grief become embedded, through the ritual comforting of the mourner, to important sites in Jewish collective memory.

Furthermore, the primary vehicle associated with grief and mourning in Jewish tradition is the *shiva*, the seven-day period immediately following the funeral in which mourners receive friends and other members of the community in their home. Though the shiva is an institution essentially defined by temporal boundaries, it may also be considered a kind of "space," in which mourning is enacted and evolves (the following month [the *shloshim*] and then the entire year [*shnat evel*] are similar examples of temporally defined spaces of mourning). To be clear, by suggesting that the shiva is a kind of space, I am not referring to the physical site in which mourners receive others. Rather, the prescribed behaviors of the shiva—covering mirrors, sitting low to the floor, tearing one's garment, reciting certain prayers—transform an ordinary room in one's home into the space of the shiva for its temporal duration. This elastic relation between space and time characterizes many Jewish institutions, as well as the depiction of *makom* in allegorical and symbolic terms.

Agnon to Gurevitch: *Makom* in Modern Jewish Thought

The degree to which this traditional idea of *makom* holds sway in modern Jewish culture may be gauged by examining its appearance in modern Hebrew literature. Although Hebrew writers sought to produce a secular idiom, the presence of traditional themes and texts was inevitable, given the enormous power and authority of canonical Hebrew texts. Indeed, the story of modern Hebrew culture may be understood in part as an attempt, only partially successful, to disengage from tradition. The writer who perhaps best embodied this often ambivalent link with the classical Hebrew canon was S. Y. Agnon (1888–1970), who was born in Galicia and immigrated to Palestine in the 1930s. Agnon also lived in Berlin for many years and the idea of migration and travel, of the often enervating effects of moving from place to place, may be found in a number of his works. Agnon's story "From Lodging to Lodging," composed and set in interwar Tel Aviv, concerns a high-strung, hypochondriac narrator who cannot seem to find a place for himself. As the story opens, he follows the advice of his doctor and "moves down" from Jerusalem to Tel Aviv to take advantage of the Mediterranean sea air. Ironically, the city's business and noise, combined with the tight confines of his room, irritates his condition even further, and he continues his search for a new home, eventually renting a room in a house on the outskirts of the city. The pastoral, edenic location is remote from the city's squalor and commotion. His new landlord's personal experience resembles his own in its continual peregrinations and disappointing encounter with life in Tel Aviv and in Palestine more generally. In relating their story, the landlord's wife concludes, "We live here in our house, enjoying everything with which the Lord [*ha-makom*] has blessed us." Upon which the narrator silently reflects, "I rejoiced that God [*ha-makom*] had brought me to pleasant lodgings and an honest landlord."[9] Agnon's story deploys the midrashic synonym for God at a crucial juncture, and represents an exemplary instance of modern Jewish culture's engagement with the idea of space. Agnon's story, with its movement from Jerusalem to Tel Aviv, from the confines of a rented room to the pastoral cottage, a perpetual wandering that continues long after the protagonists have "settled the land," offers the reader a dense parable on *makom*, a deft commentary on how Jewish attitudes toward space might have changed with the great physical migrations of the early

twentieth century and its concurrent social and political upheavals. Even
as the ostensible gap between elsewhere and the Land has been closed,
the old idea of a more abstract substitute hovers.

This passage in the story as a whole points to two fundamental ten-
sions: the first concerns the passage from space to place—from space as
emblematic of, or a container for, the divine, to the lived experience of an
actual place; the second tension concerns the encounter with the land
itself, as opposed to the biblical story about the place. This encounter
raises a number of questions: How does the renewed appreciation for a
homeland—for the creation of a material, sovereign political entity—
affect the idea of space as divine? What happens when the idyllic expecta-
tions of the "Land of Milk and Honey" coincide with the experience of the
land itself, the material conditions of life in the Middle East? Agnon's
story does not offer concrete answers to these questions; instead it proposes that modern Hebrew culture, in its new material setting in
Palestine, will continue to struggle with this fundamental revolution in
attitudes toward space and place.

The dilemmas posed within Agnon's story are undoubtedly still at
the center of Israeli discourse. In an influential article that first appeared
in 1991, anthropologists Zali Gurevitch and Gideon Aran articulated
the problem of becoming native, referring to the inevitable gap between
what they call the biblical "Story about the Place" and "the Place
Itself."[10] Zionism's modern story of return is indebted to the biblical narrative of the land. The patriarchal narrative of wandering alluded to
above—beginning with God's command to Abraham to leave his homeland, stretching to its eventual conclusion as the Israelites enter the
Promised Land after Egyptian bondage and years of wandering in
the desert—was evoked by Zionism as the ancient, exemplary model for
the return of the Jews to Palestine in the modern period.[11] This return
would restore the people to the place, obviating the need for the portable
"homeland of the text." The nation's new rootedness in territory would
somehow constitute their nativeness; this bond with the land would dis-
solve the abstract connection between space and holiness, and render the
concept of *makom*—in its substitutional sense—obsolete: having returned
to the original site of revelation, there would ostensibly be no need to
continually invent proxies for it. However, in Gurevitch's view, despite
the achievements of Zionism and the establishment of the State, the
problem of nativeness endures, due to "the irreducibility of the story to
the place, and hence the unrest, the schism, perhaps, between the Israelis
and their native place, namely Israel."[12] The degree to which this "schism"
continues to trouble Israeli society is explored further in chapter 4,
"The Land."

Space and Place, the Academy and Jewish Studies

The idea of *makom* may also be productively considered in relation to what has been called the spatial turn in the academy, a reference to the emerging importance of space as a critical category in the humanities and social sciences. Michel Foucault famously inaugurated this "spatial epoch" in a 1967 lecture:

> The great obsession of the nineteenth century was, as we know, history: with its themes of development and of suspension, of crisis and cycle, themes of the ever-accumulating past, with its great preponderance of dead men and the menacing glaciation of the world. . . . The present epoch will perhaps be above all the epoch of space. We are in the epoch of simultaneity: we are in the epoch of juxtaposition, the epoch of the near and far, of the side-by-side, of the dispersed.[13]

One of Foucault's most important theoretical models was—following Freud, perhaps—archaeology, a model indicating the firmly intertwined nature of time and space, and the degree to which an understanding of one is always embedded in an appreciation for the other. The fertility of Foucault's almost casually tossed-off list (the published article retains some of the quality of lecture notes) for scholars of just about everything cannot be overstated. Concepts such as juxtaposition, globalization, and diaspora—which have become essential modes of inquiry in recent years—are all here in Foucault's suggestive remarks. In the following pages we explore the main features of this contemporary critical discourse on space.

As noted, the phenomenologically inspired work of human geographer Yi-Fu Tuan offers a foundational set of tools with which to explore the complex relation between space, culture, and nation. Tuan explores what he calls the "symbolic value" of space, noting that space may be thought of as neutral before people grant it meaning:

> 'Space' is more abstract than 'place.' What begins as undifferentiated space becomes place as we get to know it better and endow it with value. Architects talk about the spatial qualities of place; they can equally well speak of the locational (place) qualities of space. The ideas 'space' and 'place' require each other for definition. From the security and stability of place we are aware of the openness, freedom, and threat of space, and vice versa. Furthermore, if we think of space as that which allows movement, than place is pause; each pause in movement makes it possible for location to be transformed into place.[14]

In Tuan's formulations, place is viewed as more specific, local, and always-already embedded in a particular set of social, economic, and political practices. The ostensible tension between space and place may also be understood as the tension between the two faces of *makom* that deeply inform Jewish cultural notions of space. We may note here Tuan's relative accessibility as a theorist, especially his use of different and fairly transparent terms to convey both the elasticity of space and its reliance upon some human point of view (whether of an individual in her hometown or neighborhood, or a nation in its homeland). In addition to reminding us that space and place depend on one another for definition, Tuan's metaphorical comparison of "place" to a "pause" alludes to the important presence of a third category—that of temporality, or the flow of time. Not only are all places not created equal, our experience of an individual site—one's street, the house one grew up in—may evolve over time and thus effectively render it a different place. Place is thus never inert, static, or given (even in the natural domain) but always somehow produced, that is, shaped by human activity and/or attachment. Here Tuan's work veers out of the disciplinary confines of geography per se and into the realm of the human imagination, a domain whose spatial contours have been compellingly sketched by the French philosopher Gaston Bachelard in his *The Poetics of Space*. Bachelard's evocative meditations on the psychic function of space—what he calls "topoanalysis"—focus on the essential role played by the house as a kind of metaphysical container of memory, a site that may be dipped back into over the course of a lifetime.[15] Both Tuan and Bachelard describe an elastic model for considering the centrality of subjective human experience in thinking about ideas of space and place.

The fluid but basically dualistic view of space in Tuan's work has been considerably complicated in recent years, as the spatial turn has become more indebted to the social sciences. The ideas of urban theorist Henri Lefebvre are largely responsible for elucidating the terms of this complication. In Lefebvre's work, we find a rejection of any notion of absolute space, and an insistence on the idea that space is always produced through human behaviors and actions. In the urban setting, what Lefebvre calls "social space" is produced and embedded in three intertwined domains: spatial practice, representations of space, and representational spaces.[16] This "triad of the perceived, conceived, and lived" is dialectical in nature, with each domain potentially overlapping with and influencing the others.[17] Thus infrastructure such as roads and economic networks linking the individual to a larger institution such as the state are produced by the "signs and codes" of architecture and urban planning;[18] these spaces are themselves "linked to the clandestine or underground of social life, as also to art."[19]

Lefebvre's basic analytical frame has been adopted in a variety of scholarly endeavors, some of which we encounter in the chapters that follow. All this work moves against the idea of space as a transcendent, given, or abstract entity, insisting instead that space is "produced," that is, created and shaped by powerful ideological and economic forces. Within this type of analysis, space is conceived as dynamic and fluid, subject to the global flow of capital and power. David Harvey has forcefully articulated this model and expanded Lefebvre's Marxist critique of the relation between space and industrialization, especially the potentially exclusionary effects of the bond between collective identity and territory.[20]

The work of geographers such as Harvey has often depicted this attachment to place, and particularly the idea that a group's identity derives from territory, as reactionary. Instead, they point to global flows and patterns as figures of agency that offer more palatable, though often unstable, forms of identity—thus privileging concepts such as hybridity, mobility, and diaspora in a world characterized by "space/time compression."[21] Other scholars have pointed out that not everyone experiences this space/time compression in the same way: one person's zippy internet connection is another's migratory trauma. Furthermore, it may not be productive to dismiss the simple fact that people seem to need some attachment—to something—often to a specific place.[22] Even Lefebvre recognized the emotional power abiding in particular spaces: "Representational space is alive: it speaks. It has an affective kernel or centre: Ego, bed, bedroom, dwelling, house; or: square, church, graveyard."[23] The work of Michel de Certeau builds on the Baudelairian notion of the *flâneur*—the urban dweller whose creative identity draws on his ability to move freely, yet anonymously, through the city's public spaces—and further elevates the role of subjective, dynamic experience, and the "strangeness in the commonplace."[24] Working somewhat against the idea that space is only and necessarily produced by the controlling machinations of planners and economists, de Certeau encourages us to follow the performance of the individual within the parameters created by those larger entities, and argues that space is in fact ultimately created by "footsteps," from underneath, and often in spite of, the welter of systems imposed from above.

Postmodern thought has further complicated the ways in which we think about space. According to geographer Edward Soja, for example, postmodern geography will defuse the preeminence of historicism in modern thought by demonstrating the degree to which the "historical imagination is never completely spaceless."[25] Soja's work recapitulated Lefebvre's basic model and introduced the term "third space" to describe the urban landscapes of Los Angeles and other global metropolises.[26] In Soja's schema, first space applies broadly to the empirically defined sense of space that has traditionally been the object of geographic scholarship;

second space refers to more subjective, imagined spaces. Soja's third space represents an attempt both to move beyond what may be perceived as binary thinking about space and to assert the importance of individual and collective human action. To say this another way, third space—as imagined by Soja and other critical theorists—is always potentially a site of resistance. It is also potentially a contact zone, a hybrid site marking the meeting of different cultures, whether in colonial settings or under the diverse set of conditions known as diaspora, where space and place take on multiple meanings and are often detached from a specific territorial setting.[27] In a sense, Soja's work expressly spatializes the political dimension of cultural discourse produced within these mixed zones. Postcolonial theorist Homi Bhabha's phrase "the location of culture" helps us see how culture may be indebted to the material specifics of its environment.

The work of feminist geographers such as Gillian Rose and Doreen Massey further enriches our understanding of space and historical experience. Massey's reading critically unpacks the work of Harvey and Soja, bringing to bear the kind of antifoundational thinking that characterizes feminist theory as a whole. She suggests that the entire space/time divide is simply symptomatic of Western culture's endemically dualistic thinking:

> Space and the feminine are frequently defined in terms of dichotomies in which each of them is most commonly defined as not-A. There is a whole set of dualisms whose terms are commonly aligned with time and space. With time are aligned History, Progress, Civilization, Science, Politics and Reason, portentous things with gravitas and capital letters. With space on the other hand are aligned the other poles of these concepts: stasis, ('simple'), reproduction, nostalgia, emotions, aesthetics, the body. All these dualisms . . . suffer from. . . . the problem of mutual exclusivity and of the consequent impoverishment of both of their terms.[28]

These dualisms and the implicit devaluation of space as "feminine" have certainly figured in Jewish tradition. For example, the *shekhinah* [literally, indwelling] or feminine attribute of God's presence has historically been connected to Zion and powerfully coded in female terms (see the section in "Jerusalem"). In modern times, the idea of space as something to be acted upon, to be entered into and molded to fit its human inhabitants, is very much at the core of Zionist practice and attitudes toward the Land. Following Massey, my goal here is not to somehow upgrade space in the space-time equation,[29] but to examine how the relation between time and space has operated in Jewish cultures, and to offer a caveat or corrective to normative views of *makom* in Jewish culture. This book then plots the return of space as a real category in analytical discussion—not only as a metaphor for God. The utility of space as a "key word" will be sharpened as it is brought to bear on as wide a variety of situations and examples as possible, specifically in relation to other analytical categories that have shaped the study of Jewish culture: textuality, identity, religion, history, and memory. Indeed, the idea of space as a critical category arises precisely out of an argument with history, a desire to critique normative notions of Jews as a "people of history."[30] The chapters that follow seek to analyze space not as only one pole of the space-time dyad, but as an entity that is itself given to change and flux. Below we begin to examine how this theorizing of space emerged out of a contentious relation to history, a condition that is integral to the Jewish engagement with modernity.

The End of History, the Beginning of Space

The theorization of space and place described above derives, as noted, primarily from empirically grounded, pragmatic social sciences. In the phrasing of anthropological theorist Arjun Appadurai, place has been seen as a "problem," a contested discursive site, open to competing interpretations and modes of analysis.[31] What kind of cognitive distortion, or leap of intellectual faith, might we have to perform as readers in order for these analytical categories to prove productive in the largely humanities-based domain of Jewish studies? First, we have already seen how Jewish culture's foundational preoccupation with *makom* may itself be understood in terms of a tension between place and space. Nonetheless, it may be worthwhile to reflect upon the specific historical conditions that have accompanied the ascendance of space as a critical category in the academy, and more recently in Jewish studies.

Interest in space within Jewish studies was preceded by a period of vigorous debate about Jewish historiography, most famously between Yosef Yerushalmi and Amos Funkenstein. At stake was the relation between modes of historical discourse and the longstanding but problematic notion of memory. In what sorts of dwellings did Jewish memory reside? What were the parameters and meaning, even the purpose, of the Jewish historical imagination, in its specific discursive modes (biblical narrative, medieval annals, modern memory books, to name just a few)? Do memory and history work together, or is their relation one of mutual antagonism? How did the relatively new discipline of historiography compare with the rich diversity of Jewish historical forms from the past? What, in fact, as historian Moshe Rosman has posed in the title of a recent book, is "Jewish about Jewish history"?[32] These questions and more drove scholarly discourse among Jewish historians in the 1980s, a discourse that was itself related to similar debates among historians more broadly.

Trends in the writing of history had been shifting as early as the 1960s, especially in relation to the radical politics of that era. In France, the

Annales school and social history emerged in relation to Marxist theory and practice. In America, a similar trend may be identified in the way in which women's studies grew out of the feminist movement. Cultural history, more broadly construed, was influenced by poststructuralism and early postmodern thinkers such as Claude Lévi-Strauss and Michel Foucault, who stressed the degree to which all human experience is mediated by textuality (in Foucault's terms, "discourse"). Later trends, including Germany's *Historikerstreit* [historians' debate], targeted the meaning of the postwar past in relation to conceptions of history, collective memory, and nationhood. In Israel, a similar historiographical school is represented in the diverse work of the New Historians, whose reevaluation of the 1948 war has spurred new understandings of both Zionism and statehood.[33] More recently, subaltern studies have stressed the importance of empire and colonial power in the writing of history. This rise of alternative forms of historical inquiry occasioned a kind of splintering within the discipline. Ironically, the explosion of historical work seems to have precipitated a sense of the exhaustion or inadequacy of a strictly chronological sense of historical inquiry. Out of this notion of the limits of historicism, space has emerged as an essential critical category.[34]

One might ask what it was exactly that "history" could no longer describe. In broad terms, we may consider the incipient and ongoing effects of what is now known as globalization, the worldwide disruption of what were previously understood as stable, even organic, ties between people and place, and the breakdown of the historical nation-state and its territorial borders, especially the collapse of communism and the disintegration of the Eastern bloc. As part of this widely studied phenomenon, we may also consider the mass migrations of diverse populations from various parts of the globe, for both political and economic reasons. The development of new technology and information networks is another example of how relations among different kinds of spaces, and different kinds of communities—both real and virtual—became a defining feature of "the postmodern condition."[35]

An important example that may help us trace this passage from history to space in critical theory may be found in the work of French historian Pierre Nora, whose influential conception of *"lieux de memoire"* [sites of memory] represents an ambitious attempt to theorize all these ideas—history and memory, place and space—at once. The immense popularity of Nora's ideas points both to the enthusiasm with which ideas about space were embraced by American and European scholars and the degree to which they were not entirely ready to let go of history.

Nora's article "Between Memory and History: Les Lieux de Memoire" begins by noting the "acceleration of history," and asks what becomes of memory in the wake of the breakdown of traditional forms of culture and society.[36] Nora's idealized perception of memory, and the antagonistic, "brutal" effects of history, leads him to explore those devices and vehicles through which modern societies attempt to achieve some authentic experience of the past. The critical power of the article derives in large part from Nora's utopian idealization of memory, and its heroic resistance to the deleterious effects of history:

> Memory and history, far from being synonymous, appear now to be in fundamental opposition. . . . Memory is a perpetually actual phenomenon, a bond tying us to the eternal present; history is a representation of the past. . . . Memory installs remembrance within the sacred; history, always prosaic, releases it again. . . . Memory takes root in the concrete, in spaces, gestures, images, and objects; history binds itself strictly to temporal continuities, to progressions and to relations between things. Memory is absolute, while history can only conceive the relative. . . . History is perpetually suspicious of memory, and its true mission is to suppress and destroy it.[37]

As a way of resolving this supposed antagonism between memory and history, Nora introduces the term "sites of memory" to describe what has happened to our appreciation of the past in the wake of the end of "real memory." Though some of these "sites" are actual spaces—museums, memorials, cemeteries—many are not; for example, in Nora's view, holidays, commemorative volumes, the calendar year, archival collections, public speeches, and even the study of history itself (historiography) all may be considered "sites of memory," which provide access to some authentic experience of the past. This metaphorical use of space—akin to Tuan's metaphorical description of place in temporal terms (as a "pause")—is, I would suggest, a key vehicle for importing critical thinking about space in the social sciences into the humanities.[38] I alluded above to the importance of archaeology as a model for Foucault in his epochal proclamation of space. Indeed, something metaphorical also happens in Foucault's *The Archaeology of Knowledge* (1972), where the author deploys "*spatial* metaphors to portray a new kind of intellectual route into the study of history, literature, or whatever. . . . His thinking in this connection spills over from the realm of metaphor to embrace the *empirical* spaces and places existing in such messy abundance in . . . his historical works from *Madness and Civilization* (1967) onwards."[39] This volume likewise spills over between the empirical and the metaphorical, exploring both actual spaces and their prodigious symbolic value.

Nora's work, with its territorial and national dimensions, has provided a remarkably productive way of thinking about how Jewish societies have coped with the burden of history during their various geographic wanderings, and especially during the prolonged transition from traditional to more modern forms of life. Indeed, according to Maurice Halbwachs, this very distance from the object of memory was a prerequisite to the formation of a collective memory of a particular event.[40] Examples of sites of memory in Nora's sense of the term abound in Jewish tradition. The Talmud may be considered a site of memory *par excellence*: its legal and ethical imperatives—many of which are tied back to "the Land," that primary *makom* where God and place seemed more intertwined—preserve details about a certain space and a relationship with it. The Jewish calendar year is also finely calibrated to remind the observant of different events in Jewish history, both singular and momentous—Passover recalling the Exodus, Sukkot [the Feast of Tabernacles] marking and celebrating the annual harvest—as well as the more mundane and cyclical, such as the Sabbath, which commemorates the seven days of creation. These sites of memory, "enveloped in a Mobius strip of the collective and the individual, the sacred and the profane,"[41] embody the tension also inhering in the notion of *makom*, with its oscillation between material and transcendent, between place and space. The performance of these rituals expands our notion of how Jewish space may be imagined and co-constructed.

The significance of place-making in Jewish texts—and more broadly within the lived experience of Jewish cultures so shaped by these texts—lies at the heart of this study's inquiry. Conceptually, this study is informed by a sensitivity to those contemporary critical practices that suggest a more lived sense of place, of spaces produced through and within specific social, political, geographic, and economic settings. Practically, we proceed along several parallel lines of inquiry: the idea of space as a critical category, often as a metaphor or symbol for other ideas, with special attention to the depiction of space in literary texts; and the history of actual sites, and the material, lived-experience of place.

It may not be that everything can be conceived of as a space, even in the most elastic metaphorical sense. But certainly most, if not all, experiences may be examined in spatial terms. Within the contours of this sprawling sense of what we talk about when we talk about space, the present study is concerned with how space has been imagined in Jewish cultures, and the gap between this imagined space and experienced space. I also acknowledge the potential limits of this approach, foremost of which may be how to measure the ways space is experienced, especially within such a short book. However, the imagining of space is an important point of departure within Jewish culture, precisely because of its profound historical devotion to the text, and it is my hope that this book will serve as a springboard for other ways of conceptualizing and measuring spaces and places in all their attributes.

Furthermore, though Jews have formed communities and physical attachments practically everywhere, there is one site whose significance would seem to exceed any other in Jewish experience; this is the Land of Israel, with Jerusalem, historically, at its metaphysical center. The fact that Jews traditionally pray facing Jerusalem marks only the beginning of thinking about how this particular space has fundamentally shaped Jewish culture. In the next three chapters, therefore, we continue our examination of notions of space and place in Jewish culture, by focusing on three foundational sites: the Garden, Jerusalem, and the Land.

2   The Garden

What is the role of the natural world in Jewish cultures? While the book's final chapter offers a broader discussion of the role of the environment in contemporary Jewish culture, in this chapter we focus on the symbolic and privileged natural form of the garden. The garden is a hybrid kind of a spatial site, both human artifact and organic growth; it is different from other natural sites such as the desert or wilderness, where space is perceived as awesome and unmediated.[1] And though the idea of wilderness may, too, be a myth, its wildness may be understood in relation to the ostensibly controlled virtues of the garden. The garden's distinctiveness derives not only from these cultivated, domestic qualities, or the degree to which its stewardship seems to be (at least in a utopian sense) a man-god joint venture. The garden is also enormously protean, perhaps precisely because of how highly wrought a place it is. The garden is meant not only as a natural paradise, a playground of sorts, but also, from the very start, allegorical and representational, always pointing toward another state or condition, whether the quality of humanity's relationship to the divine or a nostalgic longing for one's home. While the garden may be designed to minute, particular specifications, it also lends itself as a symbol of some lost richness or pure state.

This chapter offers several frameworks in which to think about this foundational site and its various permutations in Jewish culture, with special attention to the biblical Garden of Eden, the domestic gardens of the Song of Songs, and the complex use of the garden as both site and symbol in the medieval Hebrew poetry of al-Andalus. Questions of gender and intertextuality will inform our discussion throughout, as we examine the garden's evolution as a powerful allegorical tool.[2] Part of this power emerges from the sense that the garden, as noted, is more than just a physical site. We may also conceive of the garden as a kind of "temporal space": Eden is itself located in *kedem*, a term with both spatial and temporal connotations, meaning "east"[3] as well as the past or antiquity more generally, as in *chadesh yameynu ke-kedem*, "renew us as in the days of old" (Lam. 5:25). These two meanings of *kedem*, as both location and antecedent time period, strengthen the Garden's power as an expressive indicator of both time and place.

Eden and the Song of Songs

Perhaps no space is more associated with the idea of origins or beginnings than the Garden of Eden. Appearing in Genesis 2:8, shortly after the first version of man's creation, the garden is planted by none other than God himself: "The Lord God planted a garden in Eden, in the east, and placed there the man whom He had formed. And from the ground the Lord God caused to grow every tree that was pleasing to the sight and good for food, with the Tree of Life in the middle of the garden, and the Tree of Knowledge of Good and Bad. A river issues from Eden to water the garden, and it then divides and becomes four branches." The use of the verb "planted" calls to mind freshly turned soil and other elements of the natural world. Indeed, the following verses contain specific geographic references—names of the river's four branches and different kinds of precious gems, such as gold and lapus lazili, that may be found there. The fact that Eden is also the source of a river indicates it may be mountainous terrain, its elevated height suggesting a place closer to the heavens.

The Garden of Eden is linked to other types of beginnings, symbolized through both the Tree of Life and the Tree of Knowledge of Good and Evil: the beginning of the drama of humanity, the introductory episodes of which feature interactions with a divine, omnipotent entity. To be human is to be aware; consciousness is what separates us from the animals. A desire for knowledge ultimately leads to the end of Adam and Eve's residence in Eden, and the beginning of history as we know it.

Western culture's foundational notions of gender are generated in these primal scenes. Genesis contains two versions of the creation story: in the first version, man and woman are created simultaneously—"And God created [*bara*] man in His image . . . male and female he created them" (Gen. 1:27–28)—as part of the neatly stitched series of parallel events and dualities that characterize the first creation story (night and day, water and dry land, sun and moon, fish and birds, etc.). The first couple is created both to enjoy God's natural plenty and rule over it.[4] The second version of creation is both more chaotic and focused on the creation and actions of humankind rather than those of a divine presence. Man's formation in this second instance, "out of the dust of the earth" (Gen. 2:7), seems to in some sense precipitate the creation of the Garden of Eden. The Hebrew verb *yatsar* used to describe man's creation in the second story also denotes a hands-on, tactile kind of activity. Man in this version is intimately bound to this new place, being made from its dust, not part of another order or resembling God. Only after God notices that man has a lot of work to do, tending, presumably, to God's "planting" of Eden, and that he might get lonely, does he create woman as an *ezer kenegdo*, "helpmate," but also, literally, a "helper against him." The partnership suggested is by no means a simple one. And the distinctiveness of this particular act of divine creation, like the "planting" of Eden, is again signaled by a tactile verb: "And the Lord God fashioned [*yiven*] the rib that he had taken from the man into a woman and brought her to the man" (Gen. 2:22). *Yiven* is often translated as "fashion" but derives etymologically from the verb "to build." Indeed, the term *tsela* [rib] can also refer to an architectural element.[5] The gender hierarchy of the second creation story, in which woman's creation follows and depends upon that of man, is recalled in the curse levied upon her by God after the discovery of their disobedience: that she will be ruled by her male partner.

Throughout the creation stories, two kinds of productive activity—one both human and divine (*yatsar, yita, yiven*), another (*bara*) only for God—signal the qualities that have come to characterize the Garden of Eden as a space: a fully imagined pastoral realm as well as the transcendent site of mankind's attainment of knowledge. Moreover, it is practically impossible to think about the Garden without also thinking about exile. We cannot contemplate the rich wholeness of the place without remembering its loss. And this idea of a pastoral site symbolic of some innocent and now irretrievable beginning permeates Western culture. However, unlike its central position in Christian commentary and tradition, the Garden narrative of Adam and Eve's sin and their subsequent expulsion from Eden has not featured extensively in traditional Jewish commentary. Despite rabbinic curiosity concerning a range of substantive and formal details in the text,[6] midrashic commentaries on the Garden narrative largely read it within the basic pattern of creation, revelation, and redemption common in traditional readings of Jewish history. Adam is identified with the people of Israel as a whole, the Tree of Life is the Torah (Written Law) and the failure to obey God's commandment, and the subsequent expulsion from Eden emblematizes the nation's disobedience as a whole and the subsequent condition of exile. That these midrashic commentaries were written in the fourth and fifth centuries C.E., at a time when Christianity and its institutions were an increasingly dominant social and political force in the Roman empire, further contributes to our sense of the Garden as a symbol of an irretrievable past, a period characterized (for Jews) by territorial stability and political sovereignty. While these writings do not expressly look back to Jerusalem, we may consider the twin sites of Eden and Jerusalem as two examples of lost centers, now-absent points of origins, toward which the Jewish imagination genuflects.

While God's creation of the full range of animal-kind—from "great sea monsters, and all the living creatures of every kind that creep" to "cattle, creeping things, and wild beasts of every kind"—suggests a space that is more wild kingdom than pastoral garden, Eden is largely represented as an orderly, divinely created garden whose delights have been restricted behind a "fiery sword." Perhaps its depiction as a relatively tame place is related to the evolution of human settlement in the region—including the invention of nomadic forms of herding and agriculture and the eventual construction of more permanent cities—and especially what may have been lost in the process. Evan Eisenberg suggests that Eden may in fact be a bit more wilderness than we moderns care (or dare?) to imagine: "What exactly is the fiery sword? Is it our awe of wilderness?"[7] This distinction between an appreciation for nature as pastoral and tame, and an awareness of nature's essential wildness continues to inform modern Jewish culture and is explored more fully in the final chapter.

Eden reappears, in a sense, and merges with the landscape of Jerusalem within another important biblical garden, that place depicted in *The Song of Songs*, a sequence of love poems in which the garden appears as a central locus and symbol:

A garden locked
Is my own, my bride,
A fountain locked,
A sealed-up spring.
Your limbs are an orchard of pomegranates
And of all luscious fruits . . .

You are a garden spring
A well of fresh water . . .
Let my beloved come to his garden
And enjoy its luscious fruits.

I have come to my garden,
My own, my bride,
I have plucked my myrrh and space,
Eaten my honey and honeycomb,
Drunk my wine and my milk. (Song 4:12–5:1)

Serving as a metaphor for the beloved herself, an external, nurturing force, and something possessed by the speaker/Lover, the garden in the Song has been viewed by readers as a sexual euphemism, a symbol of both fertility and female genitalia. In this poem it is depicted as "locked," withholding love and sensual delights from all but her beloved.

The Song as a whole has been read within Jewish tradition as an allegory of God's love for his "bride," "the people of Israel." While these readings may be persuasive, limiting our reading to them would miss the multiplicity of references generated by the garden and its associated imagery. This richness of meaning is, of course, at the core of any literary text, particularly poetry, and especially when read intertextually, in relation to other sources. Two images in particular from the Song recall the essential drama of Eden, and the consequences of eating from the Tree of Knowledge: Song 2:3 depicts the beloved under the shade of the apple tree where "his fruit is sweet to my mouth." Song 8:5 relates awakening under an apple tree in connection with conception and a mother figure, which resembles the "eyes opening" of Adam and Eve, where knowledge precipitates shame and then mortality. What happens when we think about the space of the garden in the Song in relation to the Garden of Eden, an archetypal space of both natural and sexual freedom?

In both Genesis and the Song, desire is the generating force that drives the narrative: in Eden, desire for knowledge that is also a kind of sexual knowledge leads to mortality and exile; in the Song, however, the desire of the couple searching for one another in various pastoral and urban settings seems to result in something more productive—a union of sorts that is both physical and metaphysical—and ultimately, in the creation of poetry itself, of human song as a cultural expression. Just as a garden may be cultivated, and nature transformed into culture, human desire may also be "cultivated" as love. Adam and Eve's desire for one another may be understood as a desire for unity, a return to some whole sense of self (if Eve was created from Adam's rib); the "success" of their union is ultimately undercut by their expulsion from Eden. The lovers of the Song, however, seem arrested in perpetual play, and their constant union and reunion alludes to the regenerative powers of metaphor and the uniquely human talent for the language arts. The situation of the garden in the Song restores our sense of nature as a hospitable backdrop to human actions; as one critic remarks, "The Song of Songs inverts the story of the garden of Eden; man rediscovers Paradise."[8]

Both Genesis and the Song of Songs are discussed here as paradigmatic versions of the pastoral, central to Jewish imaginings of nature in its cultivated state. Both texts also remind us of how the space of the garden may represent wider notions of loss, memory, and nostalgia. In the concluding sections of this chapter we turn to modern treatments of the biblical garden; first, however, we consider the appearance of the garden in a body of work that occupies a central place in the Jewish imagination, the medieval writing of Islamic and Christian Spain.

Andalus and After

All who are sick at heart, and whose cry is bitter
Moan and sigh no longer.
Enter the garden of my poems and find
Balm for your sorrow, and joy in song.
   —Moshe Ibn Ezra (c. 1055–after 1135), "The Garden"[9]

The garden depicted within Moshe Ibn Ezra's poem suggests a site constructed by the human imagination but also firmly grounded in the dilemmas and sorrows of life on earth. The garden's multifaceted quality within medieval Hebrew poetry is perhaps most pronounced in its appearance as both text and context: the garden is both subject and site of poetry making. Borrowing from the courtly tradition within Arabic poetry in Andalus, and capitalizing on European romance traditions after settling in Christian Iberia, medieval Hebrew poets—also known as "rabbi-courtiers" for their straddling of religious and secular realms— produced an enormous and variegated body of work, whose devotion to space and landscape evidences a keen sensitivity to cultural and political upheaval and transition.[10] Though the garden and its attributes are conventions featured throughout Hebrew poetry of what has become known as the Golden Age (roughly 800–1300), the geographic parameters within which this work was produced, as well as the sociocultural affiliations suggested thereby, were fluid and changeable. Indeed, the entire question of what to call this era and its writers, and how to locate them in space and place, remains a challenge. For example, in Gil Anidjar's philosophical interrogation of al-Andalus, the very parameters of what is signified through this term are exploded. Anidjar begins with the ostensibly locative phrase from the medieval Arab Jewish philosopher Maimonides, "our place in al-Andalus." Beyond any reference to an actual set of geographic coordinates, al-Andalus is, according to Anidjar, an "event":

> The singularity of such an event or set of events of language constitutes and deconstitutes al-Andalus, and continues to do so even where unexpected. Again, in this event, al-Andalus is less a geographical location (although it is also that), and more the linguistic occurrence of and as that event. Here, language does not, or does not primarily or exclusively, refer to an outside (geographical, historical, or other) but articulates rather a more complex relation to its place, to itself as taking place and as the location of its own occurrence.[11]

Anidjar's work provides a challenging frame for thinking about a generically diverse set of texts produced by medieval Hebrew writers, all of which seem conscious of the "disappearance" of the place itself, marked most conspicuously by the expulsion of Jews from Spain in 1492, and with it the "end" of al-Andalus. Our concerns in this chapter relate more directly to geography and cultural change, as evidenced in the varying depictions of space, especially the domain of the garden.

Andalus occupies a liminal position between East and West, and its imagined and physical borders extend in both time and space. Both the composers and primary audience of this poetry were Jewish figures who rose to social, economic, and political prominence within Andalusian society. The garden appears as a central motif in their work as both an ideational and actual space. Not exactly the most natural of natural spaces, the garden symbolizes an ideal of universal beauty and is associated with the richly sensual life of the court; it is depicted through language from the aesthetic realm, as both ornate and pleasing, a setting in which to indulge and honor the senses, especially through the drinking of wine and the composition of poetry.[12]

Another poem by Moshe Ibn Ezra exemplifies this use of rich language from the domain of visual artifice:

> The garden wears a colored coat,[13]
> The lawn has on embroidered robes,
> The trees are wearing checkered shifts,
> They show their wonders to every eye.
> And every bud renewed by spring
> Comes smiling forth to greet his lord.
> See! Before them marches a rose,
> Kingly, his throne above them borne,
> Freed of the leaves that had guarded him,
> No more to wear his prison clothes.
> Who will refuse to toast him there?
> Such a man his sin will bear.[14]

The patterns of the spring garden suggest a wide array of colorful, embroidered fabrics, a dazzling display of texture and hue worn expressly to honor the garden's "king"—the rose—itself shedding the leaves of its "bud-hood" and emerging to receive the speaker's toast. The "dressing" of the garden in these different manmade clothes further heightens our sense of the garden as a space that is produced by human activities, through the fashioning of poetry—a kind of language in fine clothing—and also, in this case, through the communal drinking of spirits. As scholars have pointed out, the depiction of the courtly garden with its wine and poetry parties is a stock element of these poems and indeed other medieval poetic traditions. What kind of space is suggested by these gardens that, as Jonathan Decter notes, "derive from garden poems primarily and from actual gardens only secondarily"?[15] First, the space is typified by certain activities—drinking, making poetry, flirtation. Second, these activities themselves are highly regulated, with Moslem and Jewish (mostly) men mingling. Beyond the particulars of what exactly occurs in the garden, however, these activities are all set within a seemingly stable and secure setting, in which each player—whether flower, bud, or lawn—knows their place. The poem depicts, in other words, a kind of "social order," one that largely characterized Jewish life in Andalusia. This sense of a stable social hierarchy, in which this elite group of Jews knew their place, undergirds the orderly depiction of the enclosed, courtly garden in poetry written in Andalusia.[16]

An early poem by Dunash ben Labrat (mid-tenth century), a disciple of Sa'adiah Gaon in Iraq who moved to Cordoba and was responsible for introducing Arabic poetic meters into Hebrew, also gushingly refers to the garden's pleasures and the appeal of secular court life. However, we find a sharp rhetorical turn as well, a rebuke to the reader for indulging in a life of such pleasure:

I chided him: "Be still!
How can you drink your fill
When lost is Zion hill
To the uncircumcised. . . .
The Torah, God's delight
Is little in your sight,
While wrecked is Zion's height,
By foxes vandalized.[17]

The poem raises the specter of another kind of space entirely—Zion and Jerusalem's Temple—as a counterpoint to the courtly garden paradise, an image that implicitly prompts questions of social and religious difference. As Raymond Scheindlin points out, this poem was written toward the beginning of the period in question, when ideas of cultural synthesis were fresh and may have produced some anxiety as to how Jews might maintain their own traditions within the secular world of the Arab courts.[18] Indeed, the poem's eloquent testifying on behalf of both courtly garden and Zion speaks to a general quality found in these poets and their work: the ability to be both of the "world" and their "community," between "the space of the courtly garden and the place of kinship," without feeling bereft or in "limbo."[19]

In some respects, the garden image in Hebrew Andalusian poetry may be productively compared to its presence in medieval literature more broadly. Perhaps because the garden is a hybrid site, where nature is domesticated, it lends itself to symbolizing other forms of control, or situations where order is paramount and chaos of some sort a threat. These other gardens and their poetic renderings may also be complicit in the shaping of the garden image in medieval Hebrew writing, especially after the Almohad invasion of 1147 and the dispersion of Andalusian Jewry to the Christian Iberian north, among other sites. The garden remained the site of poetry making, wine parties, and flirtation. However, newly embedded in the Christian North, it also became a way of looking back, a site of memory that represented the now-lost world of Judeo-Arab symbiosis. Like the Garden of Eden, Andalus became a lost center of sorts, as Jews found themselves in another kind of exile. In Decter's view, "As Islamic Iberia began to fade into Jewish memory, the palace garden emerged as an icon of Andalusian culture, while the desert and forest represented landscapes of exile."[20] For Hebrew poets such as Yehuda Halevi (c. 1075–1141), the garden's verdant landscape symbolized the cultural richness left behind, and their attachment to the past is conveyed through the desire to plant internal gardens: "In my heart there are flourishing plantings for you. When I remember your name I gather the finest of spices."[21] Decter's topographic readings resemble the attention to the evolution of landscape poetry within contemporary English literary studies. Scholars of romanticism, for example, understand the depictions of landscape in poets such as William Wordsworth and John Keats as cultural constructions reflecting larger patterns of change in England from a rural to an industrial society, and only secondarily as natural spaces. Similarly, the garden operates in the work of these Hebrew poets as a figure of accommodation and provides a way of thinking about exile from their Andalusian home.[22]

Some garden depictions in poetry written in the Christian north reflect this cultural transition and the fear of a potential change in social status in their new religious and political environment.[23] While many of the conventional elements and images remain in place, they are motivated to describe a tense, often morbid atmosphere, potentially in keeping with the newfound social and political situation of the poems' authors.[24] For example, the figure of the gazelle, symbol of physical and aesthetic beauty, is depicted as caught, imprisoned:

> I hear the gazelle's sigh and her wailing
> From Edom's prison, and Arabia's jail;
> She weeps for the bridegroom of her youth
> And calls in pleasing song to Him:
> "Sustain me with cakes of nuts and raisins;
> revive me with apples of your love."[25]

Edom here is identified with the Roman Empire and Christendom, Arabia with the Muslim lands of Andalus. The gazelle, trapped in between, is transfigured into the people Israel, calling to God in the sensual and fragrant language of the Song of Songs, and even—the fruit—of the temptations of Eden.[26]

In addition to these questions of space, nostalgia, and social status, the garden in medieval Hebrew poetry also retains its essential relation to sexuality and eros,[27] tropes that are often mediated through intertextual phrases or images from the biblical gardens of Eden and the Song of Songs. So, for example, a wedding poem by Yehuda Halevi announces the theme in language that is by now familiar:

> The time for lovemaking has come!
> Go down, why do you tarry
> To pasture in her garden?
>
> Her fresh pomegranates are out of sight,
> But you, don't fear when she brings them out
> From behind the veil of her vipers—For her snakes have no venom.[28]

In this "defanged," Edenic honeymoon, the garden and the bride are depicted as one in the same, both offering fertility and pleasure. The gazelle is also a figure of male homoerotic desire while women are largely silent or completely absent from these poems as both producers and consumers.[29] However, as Tova Rosen reminds us, Hebrew poets imitated conventions of Arabic love poetry for Muslim courtiers, and their objects of desire included "princesses, slave girls and young boys."[30] An anonymous undated poem uses images from both the artificial and natural realms to provide an unusually detailed depiction of a woman:

> . . . A neck like the neck of a gazelle when
> it thirsts and lifts up its eyes to heaven;
> breasts like apples of henna,
> studded at their tips with a bit of myrrh;
> a belly like white dough,
> or like a heap of wheat;
> a navel in her belly like a cistern,
> as though she were an empty well;
> very narrow hips, like the hips
> of a bee as it flits through the vineyard.[31]

Instead of the garden as a figure for nostalgia, here we find an evocation of the garden as a fertile, feminized site, whose pastoral attributes perfectly suit the admiring gaze of her male admirer-poet.

In part we have seen how the garden for the Jewish imagination is often linked with the idea of exile. Yet the Andalusian exile, like other exiles, also proved ultimately manageable. The memory work of the garden is thus part and parcel of Jewish culture's longstanding expertise regarding the conditions of diaspora, be it by the waters of Babylon and the great inventions of Hellenic Jewry in Palestine, or the newfound centers of the Iberian north. Indeed, medieval Jewish culture more generally—and the myriad and multilingual writings of Jewish Iberian authors—is evidence of the ways in which "Jews not only adapted to the conditions of exile but often flourished within it materially and spiritually, while managing to preserve a vivid sense of their distinctive national and religious identity."[32] Yosef Yerushalmi has described this condition of being "ideologically in exile and existentially at home"[33] in specific relation to Iberian Jewry, noting how Hebrew writers transposed the geography of Andalus into a kind of cognitively Jewish map: cities in the region were given names with Hebrew etymologies. Thus Toledo was really *Toledot*, or else *Toletula*, from the Hebrew *tiltul*—"migration" or "wandering." We examine this tension between "exile" and "domicile" more fully in chapter 6, "Diasporas." Here let us simply underline, with Yerushalmi, the fundamentally Jewish quality of this kind of place-making: "Such transpositions . . . are more than mere wordplay. They reveal something about Jewish mentalities . . . an intrinsic, oscillating duality. On the one hand, ongoing links to the ancient land of origin. On the other, the ability to endow the place of exile with familiarity, to perceive it as 'Jewish.' . . ."[34] So, for example, "Lament for Andalusian Jewry," by Avraham Ibn Ezra (1093–1167), uses the language of exile to refer to his hometown:

> I moan like an owl for the town of Lucena, where Exile dwelled,
>   guiltless and strong,
> for a thousand and seventy years unchanged—
> until she was expelled.[35]

The bird imagery, and a sense that these cultural constructions of landscape are of limited comfort, may also be found in a relatively late poem by Meshullam da Piera, depicting a garden from which poetry has virtually disappeared: "But though I sang, my flute did not answer, and even the birds did not raise their voices in mirth. . . . The birds voiceless among the branches, the swallow songless in my house."[36] A poem by Moshe Ibn Ezra exemplifies the "Judaization of exile":[37]

> How far yet must my feet, at Fate's behest
> Bear me o'er exile's (*galut*) path and find no rest?[38]

As in the other Andalusian poems we have examined here, exile refers not to the Land of Israel but expressly to the poet's native land, Granada, from which he must now suffer the "battle-axe of wandering" (*garzen ha-ndod*). This "fate" is also rendered in the biblical language of exile, this time with a reference to Cain's banishment from Eden. Granada and his friends there are also recalled by intertextual reference to the Land; using the well-known phrase from Psalms relating a nostalgia for Jerusalem, the poet swears: "If I forget them, may my hand forget/Its cunning," and "Beautiful Granada-land" is called *"hadar rimon"* (glorious pomegranate).[39] The pomegranate, which we have seen figure as a symbol of fertility in the Song of Songs, is one of the most privileged of all biblical fruits, one of the seven varieties of produce associated with the Land of Israel and chosen to adorn the priestly garb of Aaron in the desert wilderness. To call the Andalusian stronghold by this name, as was common, is to invest it with the dearest of associations, redolent of both the powers of exile and the promise of home.

In the following chapter we examine the image of another influential center—Jerusalem—whose history is also intertwined with distinct conceptions of space and gender. Architect Stanley Tigerman parses the relation between Jerusalem and Eden thus: "If Jerusalem is a metaphor of Eden subdivided by the four rivers, the sacred city is nature transformed into architecture."[40] After Eden and its exile, Jerusalem takes up residence at the core of the Jewish imagination.

3 Jerusalem

Eli Amir is an Iraqi-born writer who immigrated to Israel as a teen in the 1950s and became a popular novelist and well-known public figure. His 2005 novel *Yasmin* begins with a remarkable rendering of Jerusalem: on the morning of June 7, 1967, a senator from the Jordanian parliament watches the sunrise from the window of his home and notices a straggling column of dusty, tired-looking soldiers in torn uniforms walking down a nearby alley. Remembering the tremendous commotion of the previous night's battle, Al-Sayed Antoine Salome reflects upon the heroism of these fighters, no doubt members of the Iraqi brigade that has arrived to help the Hashemite kingdom defend Al-Kuds (Jerusalem). As the soldiers pause to rest with their heavy packs and weaponry, leaning against the fence surrounding his home, he opens the balcony door and greets them, expansively, vividly comparing their efforts to the great Islamic warriors of the past:

> Al Salam Aleykum and may Allah's mercy bless you, oh mighty soldiers, fighters of the holy war, oh sons of the illustrious Arab family, oh brave-souled, beloved. I, Antoine Salome, member of the Hashemite Jordanian parliament, am honored to present you with the gratitude and admiration of King Hussein. . . . Your glorious fighting is akin to the war of Caliph Omer Ibn Al-Khtab, conqueror of Al-Kuds Al-Sharif.[1] By the sword you have pushed back the contemptible, heretical, brutal, lowly Zionist enemy, pitiful and cowardly, and with the help of Allah you will throw them into the sea.[2]

His speech is greeted with stunned silence; finally, one of the soldiers approaches, removes his helmet and says: *"Ichna yahud, min hon.* We are Jews, from here, from Israel."[3]

This short scene provides the frame through which much of the novel unfolds: the jarring sense of amazement felt by Al-Sayed, "the blood drained from his face," resembles in some fundamental fashion, I would argue, the experience of the Hebrew reader of Amir's novel, who is repeatedly forced to view her own recent history, especially the first few decades of Israeli statehood, from the point of view of those Palestinians who share its territorial setting. Just as the Arab functionary is confronted with the presence of those Israeli/Jewish soldiers, "from here," so too readers of

Yasmin, by entering its fictional world, are faced with competing claims of ownership and homeland. After the city is "reunified," Palestinians, prevented from visiting the western neighborhoods of the city since 1948, are suddenly able to visit their homes in Talbiyeh, Katamon, and the German Colony with a sense of familiarity and entitlement.

The Israeli soldiers' multilingual reply to the Jordanian official points to the kind of cultural border-crossing that is one of the novel's central themes. The soldiers speak both Arabic and Hebrew; they are, perhaps, Iraqi-born like the author (and like the novel's hero, Nuri Amari, who himself speaks Arabic at home with his parents, and Hebrew in his job in a newly formed government office devoted to managing East Jerusalem). Indeed, Antoine Salome was expecting Iraqi soldiers and here they are—just not the ones he thought he would find. The use of both Arabic and Hebrew in this critical moment—indeed throughout the novel—further complicates what it means to be "from here, from Israel." The presence of Arabic in the mouths of conquerors disrupts the historically privileged bond between Hebrew and territory, and offers instead a more complex sense of how space is constituted and produced by often unpredictable social interactions.

The novel treats the potential crossing of borders through the evolving romantic relationship between Nuri Amari, a new Jewish immigrant from Iraq who serves as an advisor for Arab affairs in East Jerusalem, and Yasmin, the daughter of Abu George, a Christian Palestinian cooperating with the city's new Israeli administration. The demarcation of physical borders, in this case between East and West Jerusalem, between Arab and Jew, Palestinian and Israeli, serves as a physical corollary to the inherently unstable borders defining Israeli national identity.[4] The potential union between Nuri and Yasmin, briefly consummated, symbolizes the untenable nature of any long-term partnership in the city, deriving, the novel suggests, from the unequal power relations between occupier and occupied.

Many Jewish citizens of the city also greeted its expansion after the war with a kind of geographic vertigo, a disorienting sense of return to something once familiar—the streets of the past, even one's childhood. In his epic poem cycle "Jerusalem 1967,"[5] Yehuda Amichai depicted the profound defamiliarization experienced upon "returning" to those neighborhoods he had not seen for nineteen years: "In vain you will look for the fences of barbed wire. /You know that such things/don't disappear . . . / In vain you will look. You will lift up your eyes unto the hills."[6] Notably, the poem's sense of space is both visual—the barbed wire through which the two halves of the city had viewed one another—as well as textual: the expectant gesture of looking toward the hills alludes to the supplication contained in the verse from Psalms, "I turn my eyes to the mountains/from where will my help come? My help comes from God" (Ps. 121:1–2). Indeed, it may be difficult to write, or read, about Jerusalem *without* recourse to textual tradition—the clichéd images of the city, whether beautiful or desolate and abandoned, are so predominant as to render any attempt at unmediated representation problematic, even incomprehensible.

"Jerusalem 1967" may also be understood in relation to the rise of poetry and popular song during the war and following. This work largely viewed the war as concluding a redemptive national narrative, the closing of a modern historical cycle that began with the advent of Zionism. However, while the city's division in 1948 may have been artificially created, its "unification" had different meanings for different residents of the city, as noted in the discussion above regarding Amir's novel and Jerusalem's Palestinian population. Amichai's work contains many of the unmistakable details of a post-1967 cityscape; walls have been torn down and the Jewish and Palestinian populations begin to come into contact. The poetic speaker moves through the city's spaces, especially the gates and narrow lanes of the Old City, and seems to possess a point of view that is both celestial and subterranean: on the one hand, "If clouds are a ceiling, I would like to/sit in the room beneath them: a dead kingdom rises/up from me"; on the other hand, "[a]bove the houses—houses with houses above them. This is/all of history."[7] Indeed, a sense of uneasy possession characterizes the speaker's newfound freedom vis-à-vis the city, walking through neighborhoods whose remaining Palestinian residents are either invisible to him or described in relation to his own sense of remorse and ambivalence. It is a peculiar kind of *flânerie*, the condition so evocatively described by the French modernist poet Charles Baudelaire in which the poet-walker gets lost in the city, observing the street from a semi-detached perspective. The speaker in Amichai's poems is indeed on intimate terms with Jerusalem's spaces, but these spaces have themselves been transformed and irrevocably altered in his absence. "Jerusalem 1967" views the war and its aftermath in these personal terms, exploring the poet's relation to the city's new mapping, even as that space has itself been subjected to the violence of war and displacement.

The violent activity is also felt by the sentient entity of the city itself, which is compared to "an operation that was left open."[8] The famous Jerusalem stone "can feel pain. It has a network of nerves."[9] The city's primary populations, however, cannot communicate with one another: "The muzzein's prayer/is wasted on the new houses. The ringing/bells roll like balls and bounce back. /The shout of Holy Holy Holy from the synagogues will fade/like gray smoke."[10] Despite its political "unification," the city remains essentially characterized by otherness and

difference, features which themselves derive from the jumbling of historical layers of the past:

> I've come back to the city where names
> are given to distances as if to human beings
> and the numbers are not of bus-routes
> but: 70 After, 1917, 500
> B.C., Forty-Eight. These are the lines
> You really travel on.[11]

Jerusalem is mathematically calculated through a multidimensional
algorithm encompassing both time and space. Like one of Italo Calvino's
"invisible cities," it "consists of . . . relationships between the measure-
ments of its space and the events of its past."[12] As in Amichai's "An Old
Bus Stop" (see discussion in introduction), here, too, the mundane details
of daily life are emblematized in the bus route; the poem seems to suggest
that lurking beneath the objective grid of the bus map, the city's topography has truly been shaped by historical events related to political and
military conquest, whether or not the bus rider considers these facts as
she moves through the city. Indeed, the speaker's "return" to the city is
construed as a kind of historical redemption, those dates charting the
city's history as an important Jewish site—500 B.C. marking the end of the
kingdom of Judah and the fall of the city to the Babylonians, siege and
sacking of Jerusalem by the Romans, followed by the destruction of the
Temple, the Balfour Declaration, the war of 1948. We return in this chapter
to contemporary iterations of Jerusalem. First, however, we survey ideas
about the city as evident in biblical texts, *piyyutim* [psalms from late antiq-
uity], and the evolution of liturgy, and trace the city's appearance as a
travel destination in medieval and early modern narratives. This selection
could easily have expanded to several times its length. I have chosen to
present here some better-known texts as well as others that suggest a
more nuanced version of Jerusalem as an ambivalent center; I recom-
mend the reader to the anthologies and other volumes cited in the notes
for further reading.

Locating the Center: Heavenly and Earthly Jerusalems

Some of the earliest depictions of Jerusalem are found in biblical texts
where it appears as a foreign city, the home of the Jebusites; later conquered by David, it eventually becomes the location of King Solomon's
Temple. The Temple in biblical texts is viewed as the permanent dwelling
place of God following temporary residence in the *mishkan*, which housed
the ark during the Israelites' journey from Sinai to Canaan. The Temple
thus marks the transition from a transitory to a more territorial national

existence. The historical narratives from the Bible create a sense of Jerusalem's growing centrality as a political and religious center. This idea of a sacred center is a powerful part of many ancient traditions. Certainly there is something universal about the assignment of sacredness to a particular site, a geographic attachment that defines a community or collective group. This site is often understood as the center of the world, with its possession a special sign of God's grace and good will toward that particular group.[13] Jerusalem's location at the center of the world originated in the book of Jubilees, a retelling of Genesis written in Hebrew during Second Temple times (around the second century B.C.E.), and is, according to one scholar, a symbolic attempt to assert the political importance of the city within the Hellenic empire.[14] Mount Zion's graphic representation as the "navel" of the world emerged from this initial description and can also be found in later rabbinic literature, most famously in the commentary on Leviticus.[15] In chapter 1 we saw how the Mishnah, composed in a post-Temple world, delineated the degrees of holiness characterizing different parts of the land and various elements of the Temple. Part of rabbinic Judaism's larger project was to make the holiness of Jerusalem somehow integral to everyday Jewish life outside, and even far away from, the city itself. This was accomplished through the shape of the daily prayer service, the central portion of which mimicked the sacrificial rites of the Temple (see the next section below).

Midrashic literature also promotes the centrality of Jerusalem, vividly granting it an inordinate amount of the world's most basic qualities.[16] The possible tension between "space" and "place" discussed in chapter 1—with space signifying a transcendent category and place indicating a more grounded, material site—is manifest in attitudes toward Jerusalem; this idea is embodied in the expression "Yerushalayim shel mala, yerushalayim shel mata"—Heavenly Jerusalem versus Earthly Jerusalem.[17] The notion that heavenly Jerusalem exists until a messianic time when earthly Jerusalem will be rebuilt represents an abiding sensibility within Judaism, indicative of attitudes toward both space and history. For the religious Jew, heavenly Jerusalem always exists in some transcendent sense; earthly Jerusalem must be built by human hands, thus partaking of the mundane and trivial details of place.

Heavenly Jerusalem first appears in apocalyptic texts of the first century B.C.E.; it has a long legacy in Judaic and Christian traditions but is interpreted differently by each. What does the centrality of this idea of an otherworldly city, one constructed and existing in some netherworld, contribute to our understanding of space in Jewish culture? Might it in fact indicate a diminished or muted enthusiasm for the place itself, for actual political or territorial autonomy?[18] First, the very mention of

Jerusalem might raise the notion of a utopian state attained either in a dream or vision, or perhaps in some messianic age. Like the visitor to one of Calvino's "invisible cities," who, when presented with old postcards of the city "must praise the postcard city and prefer it to the present one,"[19] earthly Jerusalem may always pale beside its heavenly twin. At the same time, however, this ideal also alludes to the memory of Jerusalem as an originary site. Details of the memory of Jerusalem permeate Jewish sources, arguably more than the city itself. Jerusalem thus has a vexed relation to history, being part of some glorious past and representative of a messianic future. The city is also both utterly unique and serves as a symbol of certain ideas about urban life more universally. That is, like Rome—another city whose physical plan and history is irrevocably linked to religious institutions—Jerusalem is potentially a model for life on earth in relation to some set of spiritual or moral principles, especially as this pertains to those civic contracts that regulate urban life, how people live together and treat one another.

This dualistic idea of heavenly versus earthly Jerusalem is further complicated by lived historical experience. Jerusalem has been virtually synonymous with a multicultural, cosmopolitan urban identity, drawing on the overlapping yet distinctive experiences of different religious, ethnic, and national groups. The city has been shaped, both physically and metaphysically—for better and for worse—by both the idea and the fact of these differences, conflicts that have often erupted in violence. Each of these groups has left their mark on the city. Art historian Oleg Grabar notes that despite the longstanding attachments expressed in Jewish texts, there is no tradition of Jewish architectural space in the city: "Significant Jewish monumental presence appears only in the nineteenth century, partly because Jews were not directly connected to political power since the second century and partly because post-Temple Judaism did not need or require monumental expression until the modern era."[20] This relative lack of spatial presence may also account for the fact that map-making about Jerusalem seems largely a Christian endeavor; that is, though the city was no less central for both Judaism and Islam, maps are mostly from Christian tradition.[21] This lacuna is perhaps related to the status of representation within both Judaism and Islam, considered aniconic religions hostile to certain kinds of figuration. Within medieval accounts of the city, most groups mention only their own kind and do not reveal much about other kinds of ethnic or religious groups living in the city.[22] In fact, it is Jerusalem's "internal ecumenism," its tolerance of three main and somewhat competing religious traditions, that accounts for Jerusalem's special standing among religious cities.[23] "The further uniqueness of Jerusalem," according to Grabar, "is that most of its memories were Jewish, but that these Jewish memories became Christian, and Christian and Jewish memories became Moslem."[24] This imbricated interdependence—in which (in Calvino's terms) "memory is redundant: it repeats signs so that the city can begin to exist"[25]—characterizes the space of the city until this very day, and is especially apparent in the dense plethora of religious sites constituting the matrix of the city's old center, where the Al-Aksa Mosque on the Temple Mount abuts the Western Wall and the Via Dolorosa. Jerusalem also still resides at the center of the Jewish theological imagination just as the city remains an object of political contestation, and its physical landscape, including those elements of architecture and infrastructure that shape the everyday experience of its citizenry, is itself subject to the city's ever-evolving political dimension.

The enduring meaning of Jerusalem as an urban space in the Jewish imagination may be further amplified by comparing it with Eden and that space's symbolic power. Both Eden and Jerusalem serve as formative instances of two fundamental modalities of space—the natural and the urban. Unlike Eden, Jerusalem exists as an actual city, a complex instance of the urban condition in the twenty-first century. However, like Eden, it also endures as a kind of allegory, often one with dangerous power, of a whole or more authentic existence in the past. Just as to speak of Eden is to speak of exile and the memory of what was, the prophetic texts also describe Jerusalem out of a keen sense of absence and remove. Sidra Ezrahi's recent work has considered the implications of this backward glance, arguing that a foundational nostalgia for other spaces has always powered and shaped Jewish communities as they created institutions and set down roots in other locations. Long the sacred core of the Jewish imagination in exile, Jerusalem is the object of what Ezrahi calls "a diaspora poetics." Historically this mode of creative expression has been "predicated on distance from the sacred and the Real and on the creation of substitutions and simulacra evolved in the long aftermath of the destruction of the Second Temple."[26] Ezrahi's work offers a powerful model for conceptualizing those strategies of creative accommodation deployed by the Jewish imagination at work at ever-widening circles of remove from its mythic center, and also suggests the "implosion" that potentially occurs in the wake of return.[27]

Remembering Jerusalem: Liturgy as a Site of Memory

In addition to its textual dimension, the memory of Jerusalem has featured in many rituals and life-cycle events in Jewish tradition. At weddings, for example, a glass is broken to commemorate the destruction of the Temple in Jerusalem. Numerous other customs connected to funerals, fasts, prayer, and purity bear some relation to either the geographic location of Jerusalem or the memory of Temple life and its loss. Many of these festivals, tithes, and purity customs as described in Jewish law are still observed; thus, even after its destruction, the sanctity of Jerusalem is tied to its spatial location. For example, one is obligated to pray facing Jerusalem, and, when in Jerusalem, pray facing the location of the Temple. So deeply has this memory of the Temple shaped Jewish ritual practice that religious historian Jacob Neusner even asks if "the Temple's greatest service to the people of Israel was not its destruction."[28] In explaining the Temple's continuing pull and force for Jewish religious experience, Neusner points to a central tension in the Mishnah, source of many Jewish liturgical rituals, regarding space. On the one hand, he argues, it "may be studied anywhere. It is utopian." On the other hand, "Mishnah does choose to organize the world around the themes and topics of the Temple."[29]

This paradoxical combination of utopianism tempered by the particulars of a specific place is manifest throughout Jewish ritual observance. Holidays are, of course, marked by the calendar cycle and are therefore largely temporal markers. However, as discussed in chapter 1, recent scholarship has demonstrated the value of perceiving the entire spectrum of commemorative practices in spatial terms. I would propose that liturgy in general, particularly the daily Hebrew prayer service as it has evolved, provides an excellent example of a site of memory, one that points directly toward Jerusalem and the memory of Temple life. Historically, the prayer service evolved as a replacement for the daily sacrificial offering at the Temple in Jerusalem. Thus the very act of prayer constitutes an acknowledgment of absence, a recognition that congregants exist at a remove, at once geographic and historical. At the heart of the daily liturgical service is the *Amidah* or *Shemoneh Esreh* [the standing prayer, "Eighteen"], initially composed at the beginning of the Second Temple period and given final form by Rabban Gamliel II after the destruction of the Temple. The *Amidah* largely focuses on praising God and describing his mastery and dominion; the fourteenth section expressly addresses the future status of Jerusalem: "May You rebuild it soon in our days as an eternal structure, and may You speedily establish the throne of David within it. Blessed are You, God, the Builder of Jerusalem."[30]

Even when Jerusalem or the Temple is not the substantive focus of prayer, liturgical practice alludes to the memory of a space and the ancient rituals that constituted its holiness. The performance of liturgy; chanting a specific set of texts in a particular setting; the existence of a ritually defined quorum for prayer (the *minyan* of ten); the relation between prayer leader and congregants—all these suggest a space that is itself connected to early Jewish sites of prayer. However, rather than conceive of congregants imagining themselves in Jerusalem or the Temple per se, this need to replicate the performative space itself alludes to the temporal and geographic distance from those spaces. The relation between space and memory becomes even more overt and charged during certain parts of the Jewish calendar year, most notably during the autumn month of *Tishrey*, a period including the marking of the New Year and subsequent "Days of Repentance." Each holiday includes a special service or religious obligation that evokes the memory of a different place in Jewish history. So, for example, the building of the *sukkah* (tabernacle) signifies the years spent in the desert before arriving in the "promised land," and more broadly the idea of wandering or exile in Jewish tradition. Many prayers evoke the pre-Temple site of the *mishkan*, and the Torah service, in particular, recalls Mount Sinai and the reception of the law. In Jewish tradition as a whole, as we shall see, sites such as the desert—more overtly the space of exile and loss—rest on equal footing with other more "stable" sites of Jewish political or religious autonomy, such as the Temple and Jerusalem.

One last extended example will suffice: the *piyyutim* or liturgical poems of Yom Kippur, considered the holiest day of the Jewish calendar year, constitute a sustained instance of liturgy's urge to fill the void in Jewish life after the destruction of the Temple. These poems derive from a wide historical swath of literary expression—from Kalir in mishanic times to R. Meshulam of the tenth century—and are united in their repeated insistence that the recitation of certain laws can serve as a substitute for the Temple sacrifice.[31]

On Yom Kippur, the *avodah* service relates in detail the apparatus and customs of the sacrificial rituals of the Temple. The activities of the High Priest (*kohen hagadol*) were meant to expiate the sins of the entire community; the service reaches a climax as the High Priest asks for forgiveness of his own sins, after which follows a description of the other priests witnessing his prayer. As the High Priest utters God's name, the entire community would "kneel and prostrate themselves, give thanks, [and] fall upon their faces."[32] In contemporary Jewish observance, as the High Priest's benedictions are chanted, some congregants kneel and prostrate themselves when this phrase is recited. The long litany of detail contained within the High Priest's recitation, and the repetition of this catalog, describe places and practices that no longer exist; nevertheless, the body is called upon to perform in spite of, or in memory of, the Temple's destruction.

The *avodah* service, though exemplary in some ways, offers an extreme instance of the memory of Jerusalem and the Temple in Jewish thought. Its paradigmatic qualities rest in the substitution of both text and ritual for space; that is, we do not find here a reductive instance of the bible as a "portable homeland,"[33] but of prayer—with its performative, devotional, and communal aspects—as sacred space. One could also argue that the Passover seder, with its plethora of performative rituals, a tightly scripted annual event in which elements of the Temple sacrifice are recast in symbolic fashion, represents another example of how the rabbinic imagination, in this case those mishnaic texts that represent the core of the modern seder, came to grips with having to encounter the divine outside of Jerusalem and the Temple.[34] It is possible that this memory of Jerusalem and the Temple becomes more significant much later. Indeed, although liturgy develops in relation to an imagined center, the relation between that center and the diaspora is never construed as a simple hierarchy. That is, Babylonian Jews were more concerned with Babylonian Jews than with Jerusalem per se. As with the Andalusian poetry discussed in the previous chapter, the trauma of geographical displacement finds meaningful expression within those place-making rituals and texts that ground a new sense of home.

Pilgrims, Merchants, and Other Medieval Jews

The well-known poem by Yehuda Halevi, "My Heart Is in the East," describes this sense of absolute distance from Jerusalem:

> My heart in the East, and I in the West,
> as far in the West as west can be!
> How can I enjoy my food?
> What flavor can it have for me?
> How can I fulfill my vows
> or do the things I've sworn to do,
> while Zion is in Christian hands
> and I am trapped in Arab lands?
> Easily I could leave behind
> this Spain and all her luxuries!—
> As easy to leave as dear the sight
> of the Temple's rubble would be to me.[35]

The poem has been viewed as a paradigmatic statement of what might be called the problem of Jewish geography—a succinct and vivid rendering of the spiritual shock experienced by rabbinic Judaism living in the wake of the Temple's destruction, distant from Jerusalem and the existence of the *shekhinah*, a theological rendering of God's feminine presence. Yet we may remark upon a couple of things: first, the void itself produces a poetic utterance of stunningly imaginative power, comparable perhaps only to the equally well known, and similarly bereft, verse from

Psalms: "How can I sing a song of Zion in a foreign land?" which refers to the Babylonian exile. Second, as Raymond Scheindlin notes, "There is no forward motion in this poem,"[36] as the verses juxtapose perfectly balanced pairs: East–West, Zion–Christian/Arab, luxury of Spain–rubble of Jerusalem. The poet did in fact "leave Spain behind" eventually, and late in life made a pilgrimage to Jerusalem; this poem, however, concludes in open-ended fashion, with the speaker unable to fulfill his religious vows—sacrifice at the Temple?—and willing, in a hypothetical sense, to leave behind the relative physical comfort of Spain for the mere sight of the Temple's ruins. The distance in question, then, is not necessarily geographic in nature; indeed, Jerusalem may have been physically removed, but traders and merchants regularly traversed the Levant in the medieval period. Though the poem is composed in the Levant, the speaker feels his heart to be estranged from the East, because he is not in Jerusalem, and because Jerusalem is under Christian control. The poet is also writing within a liturgical tradition that turns on being in exile, distant from Jerusalem.[37] The distance alluded to should therefore also be understood in messianic terms: the city that remains at the center of the poet's theological world (his "heart") will also remain in physical ruins until some future time.

Jerusalem's ruins are depicted in an even more tactile sense in Halevi's "Ode to Jerusalem," where the speaker yearns to "throw my face down to your ground,/ fondle your gravel and caress your soil."[38] The eroticization of the city as a woman draws directly on biblical images of Jerusalem as a wanton or profligate figure. This imagining of Zion, in which the spirit of the city is personified as a woman, dates from early prophetic writing and is related to other ancient traditions that also linked women, the city, and some form of betrayal and/or degeneracy. At the same time, Zion may represent more positive notions of fertility and matrimony. As Tikva Frymer-Kensky vividly argues:

> Zion is a multifaceted figure. Mother and beloved, mourned and mourner, abandoned and returned to, daughter and bride. She is bad wife and good mother, mother of Israel and its future bride, spouse of God and future spouse of the people, city abandoned by her exiled people and city-in-exile, accompanying them to Babylon. . . . She is the persona immanent in the city. . . . She is the mother of the people, and the place of God's presence.[39]

This is a pretty tall order, and indeed we find the female ideal of Jerusalem/Zion depicted in a variety of personae—sexually promiscuous (Is. 10:32) or abandoned (Is. 49:14), and even crying out in labor (Mic. 4:10 and Jer. 4:31). A sustained instance of this depiction of Jerusalem as Zion, a female incarnation of the city who is punished for her sins, occurs in the opening verses of Lamentations:

> Alas!
> Lonely sits the city
> Once great with people!
> She that was great among nations
> Is become like a widow;
> The princess among states
> Is become a thrall.
> Bitterly she weeps in the night. . . .
> There is none to comfort her. (Lam. 1:1–2)

> Jerusalem has greatly sinned,
> Therefore she has become a mockery.
> All who admired her despise her,
> For they have seen her disgraced. . . .
> Her uncleanness clings to her skirts. (Lam. 1:8–9)[40]

Representations of Jerusalem are thus bound up with both gender and exile. Alternately called *yoshevet zion* (dweller in Zion) or *bat zion* (daughter of Zion), the city's female nature is depicted as both desired and abject, and all the more appreciable from a distance. Even the qualities of the built city—her walls and gates—speak to this ambivalence, suggesting a topography that is both seen and unseen.

While Jerusalem may appear as an object of desire in literary texts, other documents demonstrate more material bonds, those connections shaped by the mundane details of commerce and the related, perennial notion of Jerusalem as a sacred site of pilgrimage. Jerusalem, like Safed, also considered a holy city, was a site of Jewish pilgrimage throughout the Middle Ages, as much an actual destination as simply another point on extensive itineraries tracing the full arc of Jewish commercial life in the Levant. The Jewish communities of what S. D. Goitein called "a Mediterranean society" were characterized by multiple languages—including Hebrew, Arabic, Ladino, Spanish, Greek, and Turkish—and overlapping cultural affinities embedded in trade routes that created fiercely held bonds among diverse communities living thousands of miles apart. Travelogues produced by these communities record visits to Jerusalem and the remains of the Temple, usually embedded within a larger frame narrative that is itself a hybrid document. These often first-hand accounts—part demographic record listing of the populations and institutions of Jewish communities visited during their travels, part anecdotal history mentioning famous deeds and events accorded to various sites—depict the peripatetic existence of the medieval Jewish merchant class, from the undeniably wealthy with their entourage of scribes and hangers-on to the merely subsistence earners. Along the way we meet the Jewish and non-Jewish communal and political leaders whose decisions and favors often shaped their fortunes.[41]

For example, the recorded journeys of Rabbi Petachia of Ratisbon, a contemporary of the well-known Jewish medieval traveler Benjamin of Tudela, span nearly two decades (1170–1187), and the account handed down to the modern reader provides a detailed "map" of travels commencing in his native Prague.[42] They continue through Poland, Kiev, and the Ukraine, "Kedar" (Russia and the Crimea), "Targuma" (Armenia), Mosul, Nineveh, the Tigris, and the metropolis of Baghdad, the graves of Ezekiel (outside Baghdad) and Ezra the Scribe, which have become religious shrines, Shushan, Damascus, the Galilee, Rachel's tomb, Jerusalem, Hebron, Acre, and Greece. Many places are described in matter-of-fact relation to "historical" biblical accounts: Ararat is the site where Noah's ark was once carried out of the mountains but has long since decayed; at "the Salt sea of Sodom and Gomorrah," travelers may look for a pillar of salt but it no longer exists.[43] Mention is also inevitably made of Jerusalem's current condition in contrast with its past glories. A fourteenth-century text, *The Roads from Jerusalem*, describes a series of short trips possible outside the city and notes the location of the Temple Mount: "Alas, by reason of our sins, where the sacred building once stood, its place is taken today by a profane temple, built by the King of the Ishmaelites when he conquered Palestine and Jerusalem from the uncircumcised."[44]

In addition to this ebb and flow of temporary residents, Jerusalem was tied to Jewish communities in the diaspora by monetary donations collected on its behalf, contributions that provided regular financial subsidies to the city's small Jewish community. Jerusalem's Jews in the premodern period, subject to numerous, often traumatic changes in political rule, were in large part dependent upon this *chaluka* or distribution, what geniza records call "the distribution of Palestine" [*tafriqat al-maqadisa*].[45] An interesting conclusion emerges: Jerusalem may have been at the center of a theological worldview, but its actual Jewish community was small and impoverished, at best. As such, the city provided little opportunity for commercial transactions; neither was it a natural destination for families or individuals in search of promising social, financial, and/or matrimonial connections, unless perhaps their trip was made in the context of a group with other pilgrims.[46] A modern reader (Mark Twain among them) may well have gotten the impression that most pilgrims stopped there for five minutes to see the pile of rocks (the Temple) before moving on to some other more comfortable or interesting destination, such as Cairo or Damascus. Indeed, a well-known modern version of this circuit or *sivuv*, as one traveler calls his journey, can be found in Theodor Herzl's utopian novel *Altneuland* (1902), where the young protagonist, Friedrich Loewenburg, disenchanted with Jewish Vienna's cosmopolitan life and nursing a broken heart, agrees to accompany the older Prussian general Kingscourt on a voyage to parts unknown. During their journey, they make a stop in Palestine to see the "ancient homeland." Disgusted with the "dirty, neglected" alleyways of Jaffa, they traveled to Jerusalem by "miserable railway."[47] The city's initial charm by moonlight quickly dissipates: "Jerusalem by daylight was less alluring—shouting, odors, a flurry of dirty colors, crowds of ragged people in narrow, musty lanes, beggars, sick people, hungry children, screeching women, shouting tradesmen. The once royal city of Jerusalem could have sunk no lower."[48]

This fictional response to Jerusalem resembles Herzl's own reaction during his 1898 visit to the city, famously recorded in his diaries: "When I remember thee in days to come, O Jerusalem, it will not be with pleasure. The musty deposits of two thousand years of inhumanity, intolerance, and uncleanliness lie in the foul-smelling alleys. . . . If we ever get Jerusalem and I am still able to do anything actively at that time, I would begin by cleaning it up!"[49] Modern Hebrew writing about Jerusalem was no less forgiving, even as the city began to develop as a center of modern Jewish life.

Fictional Jerusalem

Given the enormous psychological and theological baggage associated with Jerusalem, not to mention its cultural and political capital, one might anticipate that the modern European encounter with the city itself would be neither smooth nor uneventful. Indeed, much early modern Hebrew writing about the city does not depict it through the rose-colored glasses of Zionist fervor, but rather with ambivalence, resentment, and even outright hostility. Dan Miron traces the beginnings of this "demystification" of the city at the hands of modern Hebrew writers, including Ahad Ha-am and Y. Ch. Brenner, describing "the binary condition of literary Jerusalem," in which all depictions of the city necessarily oscillate between some set of polar opposites, in different historical, cultural, and political settings.[50] One classic point of reference is Agnon's epic novel *Just Yesterday* (1945), in which Jerusalem appears as Tel Aviv's doppelgänger, a premodern city characterized by ethnic and religious division and in urgent need of rehabilitation. For a large portion of the novel, the city's fractured population is ironically viewed through the eyes of a dog, Balak, whose rabid state compels him to roam the city's streets in a vain search for shelter. Instead, he becomes the object of the profoundly divided sympathies of the city's residents:

> Whenever Balak appeared in the neighborhoods of the Jews, they hurled stones at him, when he moved away from them, they cast false charges at him. There was not one mouth that did not throw mud at him and not one newspaper that did not blacken his name. . . . When the Jerusalem newspapers reached Jaffa, Jaffa thought that dog was a parable, like Mendele's horse and other stories of livestock's animals. . . .
>
> Balak . . . looked at all four corners of the sky for which way he would choose. Finally, he stuck his legs to his body and started running until he came to the neighborhood of Abu Tor. . . .[51]

Indeed, Agnon's polyphonic text encourages the reader, like those secularized readers in Jaffa, to view Balak as a parable of sorts, whose movement through the city reveals a space in which modern public opinion jostles with neighborly gossip and urban myth. Despite the city's enormous physical changes in the last several decades, there are areas of Jerusalem that may be explored with Agnon's work as a guidebook, in the same spirit as James Joyce's Dublin. Like the latter, Agnon's cityscape deftly merges classical notions of the city with the furious pace of modernity, with both comic and tragic consequences (the novel's protagonist dies a painful and ignoble, even senseless, death from rabies).

The gap between heavenly and earthly Jerusalems remained a potent topic in Hebrew fiction. Hans Kipnis, the immigrant veterinarian protagonist in Amoz Oz's 1972 novella *The Hill of Evil Counsel*, parses the essential problem thus: "I have been living in Jerusalem for three years and I continue to yearn for it as though I were still a student in Leipzig. Surely there is a paradox here."[52] The landscape of Jerusalem in the 1940s in Oz's work, here and in his massive, epic memoir, *A Tale of Love and Darkness*, is indeed teeming with contradiction—awash with new immigrants, British soldiers and bureaucrats, the fragmenting remains of Jerusalem's historically cosmopolitan culture: Jews, Moslems, Christians; pilgrims, merchants, beggars. Hillel, the young protagonist whose experience shapes *The Hill of Evil Counsel*, grows up in a newly developing neighborhood located at the city's hilly, rocky edge, far from the city center, where Jerusalem can almost appear to be a "real city," equally removed from the spiritually freighted space of the Old City. Beyond his father's neatly ordered garden, "a lonely island of clear, sober sanity in the midst of a savage, rugged wasteland," the landscape plunges into a threatening abyss of both natural and human predators:

> Beyond the fence, which Father had made from iron posts and old netting and painted in bright colors, began the wasteland. Plots of scrap iron,

dust, smelling of thistles, of goat dung; and farther on, the wadi and the lairs of foxes and jackals; and still farther down, the empty wood where the children once discovered the remains of a half-eaten Turkish soldier in the stinking tatters of a janissary's uniform. There were desolate slopes teeming with darting lizards and snakes and perhaps hyenas at night, and beyond this wadi, empty stony hills and more wadis, in which Arabs in desert robes roamed with their flocks all day long. In the distance were more and more strange mountains and strange villages stretching to the end of the world, minarets of mosques, Shu'afat, Nabi Samwil, the outskirts of Ramallah, the wail of a muezzin borne on the wind in the evening twilight, dark women deadly-sly, guttural youths. And a slight hint of brooding evil: distant, infinitely patient, forever observing you unobserved.[53]

Like interwar poetic depictions of Tel Aviv, in which the civilizing force of the city's creation is pitched against the ostensibly violent chaos of the surrounding sands, Jerusalem, too, especially in its modern incarnations, sits within a largely hostile environment. While detailing the tactile specificity of twentieth-century experience, the passage displays some of the same admixture of fear, revulsion, and compelling mystery that characterize premodern views of the city. Beyond the brightly colored fence of the budding new neighborhood of the *yishuv*, the old landscape still waits in semi-ruin, waiting to be redeemed. Potentially dangerous elements of nature (fox lairs, snakes, hyenas) seemingly conspire with man-made agents, represented through the Arab shepherds and the call for prayer. The "brooding evil" that waits at "the end of the world," an almost sentient force of the landscape that animates much of Oz's work, is almost divine in its omniscience.

Postmodern Jerusalem

Like Agnon's *Just Yesterday*, David Grossman's *Someone to Run With* (2000) contains a number of scenes of Jerusalem's streets, from a dog's-eye point of view:

A month later a boy and a dog ran through the streets of Jerusalem, strangers tied to each other by one rope, as if refusing to admit they were really together. . . . They had already escaped the busy thoroughfare, going deeper into narrow, curving alleyways, and the dog still didn't slow down. . . . The dog . . . stopped in front of a green gate set into a high stone wall, and in a graceful motion, she stood on her hind legs, pushed the metal handle with her paws, and opened it. Assaf looked left and right. The street was empty. The dog breathed and pushed forward. He entered after her and was at once wrapped in a profound silence.[54]

The boy, Assaf, and the dog, Dinka, end up in the quiet enclaves of a Greek nunnery, whose sole occupant, Theodora, has not left its grounds for fifty years while she waits, in vain, for pilgrims from her native Lyxos. Theodora's home exists in complete isolation from the dirt and commotion of the city that has grown around it in the half-century since her arrival as a novice. The building represents an oasis of stasis in a narrative that otherwise rarely stops moving, over and across the city's metaphorical and physical margins—its social misfits, criminal underworld, rooftops and alleyways—until its denouement in a cluster of crumbling homes, the remains of a Palestinian village, at the city's edge. In the novel's fictional world, Jerusalem's famous historical landmarks—all the baggage described in this chapter—simply doesn't exist. Grossman's novel depicts the city's twenty-first-century face: the downtown city center contains the unmistakable mix of tourist and missionaries, but this fictional Jerusalem is unlike any other previously encountered.

Grossman's novel uses Jerusalem as the setting for a coming-of-age story, but he seems to deliberately step outside the city's worn narratives. The spatial contours in *Someone to Run With* exhibit what Doreen Massey has called a "progressive sense of place," defined and shaped by *routes* rather than *roots*: "What gives a place its specificity is not some long internalized history but the fact that it is constructed out of a particular constellation of social relations, meeting and weaving together at a particular locus."[55] Grossman's novel seems to deliberately neglect those sites of "long internalized history" in favor of a vision of the city that is less centralized, more out of focus. As mentioned above, the story's narrative is propelled by movement and by multiple searches through the city's streets. Some of these places are familiar (Jaffa Road downtown), but most are anonymously located in unremarkable neighborhoods. The village ruins serve as temporary shelter for a couple of delinquent Russian immigrant youths who protect Assaf from a vicious attack by another roaming group. We might "read" these villages allegorically: their location on the outskirts of the city akin to their place on the "outskirts" of Israeli public discourse. Similarly, Theodora's enclave, and the dismal fate of her entire island—which perished in an earthquake—may offer some dim allegory of the fate of European Jewry. But none of this is really necessary: the ruins are simply a part of the landscape, and the story consists of a search, a love story, and, finally, a happy ending. Part of the novel's achievement is that all this happens to take place in a city called Jerusalem.

The relative optimism of the city's progressive sense of place as depicted in my reading of *Someone to Run With* is belied by another idea that also describes how space is currently produced in the city: Jerusalem as a "city of collision,"[56] meaning a city whose topography has been determined by violence. In a slightly gentler formulation, Michael Sorkin has remarked upon Jerusalem's "genius for exclusivity."[57] Sorkin's comment comes within his introduction to *The Next Jerusalem*, a collection of essays by urban planners and architects, the subtitle of which pinpoints the essential quandary—"Sharing the Divided City." The essays in this volume, which emerged out of two international conferences in the city, are predicated on the principle that any future plan for Jerusalem will necessarily depend on whether the city is perceived as "divided" or "unified," and what these qualifiers mean in actual conditions on the ground for its citizens, how power is shared and space allocated. Many planners and architects who have worked in the city, Moshe Safdie among them, argue that an artificial division was created in the city's physical plane in 1948, and much of the building and planning that occurred in the nineteen-year period until 1967 was "illogical" and "irrational," going against the city's urban syntax, the ways in which various neighborhoods, services, institutions, and interest groups had previously emerged, more or less organically.[58] The general orientation of the Israeli part of the city after the 1948 armistice was westward, and both residential and commercial neighborhoods expanded accordingly. This basic position did not change after 1967, when new planning for the city was further driven by security concerns, and by what Alona Nitzan-Shiftan calls an attempt to "Israelize Jerusalem—to inscribe on the built landscape of the city not only demographic and territorial 'facts' but more explicitly, a physical image bespeaking a set of national values."[59] For example, the architect in charge of the master plan for Maale Adumim, the city-sized neighborhood built on what was then the edge of the city, on the road leading to the Dead Sea, recalls that "the decision about Maale Adumim's location was, without doubt, political."[60] According to Safdie, "since the 'reunification' the city has continued to exist as two adjacent but separate cities,"[61] what appears on maps is an "interlocking puzzle of Israeli and Palestinian islands."[62] The consequences and implications of these spatial interventions on the shape of the city cannot be overstated, and are treated more at length in chapter 4, "The Land."

Jerusalem's physical space in recent years is increasingly characterized by high-rise construction; for example, the Holyland Park and Tower project contains numerous pied-à-terre apartments occupied by foreign owners during Passover or the Jewish high holiday season, vacant the rest of the year. Recent high-profile projects include the Supreme Court (1995), designed by Ram Karmi and Ada Karmi-Melamed, a project considered a paragon of public architecture, combining modernist simplicity and functionality with broad architectural references to Jerusalem's past. The city has also become a destination for "celebrity architects" who import their idiosyncratic sensibilities to the city's built environment, ostensibly joining the urban fabric of the city to the global arena in which they work. So Frank Gehry's Museum of Tolerance, until recently under construction, may remind visitors of the Spanish city of Bilbao, home to another of Gehry's creations; and Santiago Calatrava's "Bridge of Strings" (2008), the 1,200-foot-long light-rail bridge arching over the entrance to the city near the Central Bus Station, like some fantastic prehistoric bird, has raised objections precisely due to its unambiguous modernity within the city's façade of stone. This globalization of the city's physical dimension potentially stands in tension with the unique nature of Jerusalem's cosmopolitan, yet nevertheless extremely local, past.[63] On the one hand we have seen how the city has served as a destination for pilgrims and figured as a center in a more theological sense; on the other hand, one could argue that this relative "normalization" of the city, its entrance into the global order, effaces its politically contested nature. One clear instance of this conflict may be seen in the controversy surrounding the construction of the Museum of Tolerance, after it was discovered that some portion of the structure would be built on the remains of a Moslem cemetery. The Israeli Supreme Court eventually allowed construction to proceed, but the issue remains a sensitive one, and Gehry ultimately pulled out of the project entirely.[64]

Figure 1 Model for the Museum of Tolerance, 2010, Jerusalem—the new global architecture meets Jerusalem stone. Chyutin Architects LTD.

Jerusalem of the Mind

We have focused here largely on the ways in which Jerusalem has symbolized a kind of center in text and religious ritual. It seems fitting to also consider how emanations of Jerusalem have taken root in Jewish communities abroad. For example, many contemporary buildings connected with Jewish institutions, especially in the United States, have used Jerusalem stone for some portion of their exterior façade or interior spaces. Meant to symbolize a connection to Israel,[65] what we might call a "Jerusalem of the mind" has increasingly become a standard reference for Jewish communal institutions. While it makes sense that, lacking an indigenous architectural form, American Jewish communities have adapted the material vocabulary of Heavenly Jerusalem, we can also note the perhaps unintended connotations of this pervasive use of Jerusalem stone. In addition to the more overt reverence for the distant center, no longer quite as out of reach as in generations past, the presence of Jerusalem stone in Ekvelt (roughly, "Nowheresville"), USA, may also represent another type of portable homeland, an allusion to the locative mobility of Judaism's institutions—a wink and a nod that suggests "Jerusalem is here."

4 The Land

"Go forth from your land, from your birthplace, and from your father's house to the land that I will show you" (Gen. 12:1). "*Lekh lekha*." This terse two-word command is one of the more powerful and memorable phrases in the Bible, the brief, imperative form of the verb "to go" followed by the second-person form. One almost wants to translate it as "Get yourself to." This is only the Bible's first description of traveling to Canaan, of entering the land from another place, a place described as home. The land in Genesis, a foundational text for Judaism's covenantal relationship with the Land of Canaan, the Land of Israel, is almost always encountered from the outside: not only the object of desire and destiny, but a fundamentally strange and alien space as well. The story of Israel, which seems to begin with a promise, also then begins in exile, in a deterritorialized condition, far from Abraham's homeland. This ambivalence—the promise of home in a site that is removed from one's birthplace—characterizes the wanderings of the patriarchs and matriarchs, back and forth, into and out of the Land, into and out of Egypt. Later Deuteronomic texts describe how Moses led the Israelites out of slavery and through the desert only to remain outside the land, bereft of homecoming, viewing the Land "*mi-neged*," from afar, or, more literally, against. Rabbinic tradition, emerging from a kind of internal exile within the land itself—located in the Galilee, after the destruction of the Temple in Jerusalem—produced intricate modes of existence that were themselves deeply indebted to the Land and memories of its natural cycles and devotional rites. Arnold Eisen has characterized this historical pattern of thinking about the land from the outside as moments of *galut* or exile.[1] In foundational terms, then, the Land cannot be conceived without the condition of its opposite—exile.

Though scholarship has effectively traced and debated the origins of the centrality of the land in Jewish tradition, and its trajectory from the ancient through the modern period, the veracity of this claim is not the point here.[2] However it became operative, and whatever its actual claim to truth vis-à-vis documented, historical fact, the power of this idea has exerted enormous, undeniable influence. Furthermore, even though we consider the idea of the Land within our basic rubric of space and place, it is also crucial to note that the area known variously as *Eretz Yisrael*, Canaan, Palestine, or Israel is not akin to the Elysian fields of Greek mythology, an essentially utopian construct that served as the final resting place for Greek heroes. The Land is *real*, though it is often spoken of in surreal, ambivalent terms. As reported by those sent to "scout" the land in Numbers 13: though the land is "flowing with milk and honey" (13:26), it is already inhabited by other, powerful people with "fortified" cities, as well as "men of great size . . . *nefilim* [giants]." The land, in short, is "one that devours its settlers" (13:26–27, 32). Finally, despite the covenantal promise, the land must in fact be fought for in order to be possessed, even while these victories are seen as the product of divine intervention: "I have given you a land for which you did not labor and towns which you did not build, and you have settled in them; you are enjoying vineyards and olive groves which you did not plant" (Josh. 24:13).[3] The Land remains a contested site, filled with Others and never belonging entirely to the people of Israel.[4] Eventually, possession of the Land is itself conditional upon a certain kind of ethical behavior (detailed in Leviticus and later the Prophets), characterized by a tension between involvement with local tribes and the desire to remain distinct and separate.[5]

For religious Jews, the Land remained holy, even when Jews were absent from it; the longstanding tradition of burial in Israel attests to its importance for Jewish communities in the diaspora. As previously noted regarding Jerusalem, Judaism developed rituals and other institutions that effectively served as surrogate spaces for the original set of lost centers. Numerous traditions evolved out of depictions of the biblical landscape, and its seasonal cycles are marked in communal observance in geographic locations far removed from the Mediterranean coast. The Jewish calendar year still observes those harvest holidays connected with pilgrimage and the agricultural cycles of ancient life in the Land of Israel. At the same, rabbinic writings about the land and commandments pertaining to it vary widely in their attitudes toward the relative virtue of actually residing there. These variances have been understood in relation to historical events (e.g., the Bar Kokhba rebellion and rise of messianic zeal) as well as political and cultural circumstance (the integrative model found in Hellenic-Jewish literature such as Philo and Josephus).[6] We may discern a see-sawing tension between a professed devotion to the land and these practices that effectively create alternate spaces. For example, regarding the belief system of medieval Jews, scholars have noted that "it would be just as reductive to see the theology of the land as proof (and only as proof) of the ineradicable attachment of medieval Jews to the land of Israel as it is, on the contrary, to see idealization, metaphorization, or substitution as proof (and only proof) of their detachment from it."[7] Paradoxically, the gap between the place and its symbolic rendering has not diminished in the modern period with the establishment of the state of Israel; its stubborn presence lingers and is actually revived, "newly embodied in the Zionist act."[8] The Land's importance is attested to in its imagined qualities as the "Holy Land," promised to Abraham and his descendents in the covenantal language of the Bible, and envisioned as a fertile "land of milk and honey." These imputed qualities continued to influence its treatment, even as what was once merely an object of desire, was transformed into a more mundane, and more spectacular, reality. This chapter explores a series of modern literary texts that seek to reimagine the Land, in which its reconception as "place" is indebted to, and problematized by, its relation to its theological status as "space."

Capitalizing on Judaism's utopian connection to an ancient landscape, Zionism's assertion of ownership over the land was made through both physical and discursive means. Like other nineteenth-century European nationalisms, Zionism relied on a national literary tradition to depict the bonds among otherwise disparate members of an "imagined community";[9] for Zionism, this national entity was also bound by a common history, language, and idea of reclaiming a sacred center. This chapter's focus on literary imaginings, from the late nineteenth-century Renaissance poetry of Tchernichovski to Hebrew prose fiction, gives way at the conclusion of the chapter to a discussion of contemporary Israeli discourse about space and power.

Viewing the East: From *Kedem* to *Mizrach*

Zionism was drawn to the East as an exemplary point of origins, a "homeland" that was also a new destination and a potentially rejuvenating topography. So, for example, in the work of the poet Saul Tchernichovski (1875–1943), the East—*kedem*—appears as an important point of origins and return. A prolific translator of Greek and Latin, Tchernichovski's work is replete with pagan imagery and landscape depictions, much of which refer to an ancient condition of autonomy or kinship with the land.[10]

Tchernichovski's "Facing a Statue of Apollo" celebrates the antagonism between Hellenism and Judaism and offers a potential reconciliation, a recalibrated cultural model for the modern period.

> I've come before you, forgotten god of old
> God of ancient times [*yarchei kedem*][11] and other days . . .
> I've come before you—do you know me?
> Here I am, the Jew! We have an everlasting quarrel.[12]

Addressing Apollo through his physical surrogate, the reader may imagine the poetic speaker encountering the statue in one of Europe's museums, a scene that is itself a kind of allegory for the intellectual and cultural journey taken by many European Jews, out of the shtetl, into some cosmopolitan setting, away from the *beyt midrash*—the familiar setting of traditional Jewish learning—to the street, the cafe, the public garden, the university. The poet declares his allegiance to this divine power who represents "life, heroism, and beauty" and bemoans the fact that the God of the Wilderness, conqueror of Canaan, has himself been tamed, bound by the strips of phylacteries, a ritualistic object that restrains and therefore diminishes some more authentic, primal impulse. The poem thus moves from utilizing *kedem* as a setting for an "age-old" conflict between Hellenism and Judaism to a more internalized view of *kedem*, a force perpetually residing within the normative, religious development of Judaism in the diaspora, a condition representing a repressed and still potentially vital "other."[13]

Like other romantic nationalisms, Zionism's attitude toward the East was naive, often sentimental and orientalist in spirit; while admiring the East for its potentially revivifying cultural powers, they viewed this same space with fear and ambivalence, even disgust and antipathy. At the same time, as Europe's internal Others, Jews were themselves perceived as deriving from the East, and, in antisemitic discourse, as a primitive and stubborn force, resistant to "rehabilitation" and acculturation into European societies.[14] Indeed, as scholars have recently argued, "Jews have been seen in the Western world variably and often concurrently as occidental *and oriental*."[15] This paradox was further ramified by Zionism's actual encounter with the Mediterranean landscape and its native population, as the centers of modern Hebrew culture moved out of Berlin, Warsaw, Lvov, and Odessa into Palestine. Though Zionists may have "looked to the East for a cultural alternative . . . like European colonialists, they felt the need to distance themselves from the Arabs in order to maintain the integrity of their emerging national culture. The Arab way of life and the actual Palestinian landscapes were new, different and mysterious to Zionists. . . . But the biblical associations of these landscapes made them part of traditional Jewish culture as well."[16] The East and the native Arab population were thus objects of attraction and repulsion, both a familiar model for rootedness and rivals to be feared and despised.

Art historian Yigal Tsalmona also views Zionism's relation to the East as a "particular instance" of orientalism, but he embeds this characterization within a more complex picture: the East has perhaps been seen as "the cure of the national plight of the Jewish people . . . but to an equal extent it also represents 'the other,' exterior to the Zionist Jew and identified from 'there,' whether as an alien, even antagonistic, entity or as the object of unquenchable aspiration."[17] Such a view of the East and its native inhabitants informed early modernist painting in Palestine, especially Boris Shatz's Bezalel Academy, established in Jerusalem in 1906,

Figure 2 Encountering the Levant. Nachum Gutman, *Jaffa Port*, 1926. Courtesy The Nachum Gutman Museum, Tel Aviv, and the Gutman family.

which treated the East as a repository of ancient cultural values. The work of other artists is more ambivalent. For example, while much of the well-known work of Nachum Gutman depicted the landscape in the gentle tones of a naïve idyll, some of his images also viewed the immediate surroundings as a violent, threatening space.

However, for many Jews this "return to the East," while perhaps otherwise significant in theological and political terms, may not have possessed the same culturally charged significance as it did for Europeans immigrants. For those Jews arriving in the *yishuv* (the pre-state Jewish community) and later in Israel from Egypt, Syria, Iraq, Morocco, Yemen, and Algeria, the East was not a faraway object of some nostalgic longing but their extended backyard. Instead of viewing *kedem* as a space of utopian return and otherness, these Levantine communities saw the *mizrach* as simply their home, as a continuous and coherent native place. To perceive the Jew as in fact *native* to the Levant is, as Ammiel Alcalay has argued, "a notion so foreign to the modern dogma of the Jew as eternal stranger that it might appear unthinkable."[18] Alcalay rejects the idea of Jews always being "out of place," and argues that Levantine Jews were more conditioned by their embeddedness within different, overlapping cultures. The existence of multiple points of origin is also evident in those Jewish voyages that characterized medieval and early modern Jewish life in the Levant. This spatial capaciousness toward the East—the gradual diminishing of the East as *kedem*, imaginary place and privileged time, and its evolution as *mizrach*, the here-and-now of life in the Mediterranean, has profoundly shaped the evolution of Israeli culture.[19] "The House Must Have an Opening to the East" by *mizrachi* poet Shelley Elkayam suggests how an indigenously Mediterranean poetics might find expression within the relative confines of a predominantly Eurocentric Israeli literary discourse.[20]

> The house must have an opening to the East.
> To allow in late morning,
> to come to the bones of the building—
> sun.[21]

The poem's house symbolizes Israeli culture or society, which has closed itself to the power and meaning of locality, represented through the penetrating rays of the sun. This short lyric, which recalls the compass points of Yehuda Halevi's poem "My Heart Is in the East," alludes to the importance of the East as a physical and cultural axis toward which Israeli culture must "open itself."[22] By ignoring the powerful rays of the sun, the Israeli "house" has denied the facts of its own locality; only by owning up to its true place in the East can the "bones" of the building (that is, its lifeblood, its humanity) flourish and thrive.

Writing the Landscape

Modern Hebrew literature has played an essential role in delineating and shaping an Israeli sense of place. Not only could the land not be imagined without resort to its biblical precedent: the land itself was imagined as a text. One early pioneer described the landscape as "the *Tanakh* [Bible] open before you."[23] In the following portion of this chapter, we examine some of the ways in which the "imagined geography" of *Eretz Yisrael* has informed modern Hebrew writing. The famous opening passage from Y. Ch. Brenner's novella *Nerves* (1909), one of the earliest works of Hebrew fiction written and published in Palestine, points to the difficulty of describing the land as an implicit part of the process of making it their home:

> A perfumelike smell, which came from the low clumps of acacia trees, or "mimosas," as some liked to call them, scented the air of the small Jewish colony in southern Palestine. In the expanse of sky before us a golden shaft from the setting sun at our backs gilded a cluster of faint, calm

clouds; other clouds, as calm and faint, were limned not with gold but with long, narrow swathes of orange embroidery. At its far end the sky shone in docile light with the silvery-black sheen of myrtle leaves. . . . Next to a lone, straight cypress tree, which rose from behind the acacias and some yellowish prickly pears that were stiff with needles . . . I and my companion . . . turned from the path we were walking on and strolled toward a chain of hills that ran along a gleaming horizon. The distant ruins of an ancient castle ten or twelve miles to our right seemed suddenly close by.[24]

The scene is described in lush, romantic language; the narratorial point of view gazes upon and over the landscape, and also embeds a pair of observers strolling within it. Many of the descriptors derive from the biblical geographic lexicon: acacia (*shita*), cypress (*brosh*), and myrtle (*hadas*) are all types of flora linked with the biblical landscape. Two further terms somewhat complicate this depiction—*mimosas*, a loan word from a European language, and the *tsabarim*, or prickly pears, more recent agricultural imports that would soon come to dominate the local landscape, eventually becoming an icon of the newly emergent Hebrew culture's desire to be native. These terms, and the text's insistence on drawing the reader's attention to their use ("as some liked to call them"), point to the potential instability of the entire enterprise—both describing the land and, by association, knowing or possessing it. This tentativeness is also evident in the narrative's meandering quality over the contours of the scene described, and further implicit in an admission following this passage: "A bird whose Hebrew name neither of us knew flew brilliantly by."[25] Here language is incommensurate to the actual landscape, and the narrator can do nothing more than note this gap.

Another example of this typical conflation of land and text may be found in an early poem by Avraham Shlonsky, who was a key figure in the *moderna* or first wave of Hebrew modernism in Palestine. In "Gilboa" (1927), the Hebrew pioneer-bard encounters the land before him as both soil to be tilled and text to be fathomed:

Gilboa—it sounds like *remez-drash-sod*.
And like the dove of the sages, the *shekhinah* is cooing here.
It is the scent-of-scrolls, or the name of God pronounced
from Mapu's vineyard of *melitzot*.

But it is also a living clod. And the plain meaning [*p'shat*] of brambles.
Of the mountain's rust. Of the jackal-howl at night.
It is the vision's interpretation, in the skittering of herds,
that a boy from the *akeda* sees the horns of the ram.[26]

The sound of the word Gilboa calls forth a series of learned connotations: the midrash, Bible, and Haskalah literature—the canon of Hebrew literary history—all unfold in support of the depiction, and thus the sanctification, of the mountainous terrain. Indeed, despite Zionism's secular revolt against the behavioral and circumstantial norms of diaspora Jewish life, Shlonsky's poem—and others like it—evokes the landscape in expressly sacred terms: the sensual details of the landscape mingle with both God's divine presence (the *shekhinah*) and the potentially sacrilegious act of uttering His name. The *melitzot* or "flowery language" of Avraham Mapu, author of *Ahavat Tsion* [Love of Zion] (1852), considered the first Hebrew novel, refers to its biblical landscape depictions; the vineyard is the site of the novel's romance, set in the ancient Land of Israel, but also perhaps a nod to the tangled density of Mapu's archaic Hebrew, language that Shlonsky viewed as inadequate and inappropriate. The modernist Hebrew bard must invent a new poetic language, one commensurate to the nation-building tasks of paving roads and plowing fields.

This new poetic language is measured against the four stages of mystical interpretation—*p'shat-remez-drash-sod*, meaning "literal, symbolic, homiletic, esoteric." Shlonsky distinguishes between the three more figurative forms of exegesis—symbolic, homiletic, and esoteric—and the *p'shat*, or literal meaning of a text, which is embodied in the "living clod" and the "brambles." The poem's notion of *p'shat shel dardarim*—"the plain meaning of brambles"—proposes a new relationship between landscape and language. Hebrew landscape depictions of the Haskalah were primarily allegorical (*remez-drash-sod*), and written from a distance, relying on biblical descriptions of the land; however, modern Hebrew poetry written in the Land itself would seem to have no need for that old set of depictions, given the land's physical presence. Yet Shlonsky himself would eventually admit his failure to conceive of the Land without its textual antecedents—to encounter "the Place itself" without the burden of "the Story about the Place." Indeed, Hebrew culture has remained indebted, to some degree, to its ancient literary pedigree. This "debt" points to a central dilemma facing Israel today: To what degree and in what ways is the state "Jewish"—that is, harboring an attachment and allegiance to Jewish historical experience—and in what ways has it become something else, an entity embedded in and shaped by the particular qualities of the Israeli place, and the various populations who share it?

Zionism's vision of working the land offered a romantic critique of both modernity as well as the specific condition of European Jews. It proposed that their future as a national group would depend on overcoming the fundamental alienation of urban life and developing a creative, production relationship with land. A. D. Gordon's idea of a religion of labor in which the "new Hebrew" would replace the "diaspora Jew" was predicated on this intense physical contact with the Land: "Labor is not only the force that binds man to the soil and by which possession of the soil is acquired; it is also the basic energy for the creation of a national culture."[27] The figure of the *chalutz* or pioneer encountering the land is a common tableau in modern Hebrew writing of the *yishuv*. Texts describing the pioneering ethos often depict the land as a desert awaiting cultivation and settlement. Some parts of the land even "welcome" the pioneer's advances and efforts to "tame" it; at the same time, it is potentially dangerous and wild. The native Arab presence further complicated this situation for Hebrew writers seeking to describe the natural landscape. The Arabs' ostensible rootedness in the local landscape served as both model and foil for an emergent Hebrew culture, striving to effect its own sense of place and belonging.

One further example for Shlonsky's poetry will demonstrate the central role played by space in this Zionist narrative of belonging, where ("territory is always represented as a space that has already been occupied and violently incorporated."[28] Shlonsky's poem cycle *Mul ha-yeshimon* [*Facing the Wilderness*] (1929)[29] has been read in relation to the Arab-Jewish riots of 1929, in which scores of people were injured and killed in Jerusalem, Hebron, Safed, and Tel Aviv–Jaffa.[30] Anita Shapira has described the variety of political responses to these events, differences made manifest in the terms used to describe them: a "pogrom" or a *mered* [rebellion], a distinction that figured decisively in both Jewish and British responses.[31] Poetic responses to the events of that summer form an important chapter in the history of Hebrew political poetry; poems about Hebron, Hulda, and Jerusalem drew on familiar tropes from literary and liturgical tradition in depicting these events as both victory and slaughter.

Facing the Wilderness, part of which first appeared in the journal *Ketuvim* in September 1929,[32] narrates a drama between the desert—personified as the "God of the Wilderness"—and its native inhabitants, as they attempt to resist the civilizing forces of the pioneers. The poem describes how the "city receives its form from the desert it opposes,"[33] tracing a movement between, on the one hand, urban and human forms and, on the other hand, natural forms and their more threatening aspects, which are eventually subdued by built or social forces. In the poem's opening stanzas, the land is described as dormant, having "slumbered" for "many generations." The stage is set for a drama between the land and the interlopers who disturb its rest with the instruments and sounds of building: shovels, hoes, cement, tar, hands, and song. The intervention of the pioneers is related in Shlonsky's typically musical and densely allusive style: "A ladder [*sulam*] leans against the wall . . . feet rise and descend, bucket and tin. The workers are depicted in terms reminiscent of the biblical Jacob's dream yet retain a firm tie to the material demands of building a city. Roads are compared to a belt binding the sands, just as the camels, representing nature, are tamed and cooperate in the land-building effort. This idea of barren land awaiting human intervention often figures in Hebrew poetry of this period. Yet the land does not welcome their presence, and a *hamsin* [sirocco or sand storm]—a randomly occurring natural phenomenon—is depicted as an intentional form of revenge, plotted by the "God of Wilderness" and his ministers. The landscape, once awakened, acquires a threatening aspect: a *tsabar* (prickly pear) resembles a knife at the throat. The enemy seems abstract, described as an almost immanent force. The city, on the other hand, persists in being built house by house "like fists in the chaos."

The poem's decisive moment of enlightenment, which is also an awareness of the land's potential violence, comes toward the conclusion:

> Now I knew: the wilderness
> wails a prayer of vengeance in the night
> and from afar,
> above the mighty dome of the mosque: a crescent-moon moves
> like a hatchet.

Finally given voice, the wilderness that has threatened the pioneers and their efforts is indisputably tied to the land's Moslem inhabitants, the cry of the muezzin interrupting, even drowning out, the sounds of work and building. The poem returns briefly to the biblical landscape, calling to Reuven and Shimon to aim their shovels against the wilderness. And in the final section, hands return to work, as the building of the city (and the self) continues: *pach ve-dli, dli ve-pach, mul habli, yukam krakh* [Tin and bucket, bucket and tin, facing the nothingness, a metropolis will rise]. The city is built to an "orchestra of rebellion" [*mered*], an ostensible revolution, perhaps, against the natural order, which in the land is awakened from its slumber and provoked to a state of revenge. This rebellion is emblematic of Zionism's revolutionary character and the transformation of "diaspora Jew" to "new Hebrew." In either case, the poem's view of the land is such that it can no longer be viewed in the naive terms of biblical heritage; natural space and social space are cast as mythic, even tragic, enemies, whose meeting inevitably leads to conflict and violence. Shlonsky's poem marks a turning away from a vision of the *yishuv*, and of Tel Aviv in particular, as an intimate, pastoral community, and the following years witnessed tremendous development and expansion. Drawing on the allusive tradition that connects Hebrew poetry to biblical images of the land, *Facing the Wilderness* contains a recognition of the land's otherness, its resistance to change and its indigenous possession by other people—even while these natives are rendered in derogatory terms (voiceless, primitive, violent).

To Know the Land and Remember It

One way in which the fundamental strangeness of the land was ostensibly countered by the emergent Zionist state was through *"yediat ha-aretz"* [literally, knowledge of the land]. A mash-up of geography, Bible, and civics, this discourse was developed in the new state's formal and informal educational institutions. These lessons, often delivered "in the field" during hikes or camping expeditions, were meant to instill in children, many of whom hailed from immigrant families, a familiarity with the land and an appreciation of its historically Jewish dimensions. The hike [*tiyul*]—the consummate lesson experienced "in the field"—was an act imbued with spiritual significance, a "consecration of space" joining hiker and nature in an almost mystical bond.[34] This sacralized communion with the land has clear precedents in the German romantic tradition of the *Wandervogel*, another example of how the presumed indigenous quality of Israeli culture—its easy relation to place—is actually a European transplant. Yet the widespread practice of these hikes beginning in the 1920s was undoubtedly intended to render the land as a "Jewish geography."[35] Recent work by Yael Zerubavel and Oz Almog has described the elaborate degree to which the "text" of the land as it appeared in Jewish history has been revisioned by Zionist institutions as part of the nation-building process, parallel to and no less crucial than the construction of physical infrastructure. Narratives surrounding the life and death of Yosef Trumpeldor and the deeds of ancient figures such as Bar Kokhba were shaped to promote national values of self-sacrifice and commitment to the collective. After 1948, the experience of the war supplemented and complemented memories of the ancient Jewish past.[36] The space of the land became an arena in which history was often recast to promote the nationalist values of the emergent Jewish state. The state sponsored and built numerous monuments, museums, and other memorial sites to commemorate acts of heroism and martyrdom perceived as crucial to the state's foundational narrative,[37] and instituted the annual observance of Holocaust Remembrance Day and Memorial Day to complement these spaces. These material representations were meant to secure the ancient bond between people and homeland and cast it in modern terms, and many of them focused on the physical sacrifice involved in the establishment and defense of the state.

A complex space of mourning and grief evolved in Israeli culture, related to the traditional Jewish rituals of bereavement and focusing on both the physical remains of the lives lost and specific sites of battle. This enduring relation between place and memory has become a constitutive feature of the Israeli landscape, making Israel one of the most densely built memory sites on the planet. National institutions such as Mount Herzl, where many of Israel's heads of state have been interred, and Yad Vashem, the elaborate set of indoor and outdoor spaces devoted to memorialization of the Holocaust's victims, have become part of the regular itinerary for Israeli schoolchildren as well as visitors from abroad. Scholars have analyzed the power of these sites in relation to their ability to conjure the "presence of absence," a reification of the physical sacrifice involved in war.[38] The monumental or representational quality of the site decreases in relation to the presence of the body's physical remains. Thus, military cemeteries containing graves with actual bodies are relatively spartan and uniform in design; no extraneous information is required given the presence of the body itself, which bears witness more effectively than any informational placard. Monuments marking specific battle sites are somewhat more figurative, often involving some "original" piece of military hardware such as a tank and a plaque containing some details and the names of the fallen. The most elaborate form of signification is reserved for commemoration of those who were killed elsewhere—in Europe during the Shoah—and whose bodies remained there or were destroyed. Yad Vashem's monumental and highly figurative architecture, its symbolic representations and instructional infrastructure, may all be understood as an attempt to create the presence of that (and those) which is most absent, most irretrievable. This elaborate physical and textual memory of loss is symptomatic of what I have described as a Jewish response to a lost spatial center—only in this case the normative direction of substitution is reversed: no longer diasporic Jewish communities remembering the lost center of Jerusalem, but a newly territorialized nation selectively absorbing the experience of the Shoah, and the destruction of Eastern European Jewish life, into its own narrative of heroism and statehood.

Facing the Village

The above-described institutions of memory erased and supplanted other memories, as well as physical evidence of Palestinian life in areas now encompassed by the Israeli state. An awareness of this dual erasure—of both Palestinian settlement and the memory of it—finds profound spatial expression in Hebrew writing through the image of the village. The village presents a kind of epistemological challenge to Israel's claims for itself as a Jewish state: its presence disrupts the seamlessness of exclusively Jewish claims and mocks the divide between wilderness and civilization that had characterized Israeli pioneering discourse. The villages represent a settled version of land that predates the arrival of modern Jewish settlement, and the claims their memory makes on the landscape permeate Israeli fiction.

S. Yizhar's *Khirbet Khizeh* (1949) describes the conquest of a village and the expulsion of its inhabitants by Jewish soldiers. Yizhar's vision of the village is both romantic and tragic, accompanied by a recognition that the Zionist enterprise, in this case represented through its proxy, the army, will succeed only at the expense of the Palestinian villagers and their homes. The village is emphatically indigenous, its land and inhabitants reminiscent of something vaguely biblical.[39] The authority of long-lived existence conditions its easy location in the landscape. The land surrounding the village is described as "a tapestry of peasant wisdom, the weave of generations" in which the soldier-narrator feels like "a stranger . . . totally out of place."[40] Much of the story's narrative power comes from the narrator's inner debate regarding the ethical implications of his actions, even as he attempts to distance himself from them:

> Once villages were something you attacked and took by storm. Today they were nothing but gaping emptiness screaming out with a silence that was at once evil and sad. These bare villages, the day was coming when they would begin to cry out. As you went through them, all of a sudden, without knowing where from, you found yourself silently followed by invisible eyes of walls, courtyards, and alleyways. Desolate abandoned silence. . . . And suddenly, in the middle of the afternoon or at dusk the village that a moment ago was nothing more than a heap of wretched hovels . . . burst into a song of things whose soul had left them.[41]

The passage's sense of absence, and the paradoxical way in which silence is given voice, typifies Yizhar's spatial and narrative poetics. The army jeeps and soldiers destroy the scene's pastoral repose; they are intruders; the sight of refugees, mostly elderly, women and children, being removed from the village in trucks, serves as a catalyst in the mind of the soldier-narrator: "This was what exile was like. This was what exile looked like." Though he had "never been in the Diaspora . . . people had spoken to me, told me, taught me, and repeatedly recited to me, from every direction, in books and newspapers, everywhere: exile."[42] The text presents this narrator-figure as potentially sympathetic, and his empathy is generated expressly by his viewpoint as a Jew. Only by making the Palestinians "Jewish" does the narrator achieve some sense of their plight. That is, one could argue that the Palestinians and their exile do not exist for the narrator in their own right, but only as their situation resembles an important experience in Jewish history. In the position of the "masters" now, the narrator attempts to rationalize his own participation in the displacement of the native Palestinians by recalling the Jewish refugees who will take their place: "They would plow fields, and sow, and reap, and do great things. Long live Hebrew Khizeh!"[43] But he remains unconvinced and his relationship to the land is fundamentally altered due to his encounter with "this filthy Khirbet Khizeh. This war. The whole business."[44] The story concludes with the ominous descent of God to "roam the valley, and see whether all was according to the cry that had reached him."[45] The image recalls the earlier cry of the village's accusatory emptiness, as well as God's attention to Hagar and Ishmael in the wilderness, and suggests that retribution for the soldiers' actions, and by inference the establishment of the state enabled thereby, is in store.[46]

The success of the *yishuv*, and later the state, depended on the suppression and erasure of Palestinian claims to the land. Part of this process included development of what Meron Benvenisti has called "the Hebrew map," a map of the Land of Israel that would "restore" to its natural features those names associated with its ancient patrimony. This process began as early as the 1920s, in conjunction with British colonial efforts to map Palestine and its other territories in the region, and was continued by the fledgling state with the blessing of its new prime minister, David Ben-Gurion. Thus in addition to land acquired through purchase and military conquest, this symbolic Judaization of the landscape was a statement of ownership, which involved replacing Arabic place names with approximate Hebrew alternatives: either translations from the Arabic or the invention of Hebrew names that sounded like the Arabic as well as pseudo-biblical names to suggest an ancient Jewish presence.[47]

The relative success of this Judaization of the map, and indeed of the entire landscape, may be gauged in Benvenisti's own comments regarding the "blindness" of early Zionist settlement. In a review of Edward Said's *Out of Place: A Memoir* (2000), Benvenisti notes that Said's childhood home was a mere five hundred meters from Benvenisti's own two-room apartment, but they may as well have grown up on two different planets. In other words, they grew up in the same *place*, but not in the same *space*:

> Rehavia, our Jewish neighborhood on Gaza Road, was completely separate from the Palestinian space. Only those who have experienced the dichotomous environments of Sarajevo, Beirut, or Belfast can truly comprehend the phenomenon of the "white patches" on the mental maps in the heads of the Jews and Arabs of Eretz Israel/Palestine. We were, of course, aware of the presence of the Arab neighborhoods, but they had no place in our perception of the homeland's landscape. They were just a formless, random collection of three-dimensional entities, totally isolated

from the Jewish landscape and viewed as if through an impenetrable glass wall. There, in that other landscape, were houses and people who had meaning for us only as the objects of our perceptions and political concerns, but not as subjects in their own right.[48]

One text more than any other has thematized the ways in which the Palestinian village has troubled and threatened an Israeli sense of place. In A. B. Yehoshua's *Facing the Forest* (1963), a perpetual doctoral student from Jerusalem takes a summer job as a firewatcher in an unnamed forest, hours away from the city, in an effort to choose a thesis topic. Aside from the steady stream of summertime hikers, his only companions are an Arab caretaker and his young daughter: "The Arab turns out to be old and mute. His tongue was cut out during the war. By one of them or one of us. Does it matter? Who knows what the last words were that stuck in his throat?"[49] The Arab's connection to the place runs deep: he is a native of the village upon which the forest was built. The interaction between firewatcher and this Zionist landscape par excellence—a JNF forest—makes for a compelling meditation on the ever-encroaching effects of memory and history. In his scholastic, almost monkish, immersion in the suitcase of historical texts he has brought with him, the firewatcher may himself be a textbook example of how Israeli culture confuses the Place with the Story about the Place.[50] Yet his devotion, however tentative it may be, is not to those ancient Hebrew sources. His ability to "read the landscape" as a text clearly pointing to biblical and Zionist antecedents is complicated by the potential authority of competing textual traditions, including the extensive written discourse of the Crusades, and the troubling wordless discourse of the Palestinian village, represented by the tongueless Arab. Significantly, in Yehoshua's text, the Arab is granted neither name nor voice, but his story is subsumed to the story's larger concerns and must be told, ultimately, by others, by the Israeli Jewish protagonist. In the story's violent conclusion, the pair collude in the arson of the forest, thus exposing "out of the smoke and haze, the ruined village." "Facing" the forest, a Zionist icon of settling the land, means facing the true past of the land. The protagonist, significantly, is described as having acquired a memory at the story's conclusion, and this memory perhaps brings him one step closer to being native; but it is the Arab who has paid the true price, losing first his family and village, then his own freedom, as he is arrested and presumably imprisoned at the story's end.

Yehoshua's story marks a significant moment in the (re)emergence of the Palestinian village within Israeli consciousness. Yet as some critics have pointed out, most notably and elegantly Anton Shammas,[51] the Palestinian figure is, literally, voiceless, unable to speak, and serves largely as a foil for the Jewish protagonist's struggle with memory and nativeness.

The connection between the Palestinian Arab and the space of the natural landscape is complex, embodying as it does a conflicted attitude toward the Israeli *makom* and nativeness. First, as we observed beginning with Shlonsky's *Facing the Wilderness*, the Arab is associated with the wildness of nature, and this is both admirable and objectionable: admirable because they are "rooted" and "close to the land"; objectionable because they are "primitive." Second, many ruins associated with the Palestinian landscape—be they villages, cemeteries, or religious or other communal structures—have been "re-naturalized," that is—turned into "open space" or natural parks.[52] According to Noga Kadman, nearly half of all villages "emptied out" after 1948 are currently part of national parks, nature reserves, or other public or private trails and resort sites.[53] Kadman's work, as well as that of the civil rights organization Zochrot, committed to commemorating the *nakba* (Arabic for "catastrophe")[54] in Hebrew, has helped to raise awareness of the Palestinian presence before and since 1948. One might tentatively point to a growing presence of the awareness of Palestinian space in public and popular discourse, though its significance is difficult to measure. For example, a recent popular novel by Eshkol Nevo, *Homesick (Arba'a batim ve-gagua,* 2004), offered a more benign version of both Yizhar and Yehoshua's texts, a kind of normalization of this type of discourse. The novel depicts the relationships among neighbors in a neighborhood outside Jerusalem built upon the remains of the Palestinian village El-Castel. Each house contains its own form of *"ga'agua"*—in Hebrew both longing and nostalgia: for a son killed in Lebanon, for a better marriage or job, a more successful romance, and so on. Meanwhile, among the group of Arabs working at a nearby construction site, Siddiq observes the house he was born in and plans to go back with the key and the deed to recover an object his mother had left behind when they were expelled in 1948. The novel absorbs the Palestinian narrative into its own, effectively neutralizing it, making the house the remote object of nostalgia comparable to other longings, and defusing the Palestinian right of return.

Recent anthropological work has also offered a corrective to this erasure of both space and memory.[55] For example, Susan Slyomovics's study of Ein Houd/Ein Hod documents how the expelled inhabitants of the Arab village Ein Houd have observed the growth of the Jewish artist colony upon their land, from their new home at a neighboring site. Her work provides an extensive reading of Palestinian memorial practices, including memorial books, photographs, maps, and both written and oral narratives. The process of remembering Ein Houd is juxtaposed with the memory work of Ein Hod's Jewish population, many of them refugees from Eastern Europe, especially the artist Marcel Janco and the Dada Museum that bears his name. In focusing on a single space that has become a shared "object of memory," Slyomovics forces us to consider how space is produced—physically, textually, and imaginatively—and how the same space may be experienced differently by different groups: "Indeed, if the village of Ein Houd/Ein Hod is one place where Arab and Jew meet across the divide that separates their respective historiographies, architecture, and narrative, then what is the meaning of—where is the location of—'house' and 'home'?"[56]

Zochrot organizes field trips to various sites throughout Israel and the territories, distributing informational booklets in Hebrew, English, and Arabic about Palestinian life in a particular location. The group also posts signs and informational placards documenting the location of destroyed villages, expressly challenging the Zionist erasure of their presence in both space and memory and attempting to effectively undo or reverse the Judaization of the map referred to by Benvenisti above. The story of the villages of Imwas and Yalu, for example, which were destroyed in 1967 and whose ruins are hidden beneath the verdant flora of Canada Park on the road to Jerusalem, represents physical evidence of the land's history that is no less important than the site's Roman bathhouse and Hasmonean archaeological finds.[57]

Azmi Bashara, an influential Palestinian voice and former member of the Israeli Knesset, parses the oscillating relation between Israeli collective memory and the Palestinian past in terms of space and place.[58] That is, while Israeli culture has produced *spaces* that both represent and shape its national sense of self—natural sites such as hiking areas controlled by the Society for the Protection of Nature; memorial sites such as museums; even the entire city of Tel Aviv may be considered a space produced with a national set of ends in mind—some physical remainder of the Palestinian *place* [makom] in Bashara's view has endured. I do not believe that Bashara's essay is interested in untangling the complicated strands of "the Israeli *makom*." However, the power of its argument partially resides in this appropriation of the term *makom* to describe the native, untamed physical location that anchors Palestinian memories and their claims against the powerful production of Israeli space.

Attitudes toward the relation between Israeli and Palestinian space are also evident in architectural discourse and planning policies. A comment from Thomas Leitersdorf, who was involved in the planning of Maale Adumim, Israel's largest settlement, located to the east of Jerusalem in the Judean hills, offers a revealing example of an essentialist view of Jewish and Palestinian space:

> I look upon the morphology of the Arab villages with envy. The beauty of the Arab village lies in its accumulative and somewhat irrational

nature—development progresses slowly, with each generation adding on to the existing fabric built by its predecessor.

Our approach, on the other hand, determined by the government, produces an instant city. In three years we churned out a couple of thousand apartments—all built on one concept, one system of construction and infrastructure. For them it is different. In the beginning there was a donkey track. A man builds a home, a son is born, the son gets married and they need to add something, so they add it on to the area of the street. But so long as there is still room enough for the donkey, there is no room for the car and all that entails. But if you look at this process logically, by today's standards, you can't build a city this way. You can't pass up the necessary infrastructure or traffic and you can't provide a minimum level of services. But in terms of beauty they are way ahead of us! Architecture without architects—this is the Arab village, and this is its beauty. It is always better than when an architect comes in; the architect only spoils things because the architect has to work logically and they do not.[59]

Anyone who has traveled in Israel will recognize some of the distinctive qualities of Jewish and Arab architecture contained within this description, especially within those areas where newly built settlements sit like fortresses on hilltops overlooking the sprawling built space of the village.[60] However, these comments, made by someone intimately involved in the shaping of Israeli space, posit an irreducible difference between "our approach" (rational, systematic, the car) and "them" (irrational, primitive, the donkey, the government). The only advantage the Arabs seem to possess in Leitersdorf's scheme is beauty, and this observation is noted in a wistful tone, making it a quality that seems quaint and antiquated. This single salutary trait is possessed not by those who actually built the homes but only by the structures themselves: "architecture without architects." Certainly this kind of admiration for nature's organic forms is one of the fundamentals of modern architecture; but Leitersdorf's formulation effectively erases those human hands that built these homes, not to mention the people who live in them.

The Wall: Land in Contemporary Israeli Discourse

Two topoi dominate contemporary Israeli discourse on space: the separation wall, whose construction as a security measure began in 2002, and the road and tunnel network that surrounds Jerusalem and crisscrosses the territories. For some, the wall is an effective and necessary security measure; for others, it is no less than a contemporary version of the ghetto, a physical rendering of both Israel's political isolation in the region and the abject conditions of life for West Bank Palestinians. For those Palestinians whose daily lives and livelihoods have been disrupted or destroyed, it is a political and economic disaster.[61] Likewise, for some, the roads represent convenience and safety, especially for Jewish residents of settlements and towns in the West Bank; yet Palestinian residents have limited access to these roads, and their experience of their physical surroundings and movements are circumscribed by the system of military checkpoints through which they are daily obliged to pass, and which inhibit, rather than enhance, mobility. Two different experiences of the same space emerge: the one characterized by a sense of ease, mastery, and control, the other characterized by uncertainty, fear, and powerlessness. As sociologist Michael Feige notes, "While the Jewish settlers and Palestinians may . . . share the same space, they do not share the same 'place.'"[62]

One could view the separation wall as a logical extension of the blindness discussed above, an unwillingness to "see" the land's native presence. The road-and-tunnel network, too, may be understood in relation to those populations it effectively obscures, an extreme version of what Benvenisti refers to as "white spaces"—the inability, or lack of desire, to see Others as a subject in their own right, both embedded in space and constitutive of it.[63] Both the wall and the roads disrupt the flow of the landscape, not only in terms of nature per se but in a more total and systematic way, interrupting commerce, agriculture, and the daily social relations produced therein.

Although promoted as a security measure, many see the wall as the beginnings of an attempt to demarcate a more lasting political and physical border between Israel and those areas controlled by Palestinian Authority. Tellingly, some places closely associated with Judaism's biblical patrimony—located within areas known to some as Judea and Samaria—are *excluded* from these potential future political borders, while larger, "non-ideological" settlements (such as Maale Adumim) are not. While certainly emerging from a complex web of logistical and political conditions, it is tempting to read this still-tentative division as some indication of an evolving relation to—and a distancing from—the Story about the Place, of the production of an *Israeli makom*, which is tied to the material specifics of the here and now and not its biblical patrimony.

Perhaps more than any other artifact or institution, the separation barrier points to the porousness of Israel's political borders and the deeply unstable nature of the identity of the Jewish spatial experiment.[64] We have already considered the powerful vertigo produced in the wake of the periphery returned to its center, the collision of traditional Jewish place-making activities with national sovereignty and territory.[65] While the state of Israel certainly cannot construct a national *eruv*,[66] the separation

barrier seems a physical extension of the state's spatial practices, beginning with Zionism's institutional land acquisition in Palestine in the early
part of the twentieth century. More recently, decisions relating to land
use have preoccupied the legal system,[67] and the question of the state's
Jewish character has driven media accounts of landlords in urban areas
who refuse to rent property to non-Jewish tenants, both Palestinians as
well as members of the large migrant worker population residing in Tel
Aviv's southern neighborhoods.[68] These issues demonstrate the ongoing
complexity of spatial practices in Israel, as it continues to struggle with
those blessings and burdens associated with the land in Jewish tradition.

PART II
STATE OF THE QUESTION

This section moves beyond the Terms of Debate and imagines alternative spaces. In contrast to those roots conceived by chapters 2, 3, and 4, part 2 is organized around the idea of routes. The next three chapters, *"Bayit,"* "Diasporas," and "The City," present spatial models that make it possible to draw alternative maps. These maps coalesce wherever another kind of home can be built, a new neighborhood formed, or a different order of collective memory established, one not informed solely by an attachment to the lost center of the Land. Part 2 proceeds roughly in chronological fashion—from biblical, rabbinic, and premodern texts (largely in *"Bayit"*) through the early modern ("The City") and modern periods ("The City" and "Diasporas"). These chapters explore those extensive rituals and institutions developed by Jewish communities outside the consecrated boundaries of Jerusalem and the Land, practices shaped by cultural difference and the physical presence of otherness.

5   Bayit

*But over and beyond our memories, the house we were
born in is physically inscribed in us. . . . We are the
diagram of the functions of inhabiting that particular
house, and all the other houses are but variations on
a fundamental theme.*

—Gaston Bachelard, *The Poetics of Space*

What makes a house a home? And if there is such a thing as a "Jewish
home," how might we go about determining its defining attributes? How
is this space produced and maintained, both for those who live there and
call it home, as well as in relation to people outside? And what is the relation between these conceptions of home and the memory of it,[1] and
larger configurations such as community, neighborhood, and nation?
This chapter considers the various and diverse meanings of house and
home across a spectrum of texts, with special attention to the ways in
which space is consecrated as Jewish. The term "consecrated" is used to
indicate a particular category of Jewish homeownership, one produced in
relation to categories of religious practice and belief. Some of these
practices—such as the *mishkan* [tabernacle] or the *sukkah* [harvest festival
booth]—follow on those phenomena discussed in chapters 3 and 4,
examples of how rabbinic Judaism sought to replace or accommodate the
absence of the Temple and the condition of exile from the Land. Others—
such as the *eruv* or the synagogue—emerged in dialectical relation to
other spaces produced within the context of Jewish life in ethnically and
religiously mixed settings. Indeed, the spatial contours of home, in a physical, even architectural sense, often constitute a way of describing relations with other people and are thus one indication of how difference is
negotiated in the public sphere. So, for example, the experience of home
is often bound up with the house's physical attributes, its interior structures as well as its relation to the street and other surrounding homes.
This burden placed upon the language of home can be seen as Jewish culture began to form and flourish in the Babylonian and Persian diasporas;
as Jews and Jewish culture spread geographically, some notions of home

persisted, while others evolved or withered. The idea of home has signified in broader, often paradoxical ways, as Jewish communities found themselves "at home" in diverse and far-flung locations. At the end of this chapter we begin to consider ways of thinking about home and homeland that are less bound to collective, religious beliefs, and more grounded in the "articulate objects" of the contemporary Jewish home,[2] as a way of introducing the manifold sense of home discussed in the following chapters, "The City" and "Diasporas."

Starter Homes in the Desert: *Mishkan* and *Sukkah*

The Hebrew word *bayit* means both house and home, exemplifying a tension between place and space: the fraught and delicate relation between actual, material space—abodes, domiciles, and the physical existence of communities across time and geography—and the symbolic, often metaphorical domain of being "at home."[3] The relation between *bayit* as a physical structure and the more abstract notion of belonging or rootedness may itself be construed in different, even oppositional, ways. For example, we can consider home as a site that has been transformed into "one's own," in Tuan's terms—as space made into place. As Tuan notes, "A house is a relatively simply building. It is a place, however, for many reasons. It provides shelter; its hierarchy of spaces answers social needs; it is a field of care, a repository of memories and dreams."[4] "Home" indicates a unique and imbued place of belonging, as opposed to the empty, affectless space of the house, itself merely an architectural shell waiting to be filled with the signs of actual and/or metaphorical belonging. On the other hand, home may equally be understood as a more abstract, symbolic category, something malleable, adaptable, even portable, a feeling or a sensation that may be created, and either magnified or decreased, by the effects of human agency, as opposed to "house," which is the physical, material object, calling to mind the tangible specifics of kitchen, basement, roof.

Historically, within Judaism, the physical landscape most associated with some idea of a collective home has been the biblical topography of the ancient land of Israel and especially, as we have seen, Jerusalem and its Temple. The landscape of the desert, however, serves as an important counterpoint to the agrarian autonomy of Jerusalem and its surroundings. On the one hand, it may seem somewhat antithetical to include the desert in this chapter on home; on the other hand, the desert is precisely that site that reveals the power of Jewish place-making at its most creative, in which potentially exilic space becomes a kind of home. The desert was the crucible in which the Jews became a nation and received the Torah, even while it is also remembered as a terrain of tremendous strife. Indeed, scholars have pointed to a duality of sentiment in writing about the desert: on the one hand, the desert is the site of exile, possibly punishment; on the other hand, the desert is seen as a place of purification through suffering, of escape from the corruption of the city, and therefore worthy of being the space where the law is given.[5] The desert is the space of both "before" (entry into Canaan) and "after" (slavery in Egypt). Despite the hardships of slavery and the promise of the land—ostensibly that same land promised in the covenant—the hearts and minds of the people of Israel looked back in longing, a condition that led to their being "condemned" to wander for forty years until . . . they grew up. The desert generation is one of prolonged adolescence, during which the people must overcome their immature attachments to the past, as well as their fear of the land they approach, "one that devours its settlers" (Num. 13:32). These ambivalent reports about the land, a growing nostalgia for Egypt as well as what may have been less than ideal conditions in the desert, lead to what God calls the "incessant muttering of the Israelites against me" (Num. 14:35), which in turn sets up the divine punishment and promise: adult members of the desert generation will not be allowed to enter the land but will die in the desert. Indeed, as they approach the land, their rebelliousness and its relation to the wilderness sojourn is again recalled: "Know then that it is not for any virtue of yours that the Lord your God is giving you this good land to possess, for you are a stiff-necked people. Remember, never forget, how you provoked the Lord your God to anger in the wilderness: from the day that you left the land of Egypt, until you reached this place [the Jordan River], you have continued defiant toward the Lord" (Deut. 9:5–6). All this points to the desert as a psychologically rich site, one characterized by conflicting desires and the tension between promise and delivery, between present conditions and future possibilities.[6]

Though the desert experience resembles other biblical narratives, desert wandering seems more movement for movement's sake, rather than a sojourn with a fixed goal, or with the possibility of striking permanent roots. The desert is functional: it is the site of God's most open and extended meetings with Israel and her leaders, including the receiving of the law, and in this the desert's sacredness abides. The biblical text tells us that these meetings took place at Sinai and thereafter in the *mishkan*, an elaborate and extravagant mobile construction—part tent, part enclosed wooden structure—that God instructed the Israelites to build so that he could "dwell amidst them" (Exod. 25:8). The *mishkan* signified God's visible presence, hidden in a cloud, to the Israelites and it was the center of their cultic world. The structure itself, like the Temple, consisted of various compartments and layers of sacredness, the innermost Holy of Holies containing the tablets of the law. Commentators agree that the size and ornate quality (precious metals, expensive clothes) of the *mishkan* seem out of proportion and unlikely for a nomadic people newly freed from slavery.[7] Though Bezalel, the *mishkan*'s chief architect, goes down in Jewish history as both artisan and master-builder, the *mishkan*'s meaning lies primarily in its symbolic value as a place of encounter between God and the people (Exod. 29:42–45). According to midrashic sources, the *mishkan* makes God mobile, enabling him to be in more than one place.

In the desert, the *mishkan* is related to, and sometimes synonymous with, another structure called the *ohel* (tent) or *ohel mo'ed* (tent of meeting), which according to some texts is located outside the Israelites' encampment but also serves as a site for meeting with God.[8] Both terms appear together in poetic expressions (Is. 54:2 and Jer. 30:18), most famously in the blessing uttered by Bil'am in Numbers 24:5: "How goodly are thy tents, Jacob, and thy tabernacles, Israel," a line that became part of the daily liturgy. Bil'am is looking out over the tents of the Israelite encampment. Rabbinic interpretations suggest that "tents" refers to schools and "tabernacles" to synagogues. This interchangeability of spaces is an interesting example of the substitutive flexibility of the Jewish spatial imagination.

The memory of the desert as a productive and positive site is recalled in the holiday of Sukkot [Feast of the Booths], when meals are traditionally eaten in improvised booths or huts constructed following the commandment in Leviticus 23:43, and in accordance with talmudic instructions as to size and permitted materials. Work ceases during the eight-day holiday, and other rituals connected to the agricultural cycle are observed. The *sukkah*, whose roof is covered with branches but left relatively open to the sky, is traditionally seen as a reminder of the Israelites' years of wandering in the desert before entering the Land of Israel. Like the *mishkan*, the *sukkah* consecrates Jewish space within a community on the move. While both are ultimately impermanent places, their holiness is nonetheless inviolable. Indeed, inasmuch as the desert is considered a sacred site, "the sacredness . . . is both localized and temporary."[9] In rabbinic sources, however, the *sukkah* obtains more distinctly homelike qualities, and may be understood as another rabbinic attempt to carve out some sort of space of control within the mixed neighborhoods of Roman antiquity (see discussion below).[10] However, both the *mishkan* and the *sukkah* are prototypes of a kind of mobile sacredness that echo profoundly to this day in Jewish cultures.

The desert thus enters the Hebrew imagination as an ambivalent space. According to Ranen Omer-Sherman, who has elegantly argued that we recognize the desert's power as a site of creativity and regeneration, "The same Hebrew prophet who might curse the people with the 'barrenness' of the wilderness might also recognize it as a site of an exalted spiritual state, glancing back enviously toward the forty years of wandering as a period in which the people shared a special intimacy with the deity who accompanied them."[11] Omer-Sherman urges us to view the desert as not simply a hiatus, a "no-place" in between, but as productive, a place where the imagination can flourish and where the divine spirit has often seemed more proximate and promising, less remote and threatening. He describes how the desert has figured as a profoundly imaginative site for modern Hebrew writers such as Chaim Nachman Bialik, whose epic long poem "The Dead of the Desert" recasts the experience of the desert generation in terms of the national revival, and Shulamit Hareven, whose novels recast biblical narratives of nation-building in light of Israeli political norms. Discussing how the philosophical work of Edmond Jabès has treated the desert as a regenerative site, Omer-Sherman notes that the "universality of desert space serves as an urgent reminder to many Jewish writers that exile and alienation remain the essential human condition in spite of the ostensible transformations wrought by Zionism and other territorial nationalisms."[12] The desert endures as a both a spatial and temporal counterpoint to the Land, a reminder of other possible modalities of consecrating space and creating home.

House, Home, Woman, Nation

The term *bayit* has an enormous linguistic range in biblical texts, where it is often tied to the Temple in Jerusalem, most notably in the phrases *beyt hamikdash* (house of holiness) and *har habayit* (the Temple Mount, literally, "mountain of the house"). *Bayit* is also used to signify the nation: *beyt yisrael*—the house of Israel. This is especially common in the prophetic texts, as the people are castigated for their faithlessness or immoral ways. For example, in Ezekiel, the prophet is told to speak to the "House of Israel [who] will refuse to listen to you, for they refuse to listen to me, for the whole House of Israel are brazen of forehead and stubborn of heart" (Ezek. 3:7). The prophet is appointed as a "watchman for the House of Israel" [*shomer beyt yisrael*] (Ezek. 3:17), a term whose resonance and power would later be taken up by modern Hebrew writers, who sought to create a new canon of writing that would embody the same ethical authority of the prophetic texts. In Jeremiah 9:24, we learn the nations that are uncircumcised (Egypt, Judah, Edom, the Ammonites, Moab, and all the desert dwellers), but also how "all the House of Israel are uncircumcised of heart," meaning that they are ignorant of God's commandments: "Hear the word which the Lord has spoken to you, O house of Israel" (Jer. 10:1). This usage of an architectural term to describe the nation—a kind of "edification" of the people—is cognitively linked with the other central use of the term *bayit* in Jeremiah, where it refers to the destroyed Temple in Jerusalem. It is in exile, at a remove from the original sense of *makom* and from the theological and cultic center of Jerusalem and the Temple, that the nation is rendered in spatial terms, perhaps to suggest a coherence and stability at odds with an otherwise transient and unstable sense of their relation with God.

Rabbinic texts also attach the architectural sense of *bayit* to a variety of settings. Domestic and public spaces constituting the Jewish landscape of home in late antiquity are reflected in the vast and diverse set of texts of the Talmud. These include the study house, synagogue, court, and bathhouse [*beyt midrash, beyt kenesset, beyt din, beyt hamerchatz*], offering a glimpse into how rabbinic Judaism negotiated the political and cultural geography of late antiquity. Indeed, the texts of rabbinic culture offer an extended meditation on how to be "at home" in a post-*makom* world, where the rabbis perceived themselves and their followers as physically outside of "the land," and also living among "others" who did not share their religious beliefs and practices.

In a previous chapter I described the Talmud as a "site of memory," a textual repository of laws, customs, and stories relating to the ancient Land of Israel, and to the special tie among the people, God, and the land that is emblematized in *makom*. In fact, the Talmud is not a single unit but consists of texts written in a variety of periods and locations. The Mishnah, composed over a span of more than a hundred years and redacted by Judah Hanasi in 220 C.E., was produced in the Land of Israel, as was the *Talmud Yerushalmi* (Jerusalem Talmud), a set of commentaries on the Mishnah that was itself composed and compiled in the fourth and fifth centuries. The *Talmud Bavli* (Babylonian Talmud) dates from a century or so later and, though produced in Babylonia, comments on those mishnaic texts relating to the Land of Israel and also contains extensive portions of the Jerusalem Talmud. While this is not the place to fully explore the textual implications of these geographic shifts, suffice it to say that all these corpora are rooted in the specifics of the material environments in which they were produced, and one constitutive difference between them involves location.[13] Isaiah Gafni even identifies a form of what he calls "local patriotism" particular to the Jews represented in the Babylonian Talmud, which "project[s] the land of its provenance as something akin to a second Jewish homeland."[14] These and other spatial preoccupations found in rabbinic writing inform this chapter's main arguments.

One of the more intriguing spatial associations in rabbinic literature is the use of the term *bayit* in connection with women and women's bodies. For example, in the Babylonian Talmud we find the following enigmatic yet somehow decisive statement: "Rabbi Yossi said: During [all] my days I have never called my wife 'my wife' and my ox 'my ox.' Rather, [I have called] my wife 'my house' and my ox 'my field.'"[15] This statement seems to go beyond semantic equivalence to a more fundamental homologous relation or substitution between "my wife" and "my house," on the one hand, and "my ox" and "my field," on the other. Though this congruence of women with the domestic household is found in other ancient Mediterranean cultures, it is especially pervasive in rabbinic texts dealing with the female body and sexual relations. Besides the use of the term *bayit* to refer to a wife, rabbinic texts deploy elaborate architectural metaphors describing female sexual organs in terms of a house, with "interior" and "exterior" rooms—a "chamber," a "vestibule," and an "upper chamber"— each defined by different degrees of purity or impurity (e.g., proximity to menstrual blood).[16] Thus one midrashic commentary on the creation story says that God "constructed within her [the woman] more storage rooms than in the man, wide below and narrow on top so that she would be receiving embryos."[17] We examine further the relation between gender and space in the section below on the rabbinic neighborhood. Here we simply note that these associations square with the above-mentioned tendency of Western philosophical tradition to view space as static, something to be acted upon (in this case "occupied" or "filled") and therefore essentially "female."

Empire and the Spaces of Rabbinic Culture

Before thinking more concretely about space in rabbinic texts, we should consider the unique way in which these influential writings were created. Recent scholarship has attempted to understand and describe the special status of rabbinic authorship, especially in contradistinction to more modern conceptions of authorship.[18] Scholars now generally agree that the group we call "the rabbinic sages" were an elite group whose writings, as diverse and contradictory as they may be, largely represented a minority view within the communities of Jews living in Greco-Roman lands in late antiquity. Whether the rabbis yielded actual social or religious authority—that is, the degree to which the interpretive views set forth in rabbinic texts, which included instructions about how to live, were actually proscriptive, and not just an idealized vision—remains a matter of debate. According to Seth Schwartz, "Rabbinic legislation was utopian in that it was directed at a nation that no longer existed, and whose former members had no reason to recognize the laws' authority over them."[19] One could argue that the existence of a sustained series of arguments against certain activities—for example, idolatry—is evidence enough that the practices in question existed and were perhaps even widespread. Similarly, one could view the elaborate nature of descriptions for measuring and implementing the *eruv*, a boundary that allows for certain otherwise prohibited activities on the Sabbath (see below), as a recognition of the existence of gentile and Jewish "others" within one's immediate environment, populations whose daily rituals and customs differ with those described in rabbinic texts.

Indeed, one way of reformulating the question "Who were the rabbis?" is to ask—in the spirit of this volume—"*Where* were the rabbis?" The rabbis in Roman Palestine were urban; they lived in what we today might call neighborhoods. Though there are certainly agricultural references in their writings, they themselves were city-dwellers, and much of what they describe and proscribe, in terms of social behavior, occurred in an urban or semi-urban environment. This environment, as revealed in both archaeological sites as well as textual documentation from the period, included connected networks of houses and other institutions, such as courtyards, market squares, study houses, bathhouses, and, eventually, synagogues. Recent work in Jewish studies has begun to consider the relation between these two realms, that is, between text and artifact, specifically in the domain of space, those spaces described and inhabited by the rabbinic elite. If the rabbis in fact existed as a marginal group within the ethnically and religiously mixed urban centers of the Galilee, themselves part of the network of the Roman empire, then their writings offer an exemplary instance of how a language's spatial dimension—writing that describes one's space, one's home—may be read as an attempt to create a stable sense of self, in this case, a nominally Jewish self, in contrast to Greek, Roman, and Christian selves, and also in relation to other groups such as the Samaritans who were more intimately connected to the evolution of rabbinic Judaism.

Finally, though the corpus of texts referred to here was produced from the second through the seventh centuries of the common era, it could be that these rabbinic views only came to have wider, regulatory meaning or impact as late as the eighth or ninth century, with the rise of a Jewish center of learning in Baghdad, itself an economic and political center. Even from this brief account, we can see how the question of geography impacts our understanding of rabbinic culture. This recognition has been marked in Jewish studies by an emergence of the term "late antiquity," as opposed to "rabbinic," to describe the period in which this body of literature was produced. This usage of the term late antiquity reflects an awareness of the embeddedness of Jewish culture within the large domain of empire. According to Schwartz, the rabbis had a

loose periphery of supporters . . . who in most respects lived normative Greco-Roman lives and whose Jewishness was strictly compartmentalized (e.g., perhaps they refrained from eating pork and circumcised their sons but participated without hesitation in public festivals . . .). Most Jews seem to have lived mainly as pagan and looked primarily to the Roman state and city councils as their legal authority and cultural ideal, but even they may have retained some sense of being not quite fully Greek.[20]

Simply put, we may ask what was "Jewish" about Jewish life in Greco-Roman culture. On the one hand, Jews shared their status as a minority with other cultural and ethnic groups; on the other hand, they maintained some sense of difference, some sense of historic past, nostalgic or otherwise, that enabled them to regroup in collective terms at some point around 350 C.E. in the northern Galilee, in cities such as Tiberias and Sephoris.[21] In considering what might constitute Jewishness in this period (beyond a legal difference vis-à-vis the institutions of citizenship and empire), some scholarship has sought to locate various genres of Jewish writing—halakhic (legal) or midrashic, for example—in relation to contemporaneous Greek and Latin discourse. All this suggests rabbinic culture was produced by an educated elite, itself a minority within a minority group.

Finally, though we have until this point largely referred to Jewish life in late antiquity in terms of its textual "remains," there exists a tension between this literary, discursive evidence, and the physical, archaeological remains of the same lengthy historical period. Modern understandings of rabbinic culture have indeed been shaped by both text and artifact and by the perceived gap between these two enormous bodies of knowledge. Furthermore, both text and artifact come to us in relative degrees of coherence from a long time ago, and each and every case must be "read" within their historical context and, increasingly, in relation to one another.

The Rabbinic Neighborhood

Reading rabbinic Judaism as a culture produced by Jews living under a Roman regime has opened up the idea of Jews as "colonized" subjects, making use of the devices and habits of a colonized minority culture. To what degree may we think of the rabbis as a colonial elite, navigating dueling allegiances to different claims of identity; what kinds of discursive strategies can we locate within talmudic texts that might reflect this sense of "minorness"? Though we may accept the potential limits of such a model, reading as it does more modern ideas of nation back into the differently calibrated arena of empire, viewing the Jews' "peculiar sort of 'nationalist project'" through the metaphorical and actual lens of space has proved especially fruitful. According to Cynthia Baker, "As the large-scale economic shifts and Roman urbanization project in the Galilee were reordering the life of village, town, and city, the emerging rabbinic elite was undertaking its own attempts to rebuild, reconceive, and reorder the 'house of Israel.'"[22] Baker finds in the depiction of women in rabbinic texts a particularly acute indicator of these two impulses—a "nostalgic vision of the house of Israel as a self-sufficient household with themselves (the rabbis) at its head" and a "recognition that . . . this house stood, and would always stand, shoulder to shoulder and courtyard to courtyard with the house of many 'others.'"[23] Space is a way of negotiating religious, ethnic, and cultural diversity, as well as shoring up a potentially vulnerable status, especially in relation to a more politically autonomous past.

While we should not look to the rabbis as architects or builders in any traditional sense, there is much to be learned from considering the built environs of Roman Palestine—the urban and semi-urban settings in which the early rabbis lived and wrote—and how typical details of this environment—houses, alleyways, markets, and courtyards—appear in rabbinic texts. So, for example, archaeological remains have revealed that houses were in fact structures that shared walls, courtyards, and alleys with other "houses." Within these interwoven settings, a wide range of public and private activities occurred; so, for example, the central square, or cardo, was more often a street than a proper square, and conceivably one could be at home and in the market almost at the same time. Even more important are places such as the courtyard and the alleyway, those sites of "overlap and indeterminacy,"[24] where Jews come into potential contact with non-Jewish neighbors. Furthermore, the doors and windows were set asymmetrically, thus thwarting direct sight lines and enabling a relative degree of privacy. Clearly, Baker says, these were houses in which different kinds of people interacted—Jews and non-Jews, men and women—and it is impossible to discern or abstract any strong principle of segregation or exclusion. Finally, Baker insists, the rabbinic house or *bayit* should never be understood as "merely a space nor. . . . an inanimate thing";[25] rather, the house, in its physical guise, is always fluid and defined in terms of the many functions it may fulfill—part private domicile, part public space. Baker's work reads text and artifact together to critique historically received notions of women as essentially tied to the home, and shows how they are written into a variety of semi-public and public sites. The study also expressly bucks the idea of the talmudic sage as "sequestered" in the study house and seeks to demonstrate how both men and women are part of public networks of commerce and exchange.

The *eruv* ["mixture"] is another example of a spatial institution that attempts to carve out a Jewish space within the diverse, semi-urban environs of late antiquity, in this case mixing the permissible with the forbidden. Delineating the physical boundaries within which one may carry objects without violating the precepts of the Sabbath, the term *eruv* refers to the food or bread left in various locations in one's neighborhood: "The

Sages . . . ordained that if the inhabitants of all these homes [sharing a common courtyard] put food in one communal place before the Sabbath, they are considered one extended household and may carry within the courtyard."[26] Though rabbinic texts describe several types of *eruv*, the colloquial usage of the term refers mainly to the *eruv chatserot* (the above-described *eruv* of the courtyards, which functions on the Sabbath). The essential function of the *eruv*—the expansion of private space [*reshut ha-yachid*] into public space [*reshut harabim*]—allows for activities such as carrying or certain forms of transport, ordinarily forbidden for Jews on the Sabbath. *Eruv* refers both to the item of shared food that symbolically determines the expanded private domain as well as the perimeter marked therein. These behaviors are allowed due to the fact that some substantial area—such as the immediate neighborhood or even an entire town—is conceptually converted into an extension of one's own home. In rabbinic texts, the physical elements determining an *eruv* may include courtyards, alleys, and other kinds of openings.

What is the relationship between the *eruv* and the space in which it is constructed, indeed the space the *eruv* itself produces? On the one hand, even an area that is home to only pious Jews would still require an *eruv* if residents wished to carry items between private homes.[27] On the other hand, rabbinic texts describing the *eruv* also indicate expressly mixed neighborhoods, areas where Jews live near and with non-Jews, as well as other kinds of "non-rabbinic" Jews.[28] The concept of *eruv* has normatively been understood as facilitating the Sabbath in such a neighborhood. That is, the *eruv*'s spatial dimension has been subordinated to the temporality of the Sabbath. However, as we have seen, scholars have recently begun to reevaluate rabbinic culture in more critical terms. Like Baker, Charlotte Fonrobert reads the extensive mishnaic and talmudic depictions of the *eruv* in light of spatial theory, especially theorists of nationalism and the diaspora. While one may legitimately ask how postmodern theories of globalization may shed light on ancient society, Fonrobert's work seeks to transform our own view of how the rabbis understood space, and themselves as Jews in it:

The rabbinic theorizing of the eruv community, or the ritual system of the eruv, can be read as a powerful way to think about the importance of neighborhood for conceiving community. This . . . has particular importance in a diaspora situation. . . . The eruv construct[s] a collective identity with respect to space, but it does so in the absence of having control or any form of sovereignty over that space. On the contrary, it maps a collectivity symbolically into space over which it does not claim control, political or otherwise.[29]

Thus, while accepting that the *eruv*'s primary function is to enable the Sabbath, Fonrobert insists that it also inevitably points to larger questions that "structure the relationship between insiders and outsiders" and "operates as a boundary-making device" and ultimately as "a mechanism of exclusion and separatism or of integration."[30] While the Sabbath may be the driving force behind the institution of the *eruv*, the amount of energy expended in describing it suggests that something else is also going on, specifically the mapping of social space, of relations among different kinds of Jews, and between Jews and non-Jews. It turns out, then, that space is actually a pretty important category in rabbinic writing, perhaps equally important to time and history. We explore the continuing meaning and symbolic power of the *eruv* as a spatial device in a later chapter. Here we turn to another omnipresent component of the public sphere in which rabbinic literature was produced—sculptures and statues that were part of the Roman street.

Sculpture in the Public Realm

As indicated, the potential tension between text and artifact, between literary and material culture, has been at the heart of much recent scholarship in Jewish studies. Views that locate a "seamlessness between the archaeological evidence and rabbinic sources" have generally been debunked.[31] One particular discrepancy has generated an enormous amount of critical discussion, and even seems to feature self-referentially as a topic in rabbinic literature, an indication that the rabbinic authors may have even anticipated the need for reconciling the gap between textual proscription and the reality of their own lived experience. I refer to rabbinic injunctions against idolatry [*avodah zarah*, "worship of foreign gods"], deriving from the Second Commandment's prohibition on "graven images," a prohibition that would seem to be one way of maintaining Jewish identity within a mixed environment. How did the rabbis live in a culture whose public spaces were dominated by images of pagan gods, and what kind of accommodation was necessary? One well-known text that may help illuminate this issue appears during the mishnaic discussion of idolatry. When asked by Proklos ben Philosophos how he could bathe inside a bathhouse containing a statue of Aphrodite, Rabban Gamliel replies:

> I did not enter her territory; she entered mine. You do not say "the bathhouse is made as an ornament for Aphrodite," but "Aphrodite is made as an ornament for the bath-house." Furthermore . . . you would not enter your temple naked, having just ejaculated, and urinating before the goddess. And yet here she is set over the drain and everyone urinates before her.[32]

The presence of a sculptural icon, a statue of the goddess Aphrodite, is but one example of the numerous statues and icons that were a part of the urban street in Roman Palestine and a potential problem for the rabbinic observer. The public site in question here is the mixed, though male, space of the bathhouse (and in its maleness, it resembles the study house). One way of thinking about Rabban Gamliel's response is in terms of the spatial qualification he makes, distinctions that may be read as a demarcation, or an attempt to delineate, a sense of Jewish space. Just as the *eruv* effects a transformation of "a neighborhood . . . into a more or less intentional community by ritualizing it or inscribing it with a ritual structure,"[33] so the rabbinic response to Greco-Roman sculpture similarly scripts a Jewish space that in effect overlaps with that of their pagan environs. The space, indeed, is in the eye of the beholder—Roman for those who respect the statue, Jewish for those who urinate at her feet. Given the potential nexus of text and artifact, we may think of textual appropriation as akin to spatial appropriation—in this case, the interpretation of what appears to be a "Roman space" in Jewish terms. Both ritual and text represent attempts to sacralize, or somehow fashion, a "pure" Jewish space.[34]

Performance Space: *Beyt Kenesset*

The most ubiquitous spatial institution expressly devoted to worship and the maintaining of tradition is the *beyt kenesset* or synagogue. The notion of a *"mikdash me'at"* (Ezek. 11:16, "small sanctuary"), in which God was a "diminished presence," came to refer to those spaces used by Jews when they were scattered in faraway lands, clearly binding them to the Temple and its characteristic purity and sanctity. Functioning as one of the centers of Jewish life, the synagogue seems to have emerged during this period in which Judaism became "Judaism."[35] Though the synagogue qua synagogue receives relatively little mention in early rabbinic sources,[36] structures called "holy places" existed as early as the third century B.C.E., and certainly by the Second Temple period, and some of these places involved reading or recitation of Torah. What is the relation between these early holy places and those later archaeological remains from the third to the sixth century C.E. of structures in the Galilee and elsewhere in the Babylonian and Mediterranean diasporas? Some scholars see a continuum. For example, Stephen Fine's archaeologically driven work builds on that of earlier historians of religion who studied the location of the sacred in the ancient world, especially Jonathan Z. Smith's influential critique of normative ideas of the sacred.[37] Smith viewed sacredness as increasingly mobile or "locative" during the Hellenic period, and always embedded in a dynamic system of social change.[38] The emergence of "holy places" (what eventually became, in this view, synagogues) was part of this wider phenomenon. Fine suggests that we understand the appearance of Jewish "prayer places" as early as the Second Temple period within the context of other examples of decentralized cultic practice in Greco-Roman culture. For Jews, wishing to practice their ancestral prayers to God, the Bible became a kind of cult object, the scrolls endowing the place with holiness.[39] Other scholars view these same sites as functionally different spaces altogether, arguing that the synagogue emerged concurrently with similar Christian institutions, especially the church as a site of communal gathering, worship, and religious authority. In any case, early synagogues eventually came to "embody historical memories," a quality overtly expressed through their physical orientation toward Jerusalem, a "physical expression of attachment to Jerusalem and the Temple—despite the fact that each building's orientation and architectural style were almost exclusively borrowed, selected and adapted from the material culture of the surrounding world."[40] The relative sanctity of different elements of the synagogue's built structure is described in a mishnaic text:

> If the representatives of a town sell the town square, they must use the proceeds to purchase a synagogue; if they sell a synagogue, they must purchase an ark; if they sell an ark they must purchase wrappings for the Torah scrolls; if they sell wrappings, they must purchase Books of Scripture; if they sell Books of Scripture, they must purchase a Torah scroll.[41]

The progressively microscopic rendition of synagogue spaces recalls other rabbinic depictions of the Temple and Jerusalem, where their sanctity is also measured via a series of physical steps inward.

In thinking about its origins, the question arises of how the synagogue "learned from" ritual sites connected to other traditions, whether that of local cultic traditions or that of the Roman Empire and emergent Christian rituals. The Dura Europos synagogue in Syria contains numerous frescos depicting scenes from Jewish history. Like those found in other archaeological remains discovered in the city, such as Christian and Mithrian sites of worship, the wall paintings date from about 240 C.E. and contain narrative scenes documenting the worship of local deities and other religious rituals. In fact, the frescos at Dura may be considered in the same light as the strategies of accommodation represented by the *eruv* and in the talmudic discussion of Aphrodite in the bathhouse; that is, it would be naive to believe that rabbinic Jews didn't notice the elaborate visual displays of power, divine and otherwise, in the Roman street, as well as in private homes and semi-private sites of worship. Indeed, as we have seen in our discussion of space and rabbinic literature, these texts are rooted in the spatial environment in which they were produced. Furthermore, their authors seem to have understood how space could shape a specifically rabbinic or Jewish identity, in relation to other concurrent forms of cultural and religious affiliation. Indeed, art historian Jas Elsner has argued that the frescos may be viewed as a form of "cultural resistance," a physical "internal affirmation of Jewish identity"[42] for the benefit of Jewish worshippers within a wider environment characterized by parochial and imperial representations of divine power. According to Elsner,

> There is no doubt that the Synagogue frescoes actively promulgate Judaism by denigrating other religions. . . . In particular, the Jewish frescoes strike at the two key items in pagan religious practice . . . namely, the idolatrous worship of polytheistic deities in the form of statues and the specific act of sacrifice. . . . The direct cultural resistance of the Synagogue frescoes is against local pagan religion . . . but implicitly the Synagogue was asserting the monotheistic and exclusive supremacy of a God who had nothing to do with the Roman Empire.[43]

It is perhaps futile to search for the precise origins of the synagogue. Instead, we may view it as a space whose development unfolded in some relation to Jerusalem and the purity and rituals of the Temple, as well as the surrounding institutions of the Greco-Roman landscape.[44] What we can note, however, is that this space, whose centrality for Jewish religious and cultural practice is undeniable, began as a hybrid location, a site that evolved in relation to other similar kinds of spaces, and which bore the traces of those "other" spaces from the start. This consciousness of "other" terrains continues to characterize the production of Jewish space, especially perhaps for those iterations that seek to describe a sense of home or belonging. While the theological presence of a lost sacred center remained formative, diaspora Judaism continued to invent many rituals and customs to delineate both sacred Jewish space and the separateness of Jewish communities in relation to their neighbors.

How Much Home Does One Need?

Jean Amery's autobiographical essay "How Much Home Does a Person Need?" traces his journey as a survivor and refugee after World War II.[45] He poses the question from a very particular point of view and regarding a specific set of conditions. But the process of creating a home—both quantitatively assessed and qualitatively conjured—remains both highly idiosyncratic and often deeply communal. Broadly speaking, Jewish cultures have devised more and more ingenious ways of creating home, of building "domiciles within exile."[46] The Jewish home became that site where the "minority culture" of the Jews was most assiduously preserved. Rituals regarding the private home have been diversely performed across a wide spectrum of interpretation and observance. For example, the most mundane symbolic practice through which a house becomes a home, and specifically a Jewish home, is the fixing of the mezuzah to the outermost doorframe.[47] The practice—deriving from Deuteronomy 6:5–9, a passage recited within the *Shema* prayer—is included in a series of commands whose performance is required in a set of specific spatial locations: "Teach them [e.g., God's commandments] to your children and speak of them while you sit in your home, while you walk on the way, when you retire, and when you arise. . . . And write them on the doorposts of your house and upon your gates." The precepts are thus for private and public consumption, and specifically for both the innermost part of the home (the bedroom) and its outer perimeter (doorposts and gates). For religiously observant Jews, the mezuzah might serve as a visual reminder of God's commandments, containing as it does a small scroll with excerpts from Deuteronomy. For others, the mezuzah simply marks the house as a place where Jews live. Furthermore, the placement itself of a mezuzah on a front doorframe may bear no relation to what goes on inside. For religious Jews, a home might not be Jewish without certain behaviors prescribed by Jewish law, such as keeping kosher, or without those objects associated with religious ritual and learning. But what if these objects— kiddush cup, menorah, mezuzah—are treated as art objects and not used ritually? Surely they are still signs of Jewish affiliation, but they become part of a repertoire of material practices not necessarily connected to religious belief. These material practices might include the reading of certain books, informal conversation involving the transmission of certain kinds of values, or the preparation of particular foods in settings that are more culturally than religiously defined.

Cultural anthropologist Barbara Kirshenblatt-Gimblett uses the phrase "Kitchen Judaism" to describe these material practices of cooking and eating.[48] Though coined specifically in relation to the evolution of ideas about womanhood within the American Jewish community,[49] the term draws our attention to the potentially locational quality of many Jewish practices. These material practices constitute spaces that often stand in tension with rituals imagined in textual terms, especially those deriving from religious expression. This kind of "homemaking" has had far-reaching implications for the evolution of Jewish cultures, as the productive tension between "exile and domicile" continued to shape both physical forms of settlement and cultural expression.

We continue to explore the discourse of home in relation to the following two chapters—"Diasporas" and "The City." The frame of both chapters allows us to consider the pressures of modernity and the nation-state on the idea of home. The emergence of modern Jewish national consciousness envisioned space and homeland in a variety of ways. To be sure, some of these models of home depended upon the old centers of Jerusalem and Eden; but many did not. So, for example, the idea of *land-kentenish* (Yiddish for "knowing the land") in interwar Poland shaped the connection between natural spaces and identity that focused more on the idea of the people (the "folk"), and not religious texts, as key to Jewish survival.[50] Language continued to play a large role in these new versions of home, as a way of both rooting and consecrating. For example, the name Poland, according to legend, originates in the Hebrew phrase *po-lin* [here, we rest], a reference to a temporary sojourn that turned into a thousand-year stay. Cited in various sources, one version of the legend may be found in I. L. Peretz's ethnographic study *Impressions of Journey* (1891):

> The stillness of the summer night. At the edge of the sky, the nearby forest grows dark. On its trees our ancestors engraved the names of the Talmudic tractates they finished studying on the road. When they halted, not far away, the exilarch said, "Polin"—"Here stay" in Hebrew. That is how Poland got its name; except that the nations of the world don't know how to spell![51]

Poland's Hebrew name denotes the temporary, potentially mobile qualities we have noted as salutary markers of the Jewish spatial imagination, and shares, notably, the "Jewish eyes only" quality of the *eruv*—"The gentiles can't explain why!"[52] The making of place here also resembles the practice of the mezuzah in some respects: it has explanatory power but is not prescriptive—that is, it doesn't demand that the Jews living in Poland behave in a particular way, but it indicates a divine blessing for their living there. In more than one sense, then, the condition of being "at home in exile" continues to power the Jewish cultural imagination.

6　　　Diasporas

In the words of the German Jewish philosopher Franz Rosenzweig, "To be a Jew means to be in *Golus*."[1] Exile has largely had negative connotations, indicating an express absence from a desired location. This sense of absence, of being in *galut* [Hebrew for exile, *golus* in Yiddish] and outside one's place—either by choice or through forced expulsion—has been at the core of Jewish theological beliefs and informed Jewish communal institutions: whether that exile was as physically proximate as Babylon—or the Galilee—or as distant as New York; whether actual return was realistically conceivable or a messianic fantasy.[2] And though numerous counter-narratives may also encourage a more skeptical view of this "modern dogma of the Jew as eternal stranger,"[3] the sheer amount and variety of cultural tropes devoted to this idea demand our attention.

As we have seen, however, and despite the overwhelmingly negative connotations inhering in the state of exile, be they political or theological, the condition of exile has historically been mediated by an attachment to local place. This intense relation to space is suggested in the related notion of "Diaspora," a loan word—from the Greek *dia* [through] and *spora* [to scatter or to sow], and usually indicates an involuntary dispersed condition. First found in the Septuagint, it gained currency among Jewish communities to describe their dispersal and scattering away from the mythic centers. We have seen how the power of this spatial model predicated on center and margins has informed Jewish culture and history from its inception. Indeed, the idea of diaspora has persisted in Jewish consciousness and informed Jewish cultures in a variety of settings, often beyond any relation to physical or logistical conditions. Yet exile and diaspora are not one and the same; neither are they necessarily coterminous (in time) or, for our purposes, contiguous (in space). Indeed, the fact of exile usually predates, even anticipates, the condition of diaspora; and while the idea of diaspora, as we see in the variety of primary and theoretical sources discussed in this chapter, often emerges from a displaced or uprooted situation, it also endures as a practice of putting down roots.

Many of Judaism's most important developments and historical moments have occurred in exile, beginning with God's command to Abraham to leave his homeland and journey toward a new one, and including the granting of the law at Sinai and the production of the Babylonian Talmud. As we have seen, the lesson of carrying the tabernacle through the desert seems to have foreshadowed the idea of a "portable homeland," that toolkit of cultural, social, and political talents that have enabled Jews not only to survive, but to thrive, in far-flung corners of the planet. Recent theorists such as Daniel Boyarin and Sidra Ezrahi have considered the benefits of diaspora expressly in relation to what they perceive as the dangers of political power and statehood. Furthermore, as we discuss below, the term diaspora has entered popular and scholarly discourse; an entire school or mode of critical inquiry called diaspora studies is now devoted to describing and assessing a global condition, in which populations and ethnic/national groups find themselves in and out of territory, producing evermore complex and transnational cultural forms. As against the firmly defined boundaries of self and other implied in the term exile, diaspora suggests a more tangled, hyphenated identity, attuned to the particulars of location and the possibility of an abundance of roots and affiliations.

Theorists of both *galut* and diaspora have been divided as to their relative merits and difficulties.[4] Yet even those who object to what one scholar has called the "myth of exile" admit to its power.[5] Many Hebrew texts bemoan the state of exile and all that was perceived to have precipitated it, including the "faithlessness" of Israel and conduct unbecoming of those who would possess the land. At the same time, we find the potential downside of exile given a psychological and material twist as early as the prophet Jeremiah. In a letter to the exiled community in Babylonia, the prophet conveys God's wishes: "Build houses and live in them, plant gardens and eat their fruit. . . . Multiply there, do not decrease. And seek the welfare of the city to which I have exiled you and pray to the Lord on its behalf, for in its prosperity you shall prosper. . . . When Babylon's seventy years are over, I will take note of you, and I will fulfill to you my promise . . . to bring you back to this place [*makom*]" (Jer. 29:4–7, 10). These passages characterize, I would suggest, one sort of religious Jewish predisposition toward diaspora until this very day: a nose-to-the-grindstone practicality vis-à-vis the material conditions of life in a new place, coupled with an underlying, ever-present belief that at some relatively distant date, a kind of reunion with the originary *makom* will take place.[6] As anthropologist James Clifford notes, the "empowering paradox of diaspora is that dwelling here assumes a solidarity and connection there."[7] Yet how might regard for Israel as the "true ideal home"—a "connection there"—be expressed? Is a daily liturgical statement of such devotion sufficient? Indeed, for those whose affiliation with Judaism is expressly secular in nature, even this theological devotion to Israel might remain beside the point. Finally, if diasporas have been constituted by multiple movements, as was often the case within Jewish history, how are these interim sites and locations incorporated into the narrative regarding an "original homeland"? One might consider, for example, the nostalgia for the Lower East Side on the part of upwardly mobile Jews in suburban New York,[8] a sense of longing for an old center coupled with the material presence of new roots. We continue our discussion of diaspora with these ideas of movement and multiple centers as found in travel narratives, and conclude this chapter by examining new forms of diasporism in the United States and in Israel.[9]

Traveling Jews

In this section I offer a counter-narrative to the well-known and largely negative stereotype of the "wandering Jew." This figure has long historical roots and is represented in many European cultural settings to reinforce the idea that Jews are "placeless" and, therefore, a menace to society. The figure of the wandering Jew challenged the very status of Jews as "modern" and their ability to become a part of modern national entities.[10] The antisemitism of these images is undeniable, as is their power for Jewish and non-Jewish writers alike. If we accept, provisionally, the idea of Jews as "rootless," we may also describe a more positive notion of Jewish spaces that are constituted through movement, through the existence of routes that also inscribe a relation to place. I am therefore interested less in the stigma of placelessness accorded to Jews (though its potency is undeniable) but in their productive attachment to multiple locations and their sensitivity to both mobility and the relations between ostensibly disparate places (e.g., periphery and center, east and west). If "space . . . allows movement" and "place is pause,"[11] these qualities effectively render Jews place-makers par excellence. Travel narratives are an ideal genre in which to encounter some evidence for these claims, as well as their relation to the way space marks larger questions of identity and belonging.

We have noted the ways in which the premodern Levant was characterized by the journeys of Jewish travelers, to and fro across the Mediterranean basin and beyond (see sections in "The Garden" and "Jerusalem"). Modern narratives have also capitalized on these figures of movement, depicting travel for travel's sake, as well as journeys that may well go from a specific "here" to a particular "there," but are ultimately characterized by the meaning of the sojourn itself. Travel in modern texts often frames themes of individual and collective identity, with its movement across different geographic settings and encounters with other kinds of people. Hebrew sea-travel narratives of the Haskalah, for example, some of which were translations of popular German stories, demonstrated the ability of Hebrew to describe nature in a detailed and realistic fashion, and "conveyed attitudes toward natural science, geography, and the non-Jewish world."[12] The sea voyages of the maskil Mendel Lefin (1749–1826) feature an encounter between a faraway "savage" population and their cultured traveling interlopers, in order to think about the Haskalah's "civilizing mission" vis-à-vis its own internally perceived "others," *Ostjuden*.[13] The hasidic narratives of R. Nachman offer another way of thinking about travel as an assertive act of subject-making: first, they straddle the distance between their oral origins (in Yiddish) and written transmission (in Hebrew). Second, they trace a journey whose goal is often the Land of Israel, but whose real meaning resides in the power of the spiritual journey undertaken. Both maskilic and hasidic texts thus share an essentially utilitarian notion of space—the former treat it as "nature," in which one becomes modern through an acknowledgment of geography; the latter view space as an arena for spiritual enlightenment and improvement.[14]

As I suggest above, the idea of travel asserts another form of ownership (nativeness) over space, even if that space is only an imagined geography with a tenuous relation to actual terrain. Even in narratives of relatively short, internal travels, the familiar tropes of home and exile are deployed. For example, in his memoir, the Yiddish writer I. L. Peretz recalls the distance between his hometown and the neighboring village where he studied as a child:

> Born and raised in Zamosc, I had to be exiled to Shebreshin three miles away, in order to see my city. Shebreshin was a wooden town. . . . In that squat town with its straw and shingled roofs I yearned for my city. Zamosc rose before my moist eyes in all its three-storied, metal-and-tile-roofed glory, a city that did not stretch lengthwise like a rotting fish, but was impelled upward to the sky by its ramparts.[15]

The description is notable for its attention to disparate physical qualities—the low, premodern horizon of straw and shingles as opposed to the modern verticality of metal and tile—as well as its casting of the smaller, more remote location as "exile" with the majesty of the beloved hometown recalled in the language of Jerusalem, whose worth for the speaker, his ability to "see" the city, is only recognized at a remove. Indeed, the qualities of home are best appreciated at a physical and psychological remove.

Within the modern Jewish imagination, the train appears as a paradigmatic mode of transport, a symbol of modernity, for better and for worse.[16] It is the space where Jews meet other Jews, from near and afar, as well as gentiles of all national and ethnic stripes; the train brings the city to the shtetl and shtetl dwellers back to the city, traversing the natural landscape and disrupting normative senses of both time and space. In

S. Y. Abramovitch's story "Shem and Japheth on the Train" (1890), the author's ubiquitous fictional persona, Mendele the Book Peddler, compares premodern modes of transportation, such as the horse and carriage, to the train:

> For a coach journey in former times was quite unlike today's journeys by train. Then a man was his own master and free to choose for himself. . . . But in the train there is no feeling of independence. One is like a prisoner. . . . Consider, moreover, that the passengers make up a little colony [kolonya ketana shel dalet amot], a corporate entity of their own. Time flows on for them, evening and morning, one day . . . a second day . . . a third. . . . But in contrast the railway train is like a whole city in motion, with its multitude and its uproar, its population split into classes and sects, who carry with them their hatred and envy, their bickerings and rivalries and petty deals. Such passengers may traverse the whole world without regard to the grandeur of nature, the beauty of the mountains and the plains, and all the handiwork of God.[17]

The distinctive qualities of travel by coach promote a sense of agency and independence and encourage both intimacy—the phrase *"dalet amot"* indicating the four walls of hearth and home—and an appreciation of the divinely inspired gifts of creation that constitute the natural landscape. The train, in contrast, resembles a city, described as a fractious, riotous locale, characterized by division, deception, and mercenary desire.[18]

Yiddishland

> And although I have never seen the Tiga area
> Or the river Bire—And I dreamed up this entire country
> From a thousand-mile distance—
> I listen. . . .
>
> —Kadya Molodowsky[19]

The "psychic geography"[20] described in Peretz's and Abramovitch's texts provides a Jewish map of Eastern Europe during a time of enormous change and upheaval. This terrain is memorably traversed in Sholem Aleichem's epistolary novel *Menakhem-Mendel* (1892). The series of letters between the eponymous protagonist and his wife, Sheyne-Sheyndl, who waits with diminishing patience at home in Kasrilevke, traces his largely fruitless attempts to earn a living in various mercantile schemes. Space figures in the novel as a backdrop to the convoluted plotlines, wherein Menakhem-Mendel becomes progressively more impoverished as his travels take him farther and farther from the cosmopolitan city of Odessa (where the letters begin) to the relative backwaters of Bessarabia. Place names also serve as a marker of the different kinds of *"papirlach"* (little papers), the various stocks and promissory notes that circulate as furiously as Menakhem-Mendel himself. In an early letter, part of a section called "Londons: The Odessa Exchange," he tries to explain their meaning to Sheyne-Sheyndl:

> Londons, you should know, are highly perishable. You buy and sell them on a pledge without seeing them. Every minute you have to check if they're up or down—that is, if the ruble has risen or fallen in Berlin. It all depends on Berlin, you see; it's Berlin that has the last word. The rates soar and tumble like crazy, the telegrams fly back and forth, the Jews run around as though at a country fair, and so do I.[21]

Written during a period in which Jews were largely confined to the Pale of Settlement and prohibited from living in the capital city of Kiev, one might read Menakhem-Mendel's futile relation to space and place, relayed both through his constant movement and in the fickle and ultimately worthless value of the "Londons" and "Berlins," as a kind of fictional emblem of those physical restraints placed on the Jewish population. This is not to reduce the novel to a biographical account, though some have located parallels between the financial fortunes of the main character and his author. The very genre of the epistolary novel also thematizes the kind of movement valorized in travel narratives. In creating a "kingdom" of Ashkenaz, these Yiddish texts capitalize on the strong connection between language and territory in Jewish culture, but buck against the tie between Hebrew and the memory of a singular center in the Land of Israel.

The appeal of Eastern Europe as a Jewish homeland is pronounced among Jewish nationalists at the turn of the twentieth century. Simon Dubnow's diaspora nationalism envisioned an autonomous alternative to both acculturation and the isolation of the "ghetto," calling for a vital, cosmopolitan Jewish life "among the nations" that borrowed freely from other national-cultural traditions while maintaining a distinctively spiritual essence.[22] The term *"doikeyt"* [hereness] expressed an attachment to the "here and now," as opposed to the possible future "there" of Zionism, and was used by Bundists, Yiddishists, and other diaspora nationalists to stress their native roots and objection to the idea that Jews need go elsewhere in search of territorial sovereignty.[23]

What is the relation between this sense of "hereness" and the idea of "Yiddishland," a virtual space conjured not so much by geography or turf, but by language and cultural practice? Jeffrey Shandler has explored its use across a wide variety of texts, arguing that "the term Yiddishland infers a highly contingent tenacity inherent in any spatial entity defined by language use."[24] It may become attached to "some geographically

Figure 3 Interwar street scene in Vilna—a kiosk selling newspapers of *"di yidishe velt"* (the Jewish world). From *Yiddishland*, ed. Gerard Silvain and Henri Minczeles (Berkeley, Calif.: Gingko Press, 1999).

specific locus," but it tends to persist by developing "an alternative vision that somehow thrives despite geography."[25] While this may be true, and although the "persistence of the idea of an indigenous place for Yiddish becomes much more provocative when juxtaposed against the actuality of a Hebrew-speaking Jewish polity,"[26] Yiddishland also shares important features with Jewish spatial practices that we have witnessed in this book. For example, rabbinic responses to the Greco-Roman environs that attempted to script a Jewish space within an ethnically mixed environment—in one instance through the device of the *eruv*, in another through a series of recorded interactions with sculpture in the public sphere—resemble the cultural practice of Yiddishland; both are "defined by geographical instability and contingency."[27] Indeed, we have observed that from the very origins of the idea of exile, Jewish culture has been deeply defined by such a "diasporic territoriality" (a phrase Shandler uses in relation to Yiddish).[28] An interest in theorizing diaspora cultural practices has been at the heart of academic inquiry in recent years, and it is toward these more recent developments that we now turn.

The New Diasporas

The establishment of the State of Israel, and with it the responsibilities and privileges of political sovereignty, have contributed to reevaluations of both exile and diaspora in the postwar period, evaluations which themselves reach back into Jewish history, offering revisions of these essential features of Jewish experience. Two important parallel trends may be observed: the diaspora does not disappear, as envisioned in Zionism's creed of the "negation of exile"; rather, it continues and even thrives as Israel's potential rival. And exile comes to preoccupy and haunt the experience of Jewish statehood.

Different factors have conditioned this reevaluation of exile and diaspora. For example, Jewish American thinkers may have had an affinity for Rosenzweig[29] and, thereby, an appreciation for the relative virtues of exile, a view that was not overtly political but simply an apt description of a constitutive feature of Jewish existence.[30] The long-lived nature and relative comfort of life for large segments of American Jewry, and their integration into the American mainstream across a wide spectrum of political, cultural, and social experience, surely underlies, in some sense, the relative openness to retheorizing diasporic existence. Recent scholarship has also revisited the interwar period to examine figures within the Zionist movement who promoted diasporist, nonstatist agendas;[31] the relevance of this recovery project today is undeniable and, to the degree that it emerges from the American academy, seems tied to the broader reevaluation of diaspora forms.

Unlike its relative specificity in the Jewish context, the term diaspora has come to describe an entire constellation of conditions related to displacement, global and local migration, exile and dislocation, and the accompanying economic, social, and cultural paradigms particular to these situations. The field of diaspora studies first emerged out of cultural studies in England, largely as an attempt to describe and analyze how traditional English society had been transformed by postwar migrations to Great Britain from its former colonies, especially India and the sub-Saharan continent. Scholars working in American studies on this side of the ocean have also productively engaged models of identity that privilege "hyphenated states," sensitive to the historical and ongoing relationships between American immigrant groups and their countries of origin. Diaspora studies as a whole is connected to postcolonial studies in its insistence on viewing cultural identity within a transnational frame, focusing on forms not embedded or tied to a narrow sense of nationhood or territory but instead that reach across geographic distances, describing relations produced by trade routes and other paths of global movement.

Some scholars have tried to extrapolate from the Jewish case as a model for diasporic cultures as a whole. William Safran has delineated those traits particular to the Jewish diaspora and has argued that all diasporic groups share these essential features: (1) "They, or their ancestors, have been dispersed from a specific original 'center' to two or more peripheral regions," (2) they "retain a collective memory, vision or myth about their original homeland," (3) they "feel partly alienated or insulated" from "their host society," (4) they "regard their homeland as their true ideal home," (5) they "maintain a collective commitment to the maintenance or restoration of their original homeland," (6) they wish to survive as a "distinct community" within their new country, drawing on this tie to the original homeland, and (7) their communal institutions reflect this strong bond to the ancestral homeland.[32]

Certainly we have seen many of these features operative in Judaism and across a wide swath of Jewish history. As a model, it seems to offer some flexibility for thinking about diasporic experience in a variety of geographic and national situations. However, we should ask what might be obscured by privileging this particular formulation and by accepting the Jewish model as paradigmatic. For example, collective memory is not a static, given set of understandings or agreements about the past, but in fact a dynamic response to the demands of the present, often "revisioning" elements of the past to suit the present-day needs of the group; Zionism's own revisioning of the biblical past is a classic example of this process. Furthermore, in an immigrant society such as the United States, especially in those urban centers where Jews gathered at the turn of the twentieth century, what exactly constitutes a "host society"?

If one mode for conceptualizing Jewish diaspora—and indeed a key assumption in many of the discussions in this book—has been a spatial model of center and margins, of absence and deferral, what is lost in the "ping-pong," the to-ing and fro-ing of this view? Certainly we have seen that for Jews of the Levant, the topography of Andalus retained an aura of home, even while in "exile" from it; for these Jews of the Mediterranean, Jerusalem was both theologically distant and geographically proximate. Diaspora, I would suggest, has been an essentially different experience for Ashkenazic and Sephardic Jewish communities; the differences between them were further exacerbated, by both the establishment of the State of Israel and the destruction of European Jewish life, perceptions of which echoed the "original" loss and displacement of Jerusalem and were cast in the familiar terms of *churban* [catastrophe]. As American Jews began to treat the "ruins" of Eastern Europe as a new-old kind of lost center,[33] the one-dimensional model of "here and there" lost its grip: the center could not hold. Indeed, in a powerful critique of emergent models of diapora in critical theory, James Clifford notes that we should be wary of making Jewish experience, or any model, into an "ideal type": "We should be able to recognize the strong entailment of Jewish history on the language of diaspora without making that history a definitive model."[34] Clifford continues: "Rather than locating essential features, we might focus on diaspora's borders, on what it defines itself against."[35] This attention to self-other relations may help illuminate precisely those kinds of complex spatial institutions and attitudes that have long characterized Judaism's attitudes toward space and spatial experience, with its interlocking networks of text, ritual, and travel.

And yet, as Barbara Kirshenblatt-Gimblett notes, the idea of the Jewish diaspora as an ideal type has historically had enormous influence, generating ideas, paradigms, and prototypes that have themselves shaped an entire field: "Diaspora, ghetto, stranger, and marginal man, as concepts in the social sciences, have been generalized from a reading of the Jewish predicament. . . . In the process, Jews have become the paradigmatic case for such key concepts as diaspora, whether by self-definition or within theories of diaspora more generally, and also a primary site for modeling social pathology. . . . This is not a site of privilege."[36] Kirshenblatt-Gimblett's important caveat reminds us of the particular force of Jewish diaspora, as an internally formative mode of Jewish experience, as well as a condition externally evident in those host cultures that have become home for Jewish communities. That is, we may remark upon the specific qualities and institutions of Jewish diaspora, deriving from the self-defined nature of Jewish life as a religious existence distinct from the majority religion, without treating it as a closed or finite model for Jewish history, or any other group's history, for that matter.

In fact, dislodging the Jewish diaspora from its theoretical pedestal as "the mother of all diasporas" may allow for a deeper engagement with the full spectrum of ways in which Jewish communities have experienced space and produced place. For example, Rebecca Kobrin's recent work on the Jews of Bialystok and their descendants in New York, Melbourne, and Tel Aviv spells out the variety of strategies—including newspapers and literary supplements, philanthropy and social networks—deployed by Jews to remember and maintain their ties with each other and with their *muter shtot* (mother city). According to Kobrin, Bialystokers viewed the United States not as "the promised land" but as an exile of sorts from their "nurturing, inspirational homeland."[37] Even while these immigrants began to build new lives abroad, the memory of their lost center infused their political commitments as well as their social and economic relationships, in ways similar to those in Jewish diasporas in other time periods (see the section on Andalus in chapter 2, "The Garden"). This kind of scholarship represents an attempt to think beyond Israel's dominance in the postwar period as a central mode of national Jewish survival (see discussion below).

Although the idea of diaspora has become a creative model for thinking about transnational identities, we should not confuse the utility of these theoretical models with the genuine and difficult predicament conditions of geographic displacement. As one of diaspora's most elegant theorists, Arjun Appadurai, has noted:

> More people than ever before seem to imagine routinely the possibility that they or their children will live and work in places other than where they were born; this is the wellspring of the increased rates of migration at every level of social, national and global life. . . . We may speak of diasporas of hope, diasporas of terror, diasporas of despair. . . . These diasporas bring the force of the imagination, as both memory and desire, into the lives of many ordinary people, into mythographies different from the disciplines of myth and ritual of the classic sort.[38]

The very language of diaspora has changed, and along with it the ways in which collective identities are shaped and give shape to the world. Especially as ties between nation and territory have weakened, and in some instances completely collapsed, a new vocabulary is needed to describe these conditions.

Two powerful arguments about Jews and diasporism appeared in the early 1990s; one was an ironic, at times outrageous, fictional rendering by one of the world's foremost novelists; the other was an influential intellectual model presented by two established scholars who also happened to be brothers. In Philip Roth's *Operation Shylock*, the author's doppelgänger, believing the State of Israel in imminent danger of annihilation by the Arab states, "invents Diasporism, a program that seeks to resettle Israeli Jews of European origin back in those countries where they or their families were residents before the outbreak of the Second World War and thereby avert 'a second Holocaust.'"[39] Israel's own political arrogance, cultural narrowness, and military prowess have turned it into a latter-day Goliath, whose power and blindness stand in stark contrast to the deeds and historical achievements of diaspora Jews; these virtues are expressly contrasted with the flaws of Israeli Jews by the novel's George Ziad, a Palestinian academic who is an old friend of Roth's: "These are the Jews who are superior to the Jews in the Diaspora? Superior to people who know in their bones the meaning of give-and-take? Who live with success, like tolerant human beings, in the great world of crosscurrents and human differences? Here they are authentic, here, locked up in their Jewish ghetto and armed to the teeth? And you there, you are unauthentic, living freely in contact with all mankind?"[40] One would be hard-pressed to find a more succinct rendering of the potential downside of political statehood and the stereotypical traits associated with both Israeli and (in this case) American Jews.[41] And while recognizing the purely fictional element of Roth's fantasy, one could also read the novel as an important intervention in Jewish history, an entertaining and intellectually dazzling exercise that takes on the foundational parameters of Jewish space and Jewish places.

Another theoretical rendering of diaspora has been promoted in the scholarship of Daniel Boyarin, a rabbinic scholar, and Jonathan Boyarin, an anthropologist. In their article "Diaspora: Generation and the Ground of Jewish Identity," working from a sustained critique of both universalism (derived from the Pauline Christian doctrine of "we are all one in Christ's body") and "autochthonous nationalism" (the claim for an irreducible link between an individual and place where they claim their roots), diasporism emerges as both a way of revisioning the past and a response to the present:

> We propose Diaspora as a theoretical and historical model to replace national self-determination. . . . To be sure, this would be an idealized Diaspora generalized from those situations in Jewish history when Jews were both relatively free from persecution and yet constituted by strong identity—those situations, moreover, within which Promethean Jewish creativity was not antithetical, indeed was synergistic with a general cultural activity.[42]

The virtues of diaspora—which the Boyarins suggest rather than monotheism "may be the most important contribution that Judaism has to make to the world"[43]—are inherent in the mixing and borrowing between and among Jews and their host communities, and the productive achievements recorded in Jewish cultures as a result. The authors call for no less than a revision of Jewish history, a retooling of our sense of the relative importance of the Land in Jewish experience: "An alternative story of Israel, closer, it would seem, to the readings of the Judaism lived for two thousand years, begins with a people forever unconnected with a particular land, a people that calls into question the idea that a people must have a land in order to be a people."[44] Though the essay does not expressly state as such, its arguments may suggest that Jews are always a "displaced" people, and therefore conscious of the need to turn space into place.

What is the cultural or political moment linking Roth's *Operation Shylock* with this influential article by Daniel and Jonathan Boyarin, both of which appeared in 1993?[45] They are both, I would argue, post-Intifada texts, and deeply engaged—either expressly, in the case of Roth, or more implicitly, for the Boyarins—with the kind of place Israel had become, specifically regarding its use of power and military force, especially since the first Intifada. The process had begun in Israel over a decade earlier, in the 1970s, a period that witnessed the beginning of the dissolution of whatever societal consensus had existed in the first few decades of statehood. This phenomenon has been understood along ethnic and economic lines, and especially includes the rise of mizrachi consciousness and their increasing presence in the political arena. The 1982 war in Lebanon produced the first sustained instance of large-scale protest within Israel to the government's wartime policy, and it may be linked in a broad sense to these other instances of civic contention and debate, cracks in what was previously understood as a homogenous Israeli politic. The first Intifada, beginning in December 1987, further radicalized "the situation" and everyone connected to it: the Palestinians in the territories, Israeli Arabs and Israeli Jews, and, arguably, diaspora Jews as well.

Within Israel, too, we find a reevaluation of *galut* and diasporic experience, especially in the wake of the above-described changes in Israeli society. In an influential pair of articles from the mid-1990s, historian Amnon Raz-Krakotzkin systematically links the negation of exile and its foundational status within Israeli culture and society to the problem of Israeli-Jewish identity and to the disavowal of Palestinian identity. According to Raz-Krakotzkin, Zionism's ideological negation of *galut*, and the idea that Jews "belong" in only one place, set the ground for Israel's blindness to the Palestinian presence and the negation of their political rights, as well as the "forced" negation of more traditional elements of the mizrachi past. The idea of exile, with its "coherent moral stance,"[46] constitutes a counternarrative, a powerful and potentially far-reaching model, with profound consequences for the future of both the State of Israel and Jewish diasporas. Indeed, perhaps we are witnessing, as one pair of scholars puts it, the "end of the Jewish diaspora."[47] Certainly we need new ways to think about the connection between space and identity, and especially the relation between global migrations of population, Jews included, and the new mediascapes that seem to make the world smaller, transmitting images and information across previously impassable distances.[48]

Photographs, Diaspora, Memory

Tony Kushner's epic drama *Angels in America* opens with an elderly rabbi eulogizing one of the Jewish character's grandmothers in light of her life in America. The grandmother, he says, was

> a whole kind of person, the ones who crossed the ocean, who brought with us to America the villages of Russia and Lithuania—and how we struggled, and how we fought, for the family, for the Jewish home, so that you would not grow up *here* [emphasis in original] in this strange place, in the melting pot where nothing melted. Descendants of this immigrant woman, you do not grow up in America, you and your children and their children with goyische names. You do not live in America. No such place exists. Your clay is the clay of some Litvak shtetl, your air the air of the steppes—because she carried the old world on her back across the ocean, in a boat, and she put it down on Grand Concourse Avenue, or in Flatbush, and she worked that earth into your bones, and you pass it to your children, this ancient, ancient culture and home. . . . You can never make that crossing that she made, for such Great Voyages in this world do not any more exist. But every day of your lives the miles that voyage between that place and this one you cross. Every day. You understand me? In you that journey is.
>
> So . . .
>
> She was the last of the Mohicans, this one was. Pretty soon . . . all the old will be dead.[49]

The passage offers a moving meditation on the evolving power of space in Jewish experience. The syntax is pure Yiddish, which provides both grammatical and ontological template for how language makes a home in a strange place. The trope of exile and the impossibility of homecoming is strong here, to be sure, but the dreamed for, always-out-of-reach homeland is Eastern Europe; the trauma of the journey—through the desert, as it were, the "Middle Passage" of American Jews—exists for

Figure 4 The B'nai Israel Synagogue, Alibag, Maharashtra, India, 1984. *From Diaspora: Homelands in Exile,* © Frédéric Brenner, courtesy Howard Greenberg Gallery, New York City.

the grandson as well: though he himself remains untouched by the physical and psychological difficulties of life in the "old world," the very air he breathes, and the ground he walks, is somehow not of this place—utopian, but from elsewhere—equal parts Lithuanian shtetl and the earth of that "ancient, ancient culture." The promise of America was great; the reality—arguably—even greater.

There are no better emblems of this abiding attachment to the physical trappings and emotional predisposition of diaspora than the photographs of Frédéric Brenner, brought together in his collection *Diaspora: Homelands in Exile* (2003). This remarkable series of images, produced from 1978 to 2002 in settings across North and South America, Europe, the former Soviet Union, India, Asia, Africa, and the Middle East, offers a provocative meditation on the conditions of diaspora and the utter impossibility of trying to assess any common attributes to such a diverse set of subjects, separated by class, ethnicity, and nationality.

Stanley Cavell, in commenting on Brenner's work, suggests the photograph essentially "lives in dispersion, that it invites reproduction." In other words, as artifacts, photographs inevitably defer to the original scene they purport to represent, and these representations are themselves necessarily incomplete, "partial."[50] Cavell's enigmatic connection between the photograph and diaspora will frame our concluding discussion of one of the more important Israeli novels to appear in recent years, Ronit Matalon's *The One Facing Us* (1995). Matalon, a well-known writer and critic whose poetically rendered novels have achieved both critical and popular success, has addressed compelling issues at the core of contemporary Israeli culture, including the meaning of mizrachi culture in Israel and the place of Israel in the Levant, the Palestinian question, the relation between the public sphere of politics and the domestic domain of the home, and the power of language and memory to shape the lives of individuals, families, and national groups. *The One Facing Us* focuses on the experiences of an Egyptian-Jewish family, tracing in nonlinear fashion the route of their lives from the interwar Levant, through their more contemporary sojourns in Israel, Cameroon, France, and the United States. The novel offers us a particular view of one kind of diaspora, a wideranging network of social, economic, and ideological ties that takes as its lost center—if there is one—the Jewish quarter in Cairo.[51] The novel's probing of the limits of this Jewish diaspora also includes excerpts from the nonfictional writing of Jacqueline Kahanoff, a real-life figure whose work has in recent years become an important topos for scholars working on the intersection between memory, language, and geography. Matalon's novel uses a series of photographs, especially family portraits, scattered throughout the narrative as a contrapuntal refrain, echoing in often dissonant fashion the search for roots that forms the novel's narrative core.[52] The rationale for this dependence on photographs, despite their ability to belie or betray, is stated at the novel's very beginning: "A photograph offers evidence of what is remembered, but it also intimates what might have been."[53] This ambidextrous quality of photographs, their capacity to offer a form of hyper-realism that is also, potentially, a falsehood, lies beneath their appeal as a narrative device and provides a compelling metaphor for the various paths not chosen by the novel's perpetually wandering extended family.

The novel's protagonist, Esther, the seventeen-year-old daughter of a large mizrachi family that emigrated from Cairo in the 1950s to Israel, Europe, West Africa, and the United States, embarks upon a visit to her uncle in Cameroon. Their meeting serves as a point of departure for a personal journey, undertaken in her diary, and through her own and vicarious memories of her parents, aunt, uncles, and grandparents. Above all, it is a project circumscribed by old photographs, loosely held and bartered among female members of the family. The narrative voice invites the reader to encounter the photos up close and personal, as if the author were standing over your shoulder as you viewed her family album. The photographs punctuate and interrupt the text, as well as stimulate the narrative's associative turns; they lend an air of completeness but are also intense markers of absence. This duality—the essential paradox of photography—is further compounded by the demands of fiction. The photographs seem to contribute to the novel's realism, but they are also surreal reminders of what language cannot achieve. Of the thirty photographs referenced in the novel, half are described as "missing."[54]

The novel's preeminent interpreter of photographs is Nona Fortuna, Esther's blind grandmother. "I am raised on these photographs," says Esther. "My grandmother, Nona Fortuna, raises me. She cannot see a thing."[55] Despite her blindness, Nona Fortuna deftly analyzes the photographs and the family dynamics they represent. Her uncanny ability represents a literalization of the practice of photography, as stated by Roland Barthes, whose seminal essay "Camera Lucida" provides an important intertext for the novel: "In order to see a photograph well, it is best to look away or close your eyes."[56] At stake here is the potentially reductive nature of photographs and the narrow sense of character that may result from reading them too literally. Indeed, it is Esther's father, the novel's most enigmatic and frustrating figure, who senses the degree to which a photograph can either limit the subject and extend the opportunity for multiple affiliations: "He hated the specifics of place and portrait. In Israel he was constrained to only one place and one portrait. But not in Cairo. In Cairo there were a thousand possible places."[57]

This tension between what the photograph says and what it doesn't, what is revealed and what is hidden beyond its frames, is linked to the trauma of migration; however, this diaspora of necessity also has its virtues, as its actors develop what have been called, in a very different set of historical circumstances, the "diaspora arts of resistance."[58] A model of identity that is fragmented, partial, and subject to the eye of the beholder seems to have special meaning for what the novel, citing Jacqueline Kahanoff, calls "the Levantine generation." Writing of their schooling in Egypt, Kahanoff comments: "We did not know how it happened that we Jewish, Greek, Moslem, and Armenian children were sitting together to learn about the French revolution. . . . What were we supposed to be when we grew up if we could be neither Europeans nor natives, nor even pious Jews, Moslems, or Christians, as our grandparents had been?"[59] This particular sense of loss evokes that captured in Franz Kafka's memorable image symbolizing another generation of modern Jews, feeling similarly bereft of their parents' traditional roots and equally unwelcome within the larger, secular world of modernity:

> Most young Jews who began to write German wanted to leave Jewishness behind them, and their fathers approved of this. . . . But with their posterior legs they were still glued to their father's Jewishness and

with their waving anterior legs they found no new ground. The ensuing despair became their inspiration.[60]

Indeed, the question of language is also at the center of this novel's claims regarding diasporas and homelands. Raised in a series of neighborhoods in pre- and postwar Cairo, the extended family speaks a mix of languages at home, in school, and in the street: Arabic, Ladino, French, Greek, English, Hebrew. But "none of the languages we spoke could express our thoughts, because none was our own."[61] This sense of multiple roots with no abiding affinity for a single homeland also characterizes Esther's own narrative of self, and enriches her sense of possible affiliations, a plethora of opportunity that seems to stand in direct contradiction to her American cousin Zuza, who appears late in the novel, conducting her own search for roots. Zuza's quest is presented as a pale and superficial alternative, driven by a popular nostalgia—part *Fiddler on the Roof,* part Kunta Kinte—and an almost orientalized sense of her family's Levantine past. She covets family recipes but fails to truly gauge the depths of the loss experience by her mother's Levantine generation. Most crucially, she misses the essential "what-if-ness" of the photograph, the endless possibilities suggested by the routes of diaspora, and only wants to know "just what there was—not what could have been, not what should have been, but just what was."[62] Her naive reliance on "the facts" misses the inherent instability of identity—its ability to be many things at once, and to hold ostensibly opposite qualities together. The novel's rendering of cosmopolitan Cairo provides a realistic setting for this dynamism of diasporic identity, and it is to the historical evolution of urban space in relation to Jewish space that we turn in the following chapter.

7   The City

*She had gone with Saul to buy them in Al-Shurja
market. Mounds upon mounds of suitcases. The Jews
are going, the Jews are going. It was a grand time for
tinsmiths and suitcase dealers. Liquidation sale. The
seasons of sales to the Jews were over. Earthenware
platters for Passover, palm fronds and pomegranates
for Sukkot, noisemakers and masks for Purim. There
would be no more Jews and their holidays would not
longer be felt in the market. The tin suitcases close the
season. To each one a suitcase, to each one the space
they leave behind.*

—Shimon Ballas, "Iya"

As seen through the eyes of Iya, a Muslim housekeeper, the departure of
Jews from Baghdad in the 1950s leaves the city utterly changed and bereft
of one of its most essential populations.[1] The market's character as a
Jewish space was determined by the material needs of the Jewish religious
calendar; its demise will be similarly fixed by the Jewish consumption of
suitcases for their journey, after which all that remains is their absence.
Ballas's story describes the Jewish exodus from the point of view of those
left behind, producing a tragic and deeply felt tale that traduces the
boundaries of home and exile. Iya's Jewish employers are heading to an
Israel described as a backward desert, exotic and far removed from
Baghdad's urbane, cosmopolitan life. The story's sense of Jewish experience as deeply enmeshed in an ethnically and culturally diverse space is a
recurring feature of depictions of modern Jewish urban space. So, for
example, Sasson Somekh remembers prewar Baghdad in these terms:
"On a typical day, my father would switch linguistic codes a number of
times. He would speak Jewish Arabic at home and move to Muslim
Arabic on the street; at work, he spoke English with the bank's British
managers and various dialects of Arabic with the customers. He wrote
bank records in English, and then read English and French when he came
home. In contrast to, for example, the Jews of Cairo and Alexandria, who
normally used French at home, the Jews of Baghdad spoke only Arabic

among themselves—that is, the Jewish Baghdadi Arabic dialect."[2] As noted in the conclusion of the last chapter, language has often shaped the relation between place and notions of home and belonging. In the multi-ethnic space of the city, language has played a constitutive role in Jewish attempts to carve out a space of their own in relation to the city as a whole, its institutions and other citizens.

This chapter traces the evolution of Jewish spaces, both real and imagined, within the heterogeneous, provocative, and at times threatening space of the city. We begin by examining some of the earliest forms of Jewish urban experience, including the ghetto in European cities and the Jewish quarter in cities of the Levant. While Jews in medieval and early modern Europe did not live in isolation from their Christian neighbors,[3] these areas arose and were shaped by many different historical forces. Some of these factors were internally derived and devoted to maintaining the purity of Jewish communal life, while others were externally imposed, determined by a variety of social, political, and economic motivations. The city's connection with modernity is explored here through the notions of port, court, *shtetl*, and *shtot*, spatial categories that have informed historical research both conceptually and substantively. Finally, we consider New York and the new global architecture, sites that offer different exemplary patterns of Jewish urban life. As indicated in chapter 3, the selections offered here only scratch the surface, and the reader is referred to the notes for suggestions for further reading.

However, a few general questions and principles guide our discussion: while the synonymity of Jews and modern urban experience has by now been convincingly depicted, analyzed, and argued by sociologists, historians, critics, fiction writers, and demographers, when exactly did Jews become urban? In both Christian Europe and in the Levant, urban centers evolved in the early modern period in relation to both commerce and theology. In the medieval and early modern periods, the idea of Jews as a spiritual community set apart may be understood in relation to "Christian political units such as the kingdoms of England and France [which] had begun to define themselves spiritually as well as physically."[4] However, we can find tremendous differences between the emergence of areas typified by Jewish settlement in Italy, for example, and similar neighborhoods in Berlin, and also between Lodz and London. And while the "double punch" of commerce and theology may help explain the development of a city such as Rome, something different seems at play when considering the later evolution of great cosmopolitan centers such as Vienna and New York.

In addition to the question of history—when did Jews become city dwellers—what precisely is meant by the designation "urban," and what is at stake in such a classification? Urban is often understood as a mark of acculturation and progress, an openness to new cultural and social forms, for better or worse. The characteristic Jewish space within a city was spatially delineated in a variety of forms: the Jewish street, quarter, neighborhood, mellah, ghetto. Finally, we will consider the entire idea of urban Jewish space in relation to other spaces and places discussed in this study: how might modern urban settings be related to the idea of Jerusalem, the question of sacred space and the quasi-natural domain of the pastoral? The Bible's first and perhaps quintessential urban space may be Babel, a site characterized by a polyglot mix of language and the ambitious reach of a manmade structure toward, perhaps even in imitation of, the divine: how does a city (other than Jerusalem) become sacred? How are diaspora and home used to conceptualize and describe modern urban experience?

Medieval and Early Modern Jewish Urban Forms:
The Islamic City and Christian Europe

Cities have become such a normative part of human existence, even for those not living in an urban center, that it is hard to conceive of a time when they were actually relatively new. Medieval historian Mark Cohen makes an interesting observation in this regard concerning Jewish urban life from about the tenth century or so. In comparing Jewish life "under crescent and cross," in the Islamic Levant and in Christian Europe, Cohen finds that the relative novelty of urban life played an important role in determining Jewish-gentile relations in the medieval period. In Christian Europe, towns were in fact something new and seemed a possible threat to the established agrarian order, with its stable relations among aristocrats, peasants, and the religious authority of the Church; the fact that Jews were urban dwellers created a stigma. This was not the case under Islam, where the city had always been part-and-parcel of the social order (Mohammed himself stemmed from Mecca). In contrasting these two experiences of medieval Jewish urban life, Cohen states: "To be a Jewish townsman in the Muslim world meant to be a part of an institution originally a component of the social order rather than part of an organism considered an innovation and encroachment on the power of traditional authority."[5] Furthermore, Islamic urban areas were already organized by ethnic and religious difference, so the fact that Jews eventually lived in a separate area did not mark them as essentially different as it tended to in the Christian North.

Two terms orient our exploration of urban forms in medieval and early modern Jewish history—mellah and ghetto. These terms are by no means interchangeable, and the difference between them has everything to do with the different status of Jews in Christian Europe and the Islamic city, respectively. Still, both denote spatial boundaries limiting or indicating where Jews reside in a particular urban setting. Both also allude, therefore, to certain social and psychological boundaries between the minority Jewish population, itself often ethnically mixed, and the majority non-Jewish, also potentially of mixed ethnic and/or religious composition. The term ghetto has appeared widely within both academic scholarship and popular discourse, though often indicating something substantially different from its original use or meaning. The idea of the mellah originated in premodern Fez and, like its European counterpart, seems subject to forces far beyond its metaphorical walls, including expulsions of Jews from other places and patterns of commerce and trade. Both the ghetto and the mellah represent nodules of the local that are always part of a larger network of change and continuity.[6] And neither was isolated or detached from the city as a whole; indeed, according to one historian, "the mellah was anything but isolated. Its porousness lay at the heart of intercommunal relations."[7] In this respect, the Jewish quarters discussed in the following section may be emblematic of some fundamental tension in the evolution of urban space in many different geographic and cultural settings—the desire to live with people who are like oneself, and the concomitant necessity of living with others.

In the Levant, as in Christian Europe, Jewish-non-Jewish relations existed within a system of laws regulating both space and commerce. Where Jews could live and the range of occupational tracks open to them often shaped their individual and communal relations with their non-Jewish neighbors. In the Islamic world, the protected status of Jews as *dhimmis* meant a regulated relationship with the Muslim population and its civic and religious institutions, as well as somewhat less persecution. According to S. D. Goitein, the great social historian of Jewish life in the Levant, geniza documents suggest that city space itself in Fustat (the early modern Islamic city that prefigured Cairo) was neither firmly delineated nor broken into particular units for residential or commercial use. Indeed, "living quarters and zones of commerce and industry were often combined in the same location."[8] A similar kind of fluidity characterized spatial divisions between different ethnic and religious groups who gathered in such places as the *"khara"* [quarter] or *"shuq"* [block], and the *"rab,"* a smaller subdivision consisting of a single large structure or compound of buildings. As in European cities, Jews often settled in one area because of the travel restrictions of the Sabbath. However, "Jewish houses bordered on those belonging to or occupied by Christians and Muslims, or both; Christians and Muslims lived in Jewish houses and vice versa. Some properties were even held in partnerships by members of the three religions. Jews as a rule lived in a limited number of neighborhoods, but none was exclusively Jewish."[9] In Goitein's view, "The seclusion of Jews (and other minority groups) was self-imposed and not dictated by Muslim authorities."[10] Goitein's conclusions are in essential accord with those of the Yiddish cultural historian and linguist Max Weinreich, who proposed a similar thesis regarding Jewish life in Eastern Europe. Weinreich's argument (contra much of nineteenth-century Jewish historiography), that the relative Jewish isolationism of certain areas was internally derived and related to the need for survival, not externally imposed, pointed to another important distinction: "What the Jews aimed at was not isolation from Christians but insulation from Christianity."[11]

A similar sense of place may be found in North African cities, where the neighborhood of Jewish settlement became known as the mellah. The first mellah was established in Fez in 1438 "for reasons that are not precisely clear,"[12] when Jews were expelled from the Islamic medina and compelled to live in a compound apart. Like other Moroccan cities, Fez was characterized by physical and social boundaries that hinted at coexistence and acceptance, but also a wariness between Muslim and Jewish groups. Historian Susan Gilson Miller describes the situation thus: "The walls surrounding the mellah constituted a 'metaphorical' as well as a physical divide, separating two communities who agreed to cohabit but not assimilate."[13] This combination of "metaphorical" and "physical" suggests a space that was potentially viewed by populations both inside and outside the mellah as somewhat permeable, given to flux and shaped by the behaviors of those residents who actually lived in the area.

Indeed, according to Emily Gottreich, author of a book-length study on Jewish-Muslim relations and the mellah of Marrakesh, "'Jewish space' in Marrakesh was [not] in any way confined to the mellah. Rather, Jews managed to invest nearly all parts of the city with special meaning through the activities and practices of their daily lives."[14] Furthermore, Muslims also frequented the mellah, often engaging in activities that were not permitted by Islam—including gambling, alcohol, and prostitution— a practice that later gained for the mellah a reputation as a seedy part of town. In this way, according to Gottreich, the mellah possessed "the potential structurally to harbor activities proscribed by Islamic law while remaining very much an integral, organic part of the city as a whole."[15]

For Jewish populations under both Islam and Christianity, two related phenomena arise at the same time. First, any given "Jewish space" in the city (e.g., that area or neighborhood that has been denoted, either by custom and ritual or law, as the residence of Jews) is in fact also characterized by the presence of non-Jews and their activities. Second, the Jews themselves circulated freely throughout the city, including those areas where the city itself was defined in religious terms—the Islamic city or Christian

Rome. However, it is important to note that "Jews were an extremely small minority in their host societies. Throughout the Middle Ages, large Jewish communities may have accounted for between 1 and 3 percent of the total population."[16] A great demographic shift began in the early modern period, with a relative decrease in Jewish urban settlements in the Levant—which had historically been larger and more consequential, both economically and as centers of learning—and the concomitant rise in Ashkenazi urban centers.

For Jews in Christian Europe, "more or less permanent and separate living quarters existed for much of the Middle Ages."[17] These earlier forms of Jewish urban experience were generally driven by the internal needs of the Jewish community; even when there wasn't a "Jewish street," Jews tended to live in close proximity to other Jews, as much as possible, and within range of non-Jewish neighbors as well. At first, these Jewish "streets" or "quarters" were neither entirely Jewish, nor did all Jews in a given town live in them. Authorities in Germanic lands as well as parts of Spain and Italy sought to encourage the local settlement of Jews associated with commerce and trade, thereby increasing the relative wealth and power of their own municipal governments. In Venice, allowing Jewish moneylenders to settle in the city ensured that Christians would not trespass the commandment against usury; their growing presence eventually disturbed some of the city's population, leading to a decree in 1516 establishing a specific area of where Jews would be required to live, and from which current Christian residents would be forced to leave. This area—an island previously the site of metal foundries—became known as the "ghetto," from the Italian *gettare,* meaning to pour or to cast. The term continued to appear within legislation requiring Jews to live in specific areas (in Florence and Siena) and was also internally referred to in Hebrew documents by the Jews of Padua in 1582.[18] The term then traveled or migrated to other locations where Jews lived among themselves, but not always in absolute seclusion or segregation. Therefore, when a contemporary scholar of early modern Jewish history states that "the first official ghetto is generally dated to the second half of the fifteenth century in Frankfurt,"[19] the use of the word "ghetto" may be somewhat confusing. That is, while it is historically accurate to point to the Jewish quarter established there in 1462, the use of the term itself is anachronistic.

According to Kenneth Stow, a historian of Italian Jewish life, a papal restriction of 1555 ordering Roman Jews to live together provided, at least initially, the spatial opportunity to create a "sacred" community. Though established as a form of religious segregation and a means of converting Jews, Jews converted in relatively few numbers and something somewhat surprising happened instead: "Confinement in the ghetto could in fact be exploited to turn the ghetto experience into one that 'liberated' the individual and generated a sense of personal well-being."[20] It has even been suggested that Lurianic Kabbalah and messianic mysticism more generally "allow Jews to transcend the physical limits of the ghetto."[21] Thus the space of the ghetto was produced and evolved in unpredictable fashion; while its formation was externally imposed and potentially restrictive, the ghetto—at least in some of these early iterations—proved to be another way of consecrating Jewish space. In Stow's terms, the Roman ghetto was "the Jews' *Miqdash me'at*, the small sanctuary, the equivalent of space, time, and society all wrought into one unbreakable whole. Within this unique entity, they surely must have sensed, the idea of the holy community in both is ancient and medieval conceptions could be most perfectly realized."[22] This idea is consonant with those earliest forms of Jewish space, the tent and tabernacle, which were themselves mobile substitutes for the Temple.

In Eastern Europe, Jews lived in other kinds of urban settings as well. The premodern Jewish population in Poland, for example, was largely concentrated in midsize or small towns, where restrictions on where Jews could live often contributed to densely populated areas of town, often adjacent to the main market square (*rynek*). It may be recalled that Weinreich suggests that living quarters for Jews in early modern Jewish towns usually centered around a street that was desirable because of its connections to commerce, but that Jews lived together long before this and the segregation was voluntary. That is, like other ethnic groups, it was considered advantageous to settle with one's own. Overcrowding may have developed, but "this is not to say that the very fact of living in separate quarters was considered oppressive."[23]

Unlike the ghettos of larger urban centers, these Jewish areas of town were not physically demarcated. Furthermore, while ethnic and religious groups may have been conceptually separated, architectural historian Thomas Hubka argues that "the reality of land ownership and development practices resulted in considerable overlapping between groups, including the Jewish community."[24] However, these areas themselves developed in irregular patterns, unlike the largely harmoniously laid out plans that characterized the rest of the town. In Hubka's persuasive formulation, "These Polish, formal, town planning arrangements produced an elite versus vernacular distinction in which the highly pronounced irregularity of the tightly grouped Jewish districts contrasted with the geometric regularity and more unified visual order of the principal buildings of the small towns. . . . This general planning/aesthetic distinction between Jewish and non-Jewish/Christian environments reinforced a standard polemic where Polish elites criticized the Jewish community for seeming lack of care for visual (i.e. western, Baroque) spatial order."[25]

Several important ideas about space emerge from these observations. First, in consonance with some of what we have seen in relation to the Levant and to the Italian ghettos, while separation of space is clearly the intent of some governing authority, the messiness of living cheek-by-jowl in the relative density of even semi-urban settings moves the Jewish population into spatial contiguity with non-Jewish groups. Second, the ersatz quality of some urban planning not withstanding, the aesthetic critique leveled against the Jewish community (by the presumably "enlightened" Polish elites) alludes to normative stereotypes regarding Judaism's antipathy for the visual arts, deriving from the Second Commandment prohibition on sculptural depictions (a possible form of idolatry). We may learn from this that Jewish urban spaces, whether emerging organically from within the institutions of the Jewish community or as a result of externally imposed restrictions and permitted freedoms, were produced by a combination of factors. These factors also included strongly held convictions about Judaism that potentially shaped Jewish-gentile interactions.

In retrospect, within urban Jewish experience, no spatial designation has been more abused and more provocative than the term ghetto. Historiographically, phrases such as "the ghetto mentality" or "out of the ghetto" have been used to describe different patterns of acculturation and modern experience, primarily in Eastern Europe, and later in the United States—for example, Louis Wirth's classic *The Ghetto*—where the original notion of the ghetto as a place of compulsory settlement had little civic meaning,[26] and the term referred to enclaves where new Jewish immigrants lived and gathered. The ghetto has also appeared—not entirely ironically—as an imprecise marker of the premodern condition, as in Yiddish poet Yankev Glatshteyn's famous declaration in 1938 that he is "returning" to the ghetto, to an ostensibly simpler, more intimate time, when the *dalet amos* (four walls) of Jewish learning and tradition held strong before the ostensible temptations of modernity and secularism.

Whether deployed by Jews in ambivalent, self-reflexive fashion, or in the well-known usage of the term to describe the Nazi practice of enclosed urban enclaves for Jews during World War II (with the intention of eventually murdering them), the ghetto has become a powerful spatial trope whose political efficacy cannot be underestimated. For Zionist historians, the idea of the ghetto as a punitive, exclusionary measure confirmed their negative view of Jewish life in the diaspora. Weinreich critiqued this idea that Jews were excluded from early modern European society, arguing that the idea of the ghetto as a compulsory form of exclusion was in fact invented by "nineteenth century historians who found themselves fighting for emancipation."[27] While we may now visit and explore those physical destinations that once served as Jewish neighborhoods in many European centers, their spatial significance continues to evolve. Recently, an Israeli peace activist spray-painted the remaining wall of the Warsaw Ghetto with the words "Free Gaza." The act expressly compares the Jewish partisans of the ghetto, whose status as freedom fighters in Israeli cultural mythology looms large, with the conditions of present-day Gaza and those Palestinians fighting the strictures of the Israeli regime. This mix of what constitutes, in a loose sense, a near-sacred site of the recent Jewish past with a controversial space in the Israeli present may be jarring, even offensive, to some. I would simply point to the ongoing power of certain Jewish urban spaces, years after their physical demise, and their capacity to engender a new sense of place.

Becoming Modern: Port and Court, *Shtetl* and *Shtot*

Historical scholarship often features the "court Jews" as one way of telling the story of Jewish modernity. Across a variety of settings in Western and Central Europe, these figures became close to political and financial leaders due to their wealth, business connections, and general usefulness to their non-Jewish patrons. The court Jew has normatively been viewed as one of the precursors of the Haskalah (Jewish enlightenment) and main conduits of Jewish modernity, a kind of intermediary figure who negotiated the terrain between Judaism's traditional religious forms and Europe's emergent secular domains. This influential but ultimately monolithic view of Jewish history has been challenged in recent decades by the paradigm of the "port Jew," a concept initially formulated in the pioneering work of Lois Dubin and David Sorkin, to describe Jewish populations in port cities such as Trieste, Livorno, Amsterdam, and Hamburg. These Jews were both relatively well integrated into their local settings (Dubin's "civil inclusion") and also belonged to a wider geographic domain, by virtue of the networks of trade and commerce that constituted their livelihoods.[28] The distinction between court and port suggests a way of conceptualizing space that itself moves beyond the center-margins model. While court, of course, symbolizes the idea of centralized political and economic power, port suggests something more diffuse, a node within a network that is itself determined through mobility. The fact that both serve as equally valid explanatory models for the evolution of Jewish modernity points to the importance of both geography as well as those spaces shaped by political and economic interests for an understanding of modern Jewish experience. Together, the terms port and court, *shtetl* and *shtot* offer a kind of spatial shorthand, a way of imagining the geographic and conceptual move out of the medieval and early modern spaces of the ghetto and mellah.[29]

Other kinds of urban spaces characterized a later period within Jewish modernity. The *shtetl*, the diminutive form of *shtot* (town), figured heavily in modern Yiddish writing and has been the object of numerous historical and literary studies. From the early nineteenth century, observers of Jewish life were sensitive to the particular physical and sociological qualities that distinguished a shtetl from both a regular *shtot* and a *gross shtot*, a large city. An oft-cited passage from I. Aksenfeld's 1863 novella "The Headband" describes the spaces thus:

> A small *shtetl* has a few cabins, and a fair every other Sunday. The Jews deal in liquor, grain, burlap, or tar. Usually, there's a man striving to be a Hasidic rebbe.
>
> A *shtot*, on the other hand, contains several hundred wooden homes (that's what they call a house: a *home*) and a row of brick shops. There are: a very rich man (a parvenu), several well-to-do shopkeepers, a few dealers in fields, hareskins, wax, honey, some big money-lenders. . . . Such a town has a Polish landowner (the *porets*) with his manor. He owns the town and some ten villages, this entire district being known as a *shlisl*. . . . Such a town also has a Jewish VIP, who is a big shot with the district police chief. Such a town has an intriguer, who is always litigating with the town and the Jewish communal administration. . . .
>
> Such a town has a winehouse keeper, a watchmaker, and a doctor, a past cantor and a present cantor, a broker, a madman, and an abandoned wife (an *agunah*), community beadles, and a caterer. Such a town has a tailors' association, a burial association, a Talmud association, and free-loan association. Such a town has various kinds of synagogues: a *shul* (mainly for the Sabbath and holidays), a *bes-medresh* (the house of study, for everyday use), and sometimes even a *klaizl* (a smaller house of worship) or a *shtibl* (a small Hasidic synagogue). God forbid that anyone should accidentally blurt out the wrong word and call the town a *shtetl*. He'd instantly be branded as the local smartass or madman.
>
> A town is called a *big town* if there are a couple of thousand householders and a few brick buildings aside from the wooden homes. . . . Here everyone boasts that he greeted someone from the next street because he mistook him for an out-of-towner. After all: In such a big town as this, how can you tell if a stranger is a local? There are tons of people whom you don't know from Adam.[30]

The passage displays a finely tuned sensitivity to both space and the ways in which language shapes a sense of place. Note, for example, the architectural delineations of those various religious institutions that shape the

Jewish community's life, as well as the calibrated manner in which these urban structures fit together to form larger entities, which are themselves subject to both the internal jurisdiction of Jewish leaders as well as non-Jewish figures. The speaker slightly mocks the airs of city dwellers ("that's what they call a house: a *home*") as well as those residents of more cosmopolitan centers who cannot tell a stranger from a local. The catalogue of specific sociological and economic detail accorded to each city-type mediates the generalization of each space. This kind of detail seems constitutive of the depiction of urban spaces in Yiddish fiction. Commenting on the work of S. Y Abramovitch, the Hebrew writer David Frishman famously remarked that if a flood had "effaced from the earth the entire universe of Jewish street life . . . so that no sign remained of what was," Abramovitch's work would enable one to "reconstruct the entire picture of Jewish street life in the small town [shtetl] in Russia during the first part of the nineteenth century."[31] Though there is certainly a plethora of realistic social detail to be gained here, space in Yiddish fiction also has tremendous symbolic value. The imagined landscapes of Abramovitch's fiction may in some way resemble real life, but they often reflect some essential quality of their inhabitants' demeanor or behavior.[32] Thus, for example, the residents of *Kabtziel* [Beggarsburgh] in his story "*Hanisrafim*" [Burnt Out] are characterized by their complete and utter dependence upon the kindness of other Jews to support them in their material needs. And inasmuch as the shtetl is perceived as a "Jewish kingdom" [*yidishe meluche*], it is only fitting that should disaster strike—as in the case of the fire that destroyed Kabtziel—events are described in a way that expressly, if ironically, recalls the destruction of the Temple, both in terms of the reasons for the fire (God's wrath for a sinning people) as well as the ensuing psychic and physical trauma. This ability of the shtetl to signify is intimately suggested by its size: "The miniaturization of the Jewish urban entity makes it possible to present a word that is simple, more homogenous, and more Jewish."[33] This psychic "shrinkage" of Jewish space in order to make it "purer" (more concentrated, more Jewish) resembles, in a structural sense, the centripetal force of depictions of holiness in the Temple/Jerusalem, and also in the rabbinic descriptions of the early synagogue sacred spaces.

Such a dizzying, spiral motion, I would suggest, also characterizes a very different piece of work, one that will help us begin to think about the move out of the shtetl and other early modern spaces of Jewish urban life and into the full-on wail of the cosmopolis, exemplified for our purposes by New York. I have in mind Marc Chagall's *I and the Village* (1911), a by-now iconic work depicting the mixed space of the shtetl, through various riffs on a symmetrically rendered "other": human versus animal, Jew versus gentile. The painting's world is graphically, cosmically, centered by the relational pull between the green self of the painter and the kindly returned gaze of the goat. This tethering of a hybrid-Jewish self (the green Chagallian figure wears a cross) to an animal-other—albeit the goat beloved of Yiddish folklore—suggests an intermingling of kinds that will continue to define Jewish urban spaces.

New York, Capital of the Diaspora

Moshe Leyb Halpern's epic book-length cycle of Yiddish poetry *In New York* (1919) opens with the following ironic paean to urban life:

> What a garden, where the tree is
> bare but for seven leaves!
> It appears to be amazed!:
> "Who has set me in the place?"
> What a garden, what a garden—It takes a magnifying glass
> Just to see a little grass.
> Can this be our garden, then,
> Just as is, in the light of dawn?
> Sure, it's our garden. What else?
>
> What a watchman, brusque and quick,
> Walks the garden with a stick,
> Wakes the people on the lawn
> And to hell he drives them on.
> What a watchman, what a watchman—Grabs a collar or an arm
> Of anyone who's done no harm.
> Can this be our watchman, then,
> Just as is, in the light of dawn?
> Sure, he's our watchman. What else?
>
> What a bird—quick to forget
> All the fledglings in the nest.
> Doesn't carry food along,
> Doesn't sing their morning song.
> What a bird, oh, what a bird—Doesn't lift a single wing,
> Or try to fly, or anything.
> Can this be our own bird, then,
> Just as it is, in the light of dawn?
> Sure, it's our bird. What else![34]

The newly arrived immigrant domesticates the cavernous and chaotic urban space of New York City through the image of the garden, alluding of course to the Garden of Eden, ruled by a "watchman" who metes out justice is an arbitrary fashion but is nonetheless "ours . . . what else?" The bird recalls both the weary worker who never sees her family, a staple of Yiddish proletarian verse, and the beleaguered poet, whose voice struggles to be heard within the city's commotion. The idea of a garden also implies a self-defined Jewish quarter, in this case a space imagined as a bit of Yiddishland; no matter how meager, this garden offers a measure of security and sense of self within the cacophonous space of New York City.

Halpern's is only one example from among the prodigious amount of writing produced by American Jewish immigrants about New York and its qualities as a Jewish space. Henry Roth's novel *Call It Sleep* (1934) delivers a moving meditation on immigrant life, demonstrating how space becomes place for young David through the medium of language. His home, the stairwell, the cellar, the roof, the street, the *cheder*—all these are sites produced by different languages in both a technical, linguistic sense, as well as in the broader understanding of language as a set of tools used to navigate multiple cultural, ethnic, and gendered domains. David's gradual acculturation into the language of the street suggests the implicit acculturation of the Jewish author-qua-immigrant, who eventually adopts the methods of a newly transplanted European modernism, itself an ostensibly cosmopolitan language in which the self-fashioning of the artist takes place through "silence, exile and cunning."[35]

The book opens with a sweeping view of the New York harbor, as the mother Genya and the young David arrive beneath the sunstruck figure of the Statue of Liberty: "Her features were charred with shadow, her depths exhausted, her masses ironed to one single plane. Against the luminous sky the rays of her halo were spikes of darkness roweling the air; shadows flattened the torch she bore to a black cross against a flawless light—the blackened hilt of a broken sword. Liberty."[36] The exaggerated, hallucinatory quality of their encounter with New York's promise characterizes the novel's treatment of space, which is viewed almost entirely through the eyes of David as he moves between the relative safety of his apartment (a space also fraught with his father's barely subdued violence), the stairs, the stoop, the cellar, and the roof. David's self begins to take shape and emerge within the expanding circles of street and neighborhood, especially during a key early episode in which he gets "losted." In response to a woman trying to help him, David frantically insists that he lives on "Boddeh Stritt," a location utterly clear in his own mind but, literally, untranslatable to those around him. Finally a police officer deciphers the boy's directions:

"Near the school on Winston Place? Boddeh? Pother? Say, I know where he lives! Barhdee Street! Sure, Barhdee! That's near Parker and Oriole . . .

"Y-yes." Hope stirred faintly. The other names sounded familiar. "Boddeh Stritt."

"Barhdee Street!" The helmeted-one barked good-naturedly. "Be-gob he'll be havin' me talk like a Jew. Sure!"[37]

As Hana Wirth-Nesher and other critics of the novel have observed, Roth's treatment of language reflects the different registers accorded to English and Yiddish and, later in the story, Polish and Hebrew, within David's immigrant milieu.[38] David's thoughts, in Yiddish, as well as his conversations with his mother, are rendered in almost baroque poetic diction: "Hope stirred faintly." English, however, sounds like a dialect, whether spoken by David ("Boddeh Stritt") or even the (presumably) slightly more acculturated police officer ("Be-gob he'll be havin' me talk like a Jew'"). Later, after moving from Brownsville to the Lower East Side, the tumult of the city as he emerges from his building is described as an "avalanche of sound,"[39] whose multilingual depth will be used to magnificent modernist effect in the novel's penultimate chapter, a rhapsodic treatment of the cityscape as filtered through David's brutalized consciousness, spinning under the oppressive effects of both his home life and the electric shock of the Tenth Avenue streetcar's third rail:

(*Around him now, the cobbles stretched*
Away. Stretched away in the swirling
dark like faces of a multitude aghast
and frozen)[40]

The voices of the concerned citizens who gather around the stricken boy speak the distinctive, bawdy patter of lower New York's working classes of the day, in accents including Irish, Italian, Yiddish, and a smattering of other Eastern European languages. In their shock, the faces—numerous as cobblestones—resemble the Statue of Liberty's "ironed masses." New York's public and semi-private spaces—the streetcar, the waterfront pier, the roof, the communal toilets, and backyards—are the crucible in which David's identity is formed.

After much of the neighborhood's Jewish immigrant population, and especially their children, moved out of the area, the Lower East Side served as a cultural arena in which to test and shape American Jewish identity, even for those who had never lived there, and especially after the destruction of European Jewry.[41] The power of the Lower East Side as a site of memory, an iconic point of origins and passage in American Jewish experience, is attested in the myriad cultural forms for which it serves as a touchstone. Many of these memorializing depictions of an era gone by were produced by New York's second-generation Jews, who themselves built cooperative neighborhoods in their own image in Brighton Beach in Brooklyn and on the Grand Concourse in the Bronx, spacious, green developments that were a far cry from the crowded conditions of the tenements, and further still from the Jewish districts of European cities. According to Deborah Dash Moore, who calls the "co-ops"—as they came to be known—a "model of urban community,"[42] the apartment house represented a new form of Jewish geography:

> Though the apartment house ranked below the private home in the scale of American housing values, it encouraged greater ethnic density in a neighborhood. Jewish understanding of American society demanded that Jews not live in 'ghettos,' i.e. that they live down the block from some non-Jewish Americans. The apartment house offered them this opportunity as well as the chance to move up collectively.[43]

Though we have seen that even the most seemingly impervious forms of Jewish urban settlement have been characterized by some sort of ethnic and religious mixing, the "co-op," planned and lived in by significant numbers of Jews throughout the postwar period, seems a Jewish urban space of a different order. Perhaps this imperative to live with Jews, but also down the block (or hall) from non-Jewish Americans, is what has made New York the symbolic capital of the diaspora. To be sure, the numbers speak for themselves: at last count (in 2002), there were about a million Jews in New York City, a half million more if you consider the surrounding suburbs of Long Island and Westchester County. But there is something more, a quality having to do with what can only be called the fabric of life, the warp-and-woof of the felt experience of living in New York, which as a city-space has arguably absorbed as much from its Jewish population in the last century or so as they have from it. To say that the diaspora has a capital, therefore, is not merely ironic; it also raises the possibility of the diaspora as a vital and creative site of power, not powerlessness.

The New Global Jewish Architecture

By way of concluding this chapter, I briefly consider the emergence of what may be called the new global Jewish architecture. I refer both to the prominence of Jewish architects within the last couple of decades, such as Daniel Libeskind, Peter Eisenmann, and Frank Gehry, as well as their involvement in the construction of Jewish institutions such as museums and synagogues. As observed throughout this chapter, part of becoming modern for Jews within the space of the city meant moving out of relatively restricted areas and neighborhoods; this move into a more public arena occasioned the construction of institutions such as synagogues and museums as well as an increase in those vernacular forms of urban space characterized by commerce (a "Jewish street" or shopping district). The city increasingly became a stage upon which those more affluent portions of the Jewish community could demonstrate their civic membership.[44] While early prototypes of the synagogue may have been intended to evoke the memory of the Temple and Jerusalem, synagogue architecture has generally been influenced by surrounding local traditions typical of other religious institutions. Across the gamut of geographical and cultural locations, it was thus an architecture that reflected the past as well as a sense of present membership within a specific local, civic setting.

In recent years a number of high-profile international projects have set the stage for a reconsideration of the relation between architecture and Jewish culture. I have in mind Gehry's design for the Guggenheim Museum in Bilbao, Spain, widely emulated as a model for how museums may invigorate previously derelict or neglected cityscapes, as well as his involvement with Jewish institutional projects in both Jerusalem and Warsaw. Also important in this regard are Eisenmann's Berlin's Memorial to the Murdered Jews of Europe, Libeskind's Jewish Museum in Berlin, and his connection with the 9/11 memorial site in New York City. We might ask here about both the relative preponderance of Jewish architects in the profession as a whole as well as the ways in which Jewish content or themes (e.g., historical events, religious beliefs) are expressed or contained by a building and its physical setting. In a recent study, historian Gavriel Rosenfeld argues that the two phenomena may in fact be related and explains their connection in light of the evolution of postwar architecture and several complicating, coincident factors.[45] First, he notes that Jews were only recently admitted to the guild in America in the postwar period; that is, they trained and practiced as architects for the first time in relatively large numbers. Second, an awareness of the Shoah and its consequences for architecture, which Rosenfeld locates within postmodernism's more general appreciation for history and memory, gave rise to a specific set of architectural practices. These practices were articulated most forcefully by the deconstructivist school, many of whose key members (Gehry, Libeskind, Eisenmann) were Jewish. The conclusions reached by deconstructivist architects regarding the meaning and design of buildings represented a sharp departure from modernism's postwar formalism and especially its optimism. Instead of buildings that projected strength and hope for the future, only a "dehumanized" architecture would be appropriate for the world's damaged and bleak psychological and physical landscape in the wake of the Shoah. This broken fragmented style, a direct, almost physical expression of the perceived shattered quality of humanism after the war, characterizes well-known buildings by Gehry and Libeskind, and is perhaps most graphically represented in

Figure 5 Dresden Neue Synagogue (Wandel Hoefer Lorch Architects), built in 1997 on the site of Dresden's Alte Synagogue, originally designed by Gottfriend Semper and destroyed on November 9, 1938. The contemporary synagogue incorporates elements of the original structure. Photograph by Wojtek Gurak.

Libeskind's extension to the Berlin Jewish museum, which resembles—among other things—a kind of scar on the urban landscape. The museum's central "void" keenly depicts the wrenching absence of Jewish life in Berlin, as well as the sharp degree to which humanity had devolved during the Shoah. Though most evident when characterizing Jewish institutions such as synagogues, schools, and museums, this type of design, according to Rosenfeld, typifies postwar architecture more broadly. Simply put, the Shoah did not happen only to the Jews, and its consequences may be felt in global architecture. Is this, then, the Jews' spatial legacy in the modern era?

Like the question of Jewish art, the idea of Jewish architecture should be contextualized within the social specifics of both producers (the artists or architects) and consumers (the intended audience). In the following chapter we revisit the *eruv*, the rabbinic practice of marking a Sabbath boundary, and consider its implications in a postmodern setting, as both religious practice and aesthetic performance. These recent iterations of a traditional Jewish ritual further complicate our sense of how space and place remain important markers of Jewish identity and Jewish communities.

PART III

IN A NEW KEY

The previous two sections have reviewed how Jewish cultures have imagined space and place across a variety of geographical and historical circumstances. In this concluding section, we examine two spaces that have emerged as sites of creative debate and contention in contemporary Jewish life—the *eruv* and the environment. Building on the discussion of the *eruv* in rabbinic practice in chapter 5, "*Bayit*," our investigation of the contemporary *eruv* focuses on its postmodern malleability as both ritual and aesthetic practice. Finally, the environment chapter considers not only the burgeoning Jewish environmental movement but also the idea of *sviva* (surroundings, in Hebrew) in a broader sense: what types of global place-making are happening under the umbrella of Jewishness, and how might they relate to those spatial practices historically associated with Jewish cultures? These concluding chapters depict spatial practices that are in some sense thoroughly decentered and post-*makom*. At the same time, they continue to comment in compelling fashion on their historical antecedents.

8   Eruv

*Landsman has put a lot of work into the avoidance of
having to understand concepts like that of the eruv,
but he knows that it's a typical Jewish dodge, a scam
run on God, that controlling motherfucker. It has
something to do with pretending telephone poles are
doorposts, and the wires are lintels. You can tie off an
area using poles and strings and call it an eruv, then
pretend on the Sabbath that this eruv you've
drawn—in the case of Zimbalist and his crew, it's
pretty much the whole District—is your house. That
way you can get around the Sabbath ban on carrying
in a public place, and walk to shul with a couple of
Alka-Seltzers in your pocket, and it isn't a sin. Given
enough string and enough poles, and with a little creative use of existing walls, fences, cliffs, and rivers,
you can tie a circle around pretty much any place and
call it an eruv.*

—Michael Chabon, The Yiddish Policemen's Union

Something there is that doesn't love a wall.
—Robert Frost, "Mending Wall"

Michael Chabon's novel The Yiddish Policemen's Union (2007), set in the district of Sitka, a region of Alaska that has served as a "temporary haven"
for Jews after World War II, proposes an alternate trajectory for Jewish
political and territorial autonomy. Just as "you can tie a circle around
pretty much any place and call it an eruv," it turns out a similar principle
applies to the creation of Jewish collective space. In Chabon's fictional
world, since Israel's collapse in 1948, Sitka has served as a de facto homeland for the Yiddish-speaking Jews who inhabit it. Despite their physical
distance from the mainland, Sitka's citizens are also proud Americans,
and their culture is an eclectic mix of secular and religious Judaism,

sprinkled with the realities of the surrounding topography and a sudden impending sense of doom: after sixty years, control of Sitka is about to revert to Alaska and the fate of their Jewish enclave is in question. Meyer Landsman, a local detective, is an "everyman"—a friend, a compatriot— and also a Jewish version of Raymond Chandler's noir-driven characters. During a murder investigation, Landsman seeks the advice of Zimbalist, the "boundary maven," designer and maintainer of Sitka's *eruv*.

Sitka's *eruv* points to several related qualities that are integral to the *eruv*'s power. In Landsman's wise-guy rendering, the *eruv* seems to challenge normative Judaism—"a scam run on God"—despite its origins in Jewish law. The *eruv*'s potential subversiveness and mobility vis-à-vis more established, brick-and-mortar institutions like the synagogue has made it a productive symbol for contemporary Jewish artists and thinkers. The *eruv* is both seen and unseen, powerful and regulatory, yet quite flimsy, made of just poles and string. Once mapped out and constructed, someone has to "guard the integrity of the make-believe walls and doors against weather, vandalism, bears, and the telephone company."[1] In this, the *eruv* conjures the very foundational operations of faith: whatever its physical qualities, the *eruv*'s effects are largely dependent on the belief that it exists. In a way that powerfully challenges even the most concrete forms of dwelling, the *eruv* transforms space into place. The act of making an *eruv* requires a profound leap of the imagination: elements of the city's existing nature and manmade physical landscape (anything taller or deeper than a meter, according to talmudic instructions) are conceived of as walls and doorways that then support an imaginary roof, itself the figure for transforming public space into the domestic realm: the wide noisy grid of the city becomes a home, if only for one day a week.

In recent years, the *eruv* has become a compelling reference point within discussions about Jewish culture. A marker of both community and difference, of belonging and otherness, the visible and invisible presence of *eruvs* in Jewish communities in metropolitan and suburban settings has spurred interdenominational debate within the Jewish community, as well as public controversy between Jews and their communal representatives on the one hand and non-Jews and municipal or civic institutions on the other. At the same time, the *eruv* has emerged as both trope and device in critical theory and in art. The *eruv*'s conceptual essence seems important for all these general trends. That is, the *eruv*, like other religious practices, is based more on good faith and an idea of its existence rather than any tangible, visible proof. And for conceptual artists—most, if not all, of whom are secular—the appeal of the *eruv* lies precisely in its existence as . . . a concept! The *eruv* is both virtual, symbolic, and invisible as well as three-dimensional, material, spatial, and urban.² It is undeniable to those who need it, dismissible for those who don't. Its potency also precedes, and potentially reaches beyond, that now most ubiquitous form of postmodern space—the internet. There is no need for a "virtual" *eruv*, though we may soon discover "there's an app for that." Marking the seam between personal portability and communal identity, between the traditional rubric of halakhic law and the contemporary grid and flow of Google Earth, "EruvFinder"—whenever it is invented—will surely make its way into popular Jewish practice.

As disparate as these various engagements may be, the emergence of the *eruv* in public discourse within Jewish communities, as well as within art and theory, is further related to the evolving public face of Jewish ritual practice (and perhaps American religious life as a whole). We may locate a broad historical comparison with that period in European Jewish life when urban centers saw the appearance of monumental synagogues, whose place in the public sphere—in Berlin, for example—announced the growing acculturation of Jewish city dwellers as well as their potential economic and cultural power.³ In more recent years, the growth of centers such as Makor in New York City and the Sixth and I Synagogue in Washington, D.C., as well as new museums of Jewish art in Los Angeles and San Francisco, continue to anchor the Jewish populations of certain neighborhoods, though not religiously. At the same time, we may note the growing visibility of Orthodox populations in both urban and suburban areas, and specifically the growing emphasis on freedom of movement within these communities: the existence of an *eruv* allows young parents (usually mothers) to leave the house on the Sabbath with a stroller, and thus to participate in communal prayer services and meals in alternate locations. Mobility is also part of the appeal for secular Jewish artists, who are drawn to the *eruv* precisely because it seems to embody a form of religious practice that is neither monumental nor institutional, a practice that is decentered, mobile, and unencumbered by any necessary connection to traditional sites of Jewish religious belief and practice, such as the synagogue. Our discussion of artists considers how this non-monumentalism is related to broader developments in postwar art, as well as to the historic internal ambivalence within Jewish cultures regarding the status of the fine arts.

The Contemporary *Eruv*

Eruvs function around the world today in a variety of densely populated urban and suburban areas. As discussed in chapter 5, the term *eruv* refers mainly to the *eruv chatserot* (the *eruv* of the courtyards, which functions on the Sabbath). The essential function of the *eruv*—the expansion of the home or private space [*reshut hayachid*] into public space [*reshut harabim*]— allows for behaviors such as carrying or certain forms of transport, ordinarily forbidden on the Sabbath. *Eruv* refers both to the item of shared food that symbolically determines the expanded private domain as well as the perimeter marked thereby. These behaviors are allowed due to the fact that some substantial area such as the immediate neighborhood or even an entire town is conceptually converted into an extension of one's own home. In rabbinic texts, the physical elements determining an *eruv* may include courtyards, alleys, and other kinds of openings, making it essentially a series of doorways [*tsurot ha-petach*] strung together.

Within contemporary urban settings, the relative intactness of many neighborhood *eruvs* may be checked online.[4] The definitions of the *eruv*'s physical jurisdiction can also be quite precise: the west side of the street, but not the east; such-and-such an avenue until a particular intersection, but no farther. However, the very viability of an *eruv* in a setting as large and as densely settled as even a midsize urban center has led to the question of how the public domain is constituted and measured—whether by actual geographic area or, instead, in terms of the type of activities and populations preexisting in a specific area. That is, space may be determined by geographic measure as well as by those activities associated with it. Opinions vary as to what constitutes the public domain. One view holds all the following spaces to be public: "a) Deserts; b) forests; c) marketplaces; and d) any road that opens into them—if the road is sixteen *amot* [cubits] wide and is not roofed over."[5] One could see how this kind of narrow reading would limit the kind of *eruv* permissible in the modern city. At the other end of the spectrum is Rashi's more liberal and widely accepted eleventh-century commentary indicating that public domains are constituted by a combination of physical and performative qualities: "The public domain is sixteen cubits wide, and a city in which there are 600,000 people that has no wall, or whose main thoroughfare runs straight from gate to gate—that is thus 'open' just as . . . in the travels of the tribes in the desert."[6] Here, and in the more direct reference to the tribes' travel, space is conceived in relation to other important sites within the Jewish imagination—the desert and the walled city. (The population of 600,000 refers to the number of Israelite males who, according to the Bible, left Egypt.) In any case, the openness of the terrain, whether natural or manmade, calls for the imposition of some form of spatial boundary. The rabbis also refer to something called "absolute public space," space which by virtue of certain qualities may not be converted by the *eruv* into private space: "a space so large, so populous, so open to human passage or unbounded by roofs, walls, or other enclosures, that it would stretch the fiction of a Jewish communal household beyond plausibility."[7]

There is an abundance of contemporary halakhic material related to *eruvs* in general, and to specific *eruvs* and the surrounding debates in places such as London, Jerusalem, and New York.[8] This extended and ongoing imagining of public space seems to constitute a kind of global Jewish urban planning, a "rabbinic urbanism," in the felicitous phrasing of Jennifer Cousineau.[9] Given the above-cited disparity in determining the public domain, some issues repeatedly come into play: the question of density and the ratio of Jewish to non-Jewish populations; and the use of preexisting natural or manmade landmarks such as train tracks or a river's edge to mark sections of the *eruv*.

Eruvs and their construction have also revealed the internal dividing lines within Jewish communities, especially within a city like New York that hosts a heterogeneous and relatively widely settled Jewish population. Controversy in Brooklyn, for example, has attended the presence of competing and overlapping *eruvs* determined by various groups or sects within Hasidic and ultra-Orthodox communities. For many years, disagreements over the *eruv* in Manhattan centered on the question of which of the city's natural features as an island could be used to create the series of symbolic *tsurot ha-petach* (doorways) and *mechitsot* (partitions) that make up the *eruv*. Some *eruvs* capitalized on the city's raw materials, such as its natural boundaries or a train line. These boundaries offer different patterns of opened or sealed spaces, and ways of conceptualizing noncontiguous segments as contiguous: so the supporting beams of New York's Third Avenue "El" (elevated subway) together with the track above could be seen as a kind of doorway while the river itself was also viewed as a "sealed" border whose piers resembled doorposts. The function of the *eruv* in this case was radically tied to the fate of the city's growth and the demise of those aspects of its physical landscape that had served as markers: the Third Avenue line now runs entirely underground, while the development of waterfront areas for residential construction disturbs many of the piers that were previously in plain view and even the river. Current debates regarding the permissibility of an *eruv* on the Lower East Side are particularly ironic, given the centrality of the neighborhood in American Jewish history and memory. In Manhattan, especially, the extension of the *eruv* into various neighborhoods often seems to represent not so much the presence of a Jewish community but a real estate–driven hope for one: if you build it, they (young observant Jewish families) will come.

Within these largely Orthodox communities, arguably those most affected by the recent proliferation of *eruvs* in metropolitan and suburban centers are young families, specifically young mothers who are now free to leave the house with children in strollers. Previously confined to the home due to the Sabbath prohibition of carrying (including certain forms of transport), the *eruv* has widened the spatial sphere of their Sabbath observance and with it their social and ritual participation in the life of the community.[10] As Orthodox feminist scholar and activist Blu Greenberg notes, "Although no eruv has come out of a women's protest group, I think the increase in eruvs has something to do with the new perception women have of themselves, their needs and their place in community life."[11]

From the Barnet neighborhood in London to Tenafly, New Jersey, the construction of *eruvs* has been the focus of ongoing legal debate,[12] raising broader questions about the status of religious symbols in the public domain. On the one hand, the *eruv* may be protected in the United States and Great Britain by the principle of freedom of religion: as it becomes visible, the *eruv* is similar to a Christmas tree or a menorah. At the same time, local governments have been hard-pressed to determine their exact obligation regarding their construction and upkeep (both of which are normally the responsibility of representatives of the local Jewish community, often organized specifically for this purpose). Yet municipalities have also had to allow for special attachments to utility poles in order to enable *eruv* construction, a practice that potentially discriminates, or appears to discriminate, in favor of a particular religious group. Indeed, one wonders what non-Jewish residents think about the construction of the *eruv*, usually a fairly unobtrusive string or wire hung far from the line of natural site, but often requiring some infrastructure for stability and, in some instances, public funding to maintain. Recent controversies in London indicate that the *eruv* aroused vehement opposition on the part of both Jews who viewed it as a kind of ghetto and non-Jews who objected to the perceived intrusion of religious difference in the public sphere. Indeed, the presence of *eruvs* in various communities has provoked discussion across a wide variety of legal and social forums.[13]

In Israel, as well, the *eruv* is the subject of intense public scrutiny and debate, albeit within a different social and cultural climate. In Jerusalem, where there have been a number of incidents of "*eruv* cutting," the *eruv* has been at the center of disputes between religious and secular Jews, the latter of whom oppose the idea of large numbers of Orthodox Jews moving into the neighborhood, potentially changing the nature of its social and communal infrastructure. The old city itself is walled and therefore not in need of an *eruv*. Jerusalem's *eruv* has also marked the municipality's creeping expansion into politically contested areas, as new Jewish neighborhoods are built and the *eruv* extended. In Jerusalem, the French conceptual artist Sophie Calle's work called attention to the "ready-made" quality of city life, in which the symbolic meaning of various streets and neighborhoods depends upon the lived experiences of the city's diverse population. Calle interviewed Israeli and Palestinian residents of the city and asked each to take her to a "public place that they considered private."[14] What emerges is a photographic and textual representation of a new kind of *"eruv"* or mixing—public and private, but also Jew and Moslem, East and West, old and new, past and present, men and women—a blending that defines all urban experience.

Indeed, discourse about the construction and meaning of the *eruv* frames the city as a space that is experienced differently by different groups, activities that occur simultaneously, without actually building (or destroying) anything of substantial physical measure. Perhaps the *eruv* is another portable spatial device; though produced through a specific set of geographic coordinates—doorways and sideposts—it best suits or approximates our sense of space in a postmodern world. To the extent that the *eruv* offers another way of making a home, it is a diaspora practice par excellence.

Is It Art or Is It Ritual?

In addition to Calle's Jerusalem installation, the *eruv* has been featured in a number of recent conceptual and artistic projects whose parameters move beyond the *eruv's* site-specific or religious qualities. This appropriation of the *eruv* for other purposes should be understood within the broad contemporary reinvention of Jewish ritual. Indeed, "the incorporation of old materials into new forms,"[15] a durable and age-old form of recycling, is also one definition of tradition: the preservation and conservation of old customs within new settings. Some *eruv* artists question the functional, ritual status of art within Jewish cultures. This slippage between the aesthetic and the ethical is not, it should be noted, a recent invention but a tension central to the production of "Jewish art" for centuries: are kiddush cups ritual objects or art? Are illuminated manuscripts or illustrated *haggadot* artwork or sacred texts? Jewish artists have thematized and critiqued this duality, creating work that both builds on traditional Jewish ritual and plumbs its origins. A notion of ritual as anthropomorphic rather than divinely inspired informs many of these works and "challenges the traditional views of Jewish practice, which assert a hierarchy, placing the timeless Torah and its text-related objects and rituals at the center and culturally specific ceremonial practices at the periphery." Rather than investing in the experience of more solid, brick-and-mortar institutions, "contemporary artists focus on Judaism as a lived, organic experience, not one fixed in text or custom. . . . They disconnect the actions of ritual from their symbolic intent and repurpose them for unexpected connections and harmonies."[16]

In "Sixteen Eruvin I've Walked Through," Ben Schachter re-creates the symbolic presence of the *eruv* in acrylic paint and thread on canvas, drawing on the communal resonance of the *eruv* form to raise questions of memory and personal ritual.[17] Schachter immersed himself in rabbinic material about the *eruv* and then produced these shapes from maps of *eruvs* in cities he had visited. His work alludes to the growing presence of Web 2.0 geographic media such as Google Earth, GPS systems, and Second Life. These web-generated worlds[18] ground the user in a virtual sense of space that—like the *eruv* itself—is both topographic and social, subject to the physical contours of the areas in which it is constructed and sustained by the communal need for its wholeness. "A Brief History of String," an article by fiber artist Sabrina Gschwandtner in the avant-garde journal *Cabinet*, compares the *eruv* with other types of string that have "delineated religious space, described narratives [and] denoted mathematical data."[19] Gschwandtner's free-for-all use of string as an artistic medium questions the culturally determined distinction between the fine arts and craft, and especially the association between the latter and "women's work" such as quilting or knitting. String-*eruv* art, staged expressly in museums and exhibit spaces, capitalizes on string's ability to playfully conjure the tactile relation between inside and outside, belonging and estrangement, artifice and tradition.

Other *eruv*-inspired projects don't actually use string but turn more on the *eruv*'s conceptual essence, allegorizing it as a series of physical objects or activities performed in space, which are then documented in some fashion. Maya Escobar's video project "Berlin's Eruv" contrasts the absence of an actual *eruv* in Berlin with the monumental presence of memorials and other institutions commemorating the Shoah and Jewish life before the war. Her series of interviews with Jewish Berliners, some of which take place as the subjects walk through the city's streets, attempts to create a "metaphorical eruv" that represents the city's ongoing Jewish life.[20] This filmic delineation and performance of private space within the public realm recalls the memory-work of Calle's Jerusalem *eruv* project; both highlight the idea of the *eruv* as an invisible but enduring boundary, one supported not by metal poles or flimsy wire, or even delineated by the city's natural boundaries of a river or a mountain, but by the powerful yet portable memories of the city's inhabitants.

eRuv, Elliot Malkin's 2005 "digital graffiti project," consisted of semacodes (which resemble and function as large barcodes) posted along the former site of the elevated Third Avenue train in the Lower East Side, an important link in that neighborhood's *eruv*.[21] Smartphone users could scan the semacodes and thereby access historical information about the *eruv* and the hasidic community it once served. In addition to creating a virtual rendering of one of the *eruv*'s main branches, the installation also served as conduit for information about New York more broadly, calling

Figure 6 Art, ritual, environment. Allan Wexler, *Gardening Sukkah*, 2000, shown as part of "Reinventing Ritual: Contemporary Art and Design for Jewish Life" at The Jewish Museum, New York. Columbus Museum of Art, Columbus, Ohio. Gift of the artist.

attention to its past transportation and preserving this information on the web, years before the Highline.

While the *eruv* may be related to the persistent force of religious, institutional forms in the modern world, the use of the *eruv* in this last group of art seems less invested in religious ritual per se and more devoted to the idea of art as performance rather than as artifact, as a process demanding audience participation and evoking a specific and often charged relation between artist and audience, viewer and producer. In this sense, *eruv* art is also broadly embedded in minimalism and later postminimalism, postwar movements that have sought to deflect attention away from the actual work of art to the experience and body of the viewer, and the physical arena in which the artwork is displayed and viewed. The French Situationists were similarly attuned (though from a different and more overtly political point of view) with the "situation" and "spectacle" of art, particular within urban space, and to creating or noticing patterns in city life. One outstanding example for our purposes is the "string art" of Fred Sandback,[22] whose installations typically turn the voluminous space of a large, empty room into subtle yet discreet "territories" defined by yarn and string. His posthumous installation at the Dia Museum in Beacon, New York, deploys low-strung pieces of string to slice up the space into unobtrusive sections. It is a perplexing and demanding piece, leading to reflection upon the difference between inside and outside and the ironic power of a simple piece of string to unsettle one's preconceptions about both art and space. Indeed, the string's presence draws our attention to space as a sculptural material in and of itself. Sandback coined the term "pedestrian space" to define space that was "literal, flatfooted, and everyday. The idea was to have the work right there along with everything else in the world, not up on a spatial pedestal."[23] He also claimed to practice a kind of "nomadicism" in his work, and his personal statements betray resistance to the institutional setting of museums for his work.[24] This embrace of impermanence, as well as the use of materials that seem to deliberately embrace mobility, directly parallels the sense that the *eruv* is an alternative, anti-monumental form that appeals to a post-brick-and-mortar sensibility. The irony here, of course, is that the *eruv* is certainly a rabbinic institution, and one might fairly ask: How "authentic" do we expect *eruv* theory and art to be? That is, what kind of trajectory is considered permissible when appropriating the term and its practice for areas far from actual halakhic observance?[25] The answer, of course, depends on who is asking and to what ends. The art discussed here seems connected to globalism and postmodernism more broadly conceived, including the rise of ideas about the local ("think globally, act locally") and also an increased sensitivity to diaspora forms, especially discursive and aesthetic forms that thematize notions of diaspora existence.

Finally, I want to consider the idea of the *eruv* in relation to other spaces discussed in this book. We have seen how the rabbinic *eruv* maps a space of collective Jewish identity that is dependent neither on sovereignty nor any form of actual political or territorial control.[26] What does the historical *eruv* share with other Jewish forms such as the mellah, ghetto, or Jewish quarter? Clearly one key difference has to do with its derivation—internal Jewish religious law, as opposed to that often externally imposed by non-Jewish legislative bodies. However, might there be cases in which they are physically or even symbolically contiguous? The contemporary presence of the *eruv* brings to the fore questions of multiculturalism in cities that are already characterized by diversity and difference. This helps to explain why London seems to be such an *eruv* "hotspot," with its larger and relatively new Indian populations and potentially greater Islamic presence. Architect Manuel Herz notes that "at the heart of this problem is not the question of imposing upon urban space an obscure religious practice, but rather the willingness of city authorities to sanction the city as the site of multiple readings."[27] Herz's discussion of the *eruv* in relation to Jewish architecture in postwar Munich points to the fundamental duality between space and place undergirding the Jewish spatial imagination: according to Herz, the Talmud "assumes that the city does not exist in its physical embodiment alone, and that its material elements are always pointing towards something else. Thus the *eruv* bridges two cities—one that is perceived and tangible, the other aesthetically ideal. The urban dweller appropriates the city she or he lives in. They decipher but must also write each new interpretative framework. A second metaphorical or 'mobile' city is overlaid upon the existing one by the practice of moving through the city."[28]

These contemporary theoretical readings of the *eruv* bring the textual record of rabbinic practice into conversation with diaspora theorists, especially those interested in locality and the neighborhood as a social form. Arjun Appadurai describes the formation of the neighborhood vis-à-vis its historical and physical surrounding as the "transformation of spaces into places":[29] "the production of neighborhoods is always historically grounded and thus contextual. . . . Neighborhoods are always to some extent ethnoscapes, insofar as they involve the ethnic projects of Others as well as consciousness of such projects."[30] This juxtaposition of ancient texts with postmodern theory potentially illuminates the emergence of the *eruv* in halakhic texts, and "on the ground" in late antiquity, where neighborhoods are "opposed to something else and derive from other, already produced neighborhoods."[31] As discussed in chapter 5, these ideas (like other boundaries that demarcate and shape identity) help illuminate the historical figure of the *eruv* as a self-imposed marker of Jewish difference.

Can we use postmodern texts to unpack the details of premodern urban space, especially in relation to the currently privileged space of "territory without sovereignty"? What does globalization theory and its conception of space and place have in common with rabbinic culture? For Fonrobert, the fact that the rabbis were not living in isolation in the desert, like other ideologically compelled Jewish groups such as the Essenes, but were part of mixed, semi-urban neighborhoods provides one crucial point in departure.[32] Another crucial element is the Jews' lack of dependence, in this instance, on territory for national definition. In focusing on the rabbinic use of the *eruv*, and its consequent consecration of urban Jewish space, as a *diaspora* practice, we potentially enrich our sense of the ways in which Jews are indeed a people of space, not only of time.

9   Environment

They call their God Makom, *"Place."*
And now that they have returned to their place, the
   Lord has taken up
Wandering to different places, and His name will no
   longer be Place,
But Places, Lord of Places.

          —Yehuda Amichai, "Jewish Travel,"
          in *Open Closed Open,* 2006

Yehuda Amichai's poem "Jewish Travel" poses a question regarding the essence of Jewish space: Now that the gap between space and place, between the Story about the Place and the Place itself, has been closed, how have the spatial conditions of Jews and Jewish life changed? Is there a difference between Jewish space and Israeli space, between Jewish travel and Israeli travel?[1] And if, as Amichai's poem suggests, God has merely proliferated into many Places—many *makoms*—how is this attention to multiple roots and places manifested in Jewish life? We begin to address this question by examining two different, even contradictory, varieties of modern Jewish travel: Birthright tours of diaspora Jews to Israel and Israeli backpacking trips to the Far East. Both phenomena involve young adults in intensive immersion in a foreign culture that highlights or reveals something about their identity as Jews or Jewish Israelis, respectively. Though travel in the postmodern world certainly differs in important respects from the kinds of movement discussed in earlier chapters, contemporary travel to a perceived ancestral or cultural center—and away from it—still shares some distinctive elements with premodern notions of pilgrimage, and travel more broadly construed. Finally, I would also like to suggest that the recent rise in Jewish environmentalism is another expression of a devotion to a plurality of Places (*mekomot*) that are no less sacred than the original Place. Much Jewish engagement with the environment entails normative notions of *makom*—the Earth's holiness and our place in it, an updated version of Eden, gone bad. Divergent approaches to the natural world from stewardship to exploitation, and competing notions of wilderness and the garden as models for ethical environmental practice, may be understood in relation to historical forms of Jewish place-making.

Travel Revisited: Jewish Tourism and Israeli Backpacking

Diaspora homeland tourism and Israeli backpacking to areas such as India, East Asia, and South America have emerged in recent decades as characteristic forms of travel, creating attachments to space and place that are related to, but distinct from, some of the ideas about place-making we have discussed thus far. Each raises fundamental questions about how space is created and the relation between these spaces and notions of place, identity, and belonging. Heritage tours such as Birthright are premised on some of the old longing-for-a-lost-center model; often combined with trips to "sacred" European sites related to the Shoah and to Jewish life before World War II, modern Jewish homeland tourism also entails a newly confident sense of diaspora and a revised balance between the sovereign state of Israel and Jews whose home is elsewhere. Indeed, Birthright—though related to earlier forms of Jewish educational tourism that stressed the importance of a tie to Israel—also inscribes the very condition it would seem to be mitigating against; that is, the program accepts the condition of diaspora even as it promotes an attachment, indeed a "right" to belonging in Israel as well.[2] We might see in this most emblematic encounter with Israel a recalibrated sense of the meaning of the Jewish state in American Jewish life, and a sober reevaluation of Zionism after six decades of statehood.

A revised sense of center and margins also informs the beginnings of the Israeli diaspora. Sociologists Chaim Noy and Erik Cohen have argued that certain patterns of Israeli backpacking are related to what Israelis perceive as the mobile boundaries of their own state. Due to the unstable political nature of the state's existence, Cohen argues that Israeli youth have come of age with a sense of the boundaries of the state as negotiable and given to flux. They bring this mentality to their travels abroad as well, treating their extended post-military service treks as journeys to a new frontier.[3] Anthropological work has also demonstrated how Israeli backpackers typically use certain descriptive vocabulary that extends ideas inhering in the Israeli *makom*. For example, the terminology of the occupation may describe different kinds of touring activities: *kovshim* [conquerers, derived from the same root as *kibush*, occupation] to depict the activity of hiking and touring numerous sites; *mitnachalim* [settlers] to indicate the behavior of older trekkers who might stay in fewer locations for longer periods.[4] For these young Israeli trekkers, therefore, their identities as travelers and their "native" sense of place are symbolically entwined through language, specifically language relating to place and belonging. This re-creation of "Israeli locality" is also facilitated by the extensive use of Hebrew-language signs and names for institutions such as guesthouses, restaurants, cafes, and other services catering to backpackers.[5] The existence of these enclaves in what amounts to an Israeli diaspora fundamentally disrupts the connection between culture and roots and the idea that identity may be tied to a particular physical site—even through its absence. In a sense, this export of the local to widely scattered sites resembles the portability that, as we have seen, often defined Jewish cultures historically; at the same time, these Israeli "ethnoscapes"[6] also resemble the kinds of spaces created globally by other diaspora communities who carry with them cultural traces of their homelands.

The Garden Revisited: Judaism and Ecology

Does Judaism have an antagonistic relationship to nature? An influential 1967 article in the journal *Science* pinned a large part of the blame for the world's environmental crises on the Judeo-Christian tradition, in which nature and all its riches were created "explicitly for man's benefit and rule: no item in the physical creation had any purpose save to serve man's purposes."[7] The article refers to a view of the natural world that is also implicit within a certain strata of traditional Judaic texts, exemplified by a famous section of the mishnaic collection *Pirkey Avot* [Sayings of the Fathers]. The passage in question asserts the supremacy of textual study over nature appreciation: "One who while walking along the way, reviewing his studies, breaks off from his study and says, 'How beautiful is that tree! How beautiful is that plowed field!' Scripture regards him as if he had forfeited his soul."[8] In rabbinic terms, admiration of the natural world was akin to idolatry; admiring God's handiwork could lead to worshipping it, sanctifying it, followed by the slippery slope to paganism. This view was largely internalized and incorporated within Zionism's general condemnation of diaspora Jews. Micah Joseph Berdichevski's revision of *Pirkey Avot* neatly summarizes the (re)turn to the natural world envisioned as central to the Zionist project: "Whoever walks by the way and sees a fine tree and a fine field and a fine sky and leaves them to think on other thoughts—that man is like one who forfeits his life! Give us back our fine trees and fine fields! Give us back the Universe!"[9] Recent Jewish environmentalist thought has sought to refute this supposed antagonism toward nature by retheorizing Judaism's relation to the natural world through a revisionary reading of canonical texts. Indeed, biblical texts describe different kinds of relationships to nature, from the mastery of Genesis 1:28 to notions of codependency and stewardship. For example, the promise of the land and its fertility are tied to humanity's ethical behavior. One scholar notes that the "Bible indicates a variety of ways in which nature is subservient to man, but also ways in which man is subservient to nature."[10] For those operating from within a religious tradition, the main point of contention seems to be whether God is immanent or transcendent, in and of the world, or outside it. If the former, the danger of paganism lurks; if the latter, nature is potentially devalued.[11] One scholar has argued against this kind of polarizing, either/or view of nature, calling instead for a diversity of cultural metaphors that mirrors the earth's biodiversity.[12] For Eilon Schwartz, strict adherence to one model or another—nature as either an awe-inspiring, potentially deified wilderness or a garden to be tilled and tended—diminishes our ability to fully appreciate nature and potentially leads to environmental disaster. Indeed, in chapter 2 we noted the already hybrid quality of garden, a human spatial artifact embedded in, and constituted by, the natural world. In light of Amichai's "Lord of Places," this biocultural pluralism and an insistence on how humanity and nature are intertwined constitute a neat twist on nature as a mirror of the divine: if god is manifold, then so too should be our apprehension of the environment.

Eco-Jews and *Greenkeit*: The New Jewish Environmentalism

Recent years have seen an explosion of Jewish environmental activity, both in the United States and in Israel, touching on issues such as sustainability and food cultures as well as broader concerns of social justice, both local and global. The emergence of these new Jewish forms of eco-observance—synagogues hosting organic food cooperatives and Community Supported Agriculture, JCCs sponsoring locavore cholent cook-offs, the ethical slaughter movement—seems to represent a near seismic shift in Jewish attitudes toward land and space. In a post-diaspora world, is the environment the new place where Jews feel most at home? What is connection between environmental concerns and neo-hasidic forms of Jewish spirituality? What might a "Jewish theology of nature" look like?[13] And how is Jewish environmentalism practiced? These questions and others have driven a broad range of Jewish responses to environmental crises of the past several decades and the emergence of both global and local environmental groups. What began as a set of grassroots movements in the 1970s, highlighting the commonalities between Jewish ritual observance and sensitivity to the natural world, has arrived at the turn of the twenty-first century as a set of fully engaged, cutting-edge social movements and political lobbies, whose coalition partners range from local food kitchens to members of congressional subcommittees.[14] Jewish environmentalism in the United States has come of age alongside global environmentalism and has it own corner of boutique concerns: eco-kashrut, Sabbath-friendly bike rides, and the green construction and maintenance of synagogues.[15] One might wonder if this new, environmentally committed lifestyle represents a postmodern incarnation of Isaac Deutscher's "non-Jewish Jew," those Jews who characteristically operated on the margins of society, "in society and yet not in it, of it and yet not of it,"[16] a diverse group whose cultural and social mobility inspired Yuri Slezkine's characterization of modernity as "the Jewish century."[17] These same qualities informed the involvement of many American Jews in the civil rights movement in the 1960s. At the same time, comparing these American groups with their Israeli counterparts offers us a final opportunity to consider the different meanings of space and place for Jewish cultures in disparate geographic and social situations.

In Israel, environmentalism has become increasingly attached to movements for social justice, and issues such as civil rights, public health, fair housing, clean water, and transportation. Precisely because land issues are paramount in Israel, a concern for the environment is inextricably bound up with questions about space and who controls it.[18] At the same time, this emergence of a concern for environmental justice[19] is consonant with environmentalism's evolution as a global movement. This process, dating roughly from the 1990s, has entailed the realignment of what were perceived as narrow ecological concerns with broader goals reflecting an appreciation of the environment as a sphere encompassing all kinds of human behaviors and activities. In local terms, while early Zionist approaches to nature involved an escape from history,[20] and an erasure of Palestinian memory (see the discussion in chapter 4), contemporary Israeli environmentalists often expressly acknowledge the difficulty of separating "the broader national conflict between Jews and Arabs from Israel's ecological experience."[21] For example, the extent to which the minority Israeli Arab population may be discriminated against in environmental terms—greater exposure to hazardous material or waste and "impaired access to natural resources"[22]—is part of a diverse menu of concerns currently being tackled by the over one hundred grassroots organizations composing the umbrella group "Life and Environment: The Israeli Union of Environmental NGOs."[23] This close attention to the lived particulars of place, to the production of space as an ongoing and contentious process, subject to both institutional control and individual agency, characterizes Israeli environmentalism at its best. At the same time, Israeli environmentalists are also indebted to an abiding sense of place,[24] the legacy—for better and for worse—of Zionism. We have seen how Gurevitch and others insist upon the continuing, fundamental estrangement between Israeli Jews and their place, between the Story about the Place and the Place Itself (see the discussion in chapter 1), this despite the elaborate discourses invented by the state and its institutions to instill a sense of belonging and nativeness. While this gap may have historically defined Israeli national culture, the new environmentalism represents an appreciation for the Israeli *makom* that is fully alive to the present and treats Israeli space as subject to both history as well as a particular set of contemporary, material circumstances. Together with the revamped sense of *tikkun olam* [repairing the world] that infuses Jewish environmentalism outside Israel, the new *greenkeit* signifies the latest iteration of Jewish place-making, an indication of space's enduring force within Jewish cultures.

In this volume we have explored how Jewish cultures have engaged in spatial practices across a range of historical and geographic settings, with special attention to the text as a repository of ideas about space and place. Though often viewed as the "people of the book," and as somehow lacking geography, spatial thinking has in fact permeated Jewish cultural expression. Contemporary critical models of the relation between space and place provide a way of assessing the strands common to Jewish spatial practices across time and space, and thinking about those behaviors unique to Jewish cultures in relation to place-making more generally. So, for example, the practices of portability and substitution—the *mishkan* for the Temple, holiday ritual observance for the ancient, agrarian landscape, the museum space for the *shtetl*—which have long marked Jewish diasporic existence may be understood under the broad rubric of how all communities trade on memory and symbolic constructs to create a sense of place and belonging. This "production of locality" has increasingly come to characterize cultural practice within the transnational global landscape. Considering Jewish spaces such as those discussed in this study in relation to contemporary models of place-making can only deepen our appreciation of the complexity of Jewish spatial practice, whether located within the historically privileged realm of the text or embedded in the physical landscapes of Jewish experience.

This volume has aimed to introduce readers to these and other critical questions informing contemporary scholarship about space and place, and to read these ideas back into Jewish history, exploring as wide a swath as possible of texts, places, and rituals. In thinking about this diverse but necessarily limited collection of spaces, this book has particularly explored the relation of Jewish cultures to both the idea of the Promised Land and the religious community implied therein. The volume's trajectory from "Terms of Debate" through "State of the Question" and "In a New Key" suggests a still-evolving relation between Jews, cultural practice, and the Land. As observed in an earlier chapter, initial biblical descriptions of the Land depict it from a distance, viewed "*mi-neged*" [from afar]. Some sort of displacement of this most central of spaces thus occurs with its very introduction into Jewish history. Jewish culture retains more than a residue of this initial decentering of the land. Indeed, an acknowledgment of what we might call a "post-*makom*" world informs contemporary Jewish cultural expression and will no doubt continue to shape future spatial practices. While the negotiation between diaspora and homeland remains central to Jewish cultural expression, this tension has always also produced conditions of rupture and multiplicity, whose abiding presence continues to forge a distinct imprint upon modern Jewish experience. This project thus joins the growing body of scholarship within Jewish studies devoted to exploring these multifarious connections between space and cultural identity, broadening the arena of discourse to include an expressly interdisciplinary method. It was suggested at the start of this volume that its chapters need not be read sequentially. Upon reaching these concluding paragraphs, however, the reader is urged to return full circle to the introductory pages, and also to continue one's intellectual exploration outside the boundaries of these covers, to those myriad spaces and places intimated within.

Notes

INTRODUCTION

1. By marking the term with qualifying quotation marks, I mean to acknowledge the often ideologically driven notion of canonicity. Revealing the assumptions undergirding canonicity does not necessarily, to my mind, diminish the power of the canon, but simply grounds each and every cultural artifact in its historical context.

2. See the introduction to Julia Brauch, Anna Lipphardt, and Alexandra Nocke, eds., *Jewish Topographies: Visions of Space, Traditions of Place* (Burlington, Vt.: Ashgate, 2008).

3. Yehuda Amichai, *A Life in Poetry: 1948–1994* (New York: Harper, 1995), 419.

4. Yi-Fu Tuan, *Space and Place: The Perspective of Experience* (Minneapolis: University of Minnesota Press, 2001), 6.

5. Zali Gurevitch and Gideon Aran, "Al ha-makom," *Alpayim* 4 (1991): 9–44. See the abridged translation "The Double Site of Israel," in *Grasping Land: Space and Place in Contemporary Israeli Discourse and Experience*, ed. Eyal Ben-Ari and Yoram Bilu (Albany: State University of New York Press, 1997).

6. See note 2 above and the special issue of *Jewish Social Studies* 11:3 (Spring/Summer 2005) entitled "Jewish Conceptions and Practices of Space."

CHAPTER 1 — *MAKOM*

1. Genesis Rabbah 68:8.

2. I am grateful to Malachi Hacohen for this suggestion.

3. "Just as 'Heaven' is a metonym for 'the God of heaven,' so is also Maqom [literally, 'Place'] used metonymically and refers to the God who reveals Himself in whatever place he wishes." Ephraim A. Urbach, *The Sages: Their Concepts and Beliefs* (Jerusalem: Magnes, 1975), 72.

4. If you look up the word *makom* in the Even-Shoshan Hebrew dictionary (like the *OED*, it offers expansive definitions and examples from literature), you will find that it may refer to "a specific area or space that each body/person occupies or may occupy" and the following example from the Hebrew Bible: "the place that you are standing upon is holy land" (Exod. 3:5). This primary definition is followed by several other general definitions of place including location, settlement, seat, space, and condition or status. The first example of a secondary definition is the midrashic use, where *Makom* = God.

But this consonance is hinted at, I would argue, in the very first instance, where holiness, or the divinity, is evoked to illustrate the most basic definition of space.

5. Baruch Bokser, "Approaching Sacred Space," *Harvard Theological Review* 78:3–4 (1985): 279–299, here 280.

6. The phrase is from Frances Yates's classic study *The Art of Memory* (1966; reprint, Chicago: University of Chicago Press, 2001).

7. Bokser, "Approaching Sacred Space," 290.

8. Jonathan Z. Smith, *To Take Place: Toward Theory in Ritual* (Chicago: University of Chicago Press, 1992).

9. S. Y. Agnon, *A Book That Was Lost and Other Stories* (New York: Schocken, 1996), 155.

10. Zali Gurevitch and Gideon Aran, "*Al ha-makom,*" *Alpayim* 4 (1991): 9–44.

11. Yael Zerubavel, *Recovered Roots: Collective Memory and the Making of Israeli National Tradition* (Chicago: University of Chicago Press, 1997).

12. Zali Gurevitch, "The Double Site of Israel," in *Grasping Land: Space and Place in Contemporary Israeli Discourse and Experience*, ed. Eyal Ben-Ari and Yoram Bilu (Albany: State University of New York Press, 1997), 204. For an evocative set of philosophical meditations on the meaning of *makom* in Israeli culture, see Ariel Hirshfeld, *Local Notes* [Hebrew] (Tel Aviv: Am Oved, 2000).

13. Michel Foucault, "Of Other Spaces," *Diacritics* 16:1 (Spring 1996): 22–27, here 22.

14. Yi-Fu Tuan, *Space and Place: The Perspective of Experience* (Minneapolis: University of Minnesota Press, 2001), 6.

15. Gaston Bachelard, *The Poetics of Space* (Boston: Beacon Press, 1994), 8.

16. Henri Lefebvre, *The Production of Space* (Oxford: Blackwell, 1991), 26–46. For a helpful discussion of these terms and of space and place in critical theory, see Tim Cresswell, *Place: A Short Introduction* (Oxford: Blackwell, 2004).

17. Lefebvre, *The Production of Space*, 39.

18. Ibid., 33.

19. Ibid.

20. David Harvey, "From Space to Place and Back Again: Reflections on the Condition of Postmodernity," in *Mapping the Futures: Local Cultures, Global Changes*, ed. Jon Bird et al. (London: Routledge, 1993).

21. See David Harvey, *The Condition of Postmodernity: An Enquiry into the Origins of Cultural Change* (London: Blackwell, 1989), 240.

22. See Doreen Massey, "A Global Sense of Place," in *Space, Place and Gender* (Minneapolis: University of Minnesota Press, 1994).

23. Lefebvre, *The Production of Space*, 42.

24. Michel de Certeau, "Walking in the City," *The De Certeau Reader* (London: Blackwell, 2000), 103.

25. Edward W. Soja, *Postmodern Geographies: The Reassertion of Space in Critical Theory* (New York: Verso, 1989), 14.

26. Edward W. Soja, "Thirdspace: Expanding the Scope of the Geographical Imagination," in *Human Geography Today*, ed. Doreen Massey, John Allen, and Philip Sarre (Malden, Mass.: Blackwell, 1999), 260–278.

27. See my discussion in chapter 6, "Diasporas."

28. Massey, "Politics and Space/Time," *Space, Place and Gender*, 257.

29. Ibid., 260.

30. The phrase is the influential formulation of German historian Heinrich Graetz, whose multivolume *History of the Jews* began appearing in 1853.

31. Appadurai, "Introduction: Place and Voice in Anthropological Theory," *Cultural Anthropology* 3:1 (February 1988): 16.

32. Moshe Rosman, *How Jewish Is Jewish History* (London: Littman, 2007).

33. See especially the widely read 1995 special issue of *History & Memory* edited by Saul Friedlander, including articles by Anita Shapira, Uri Ram, and Ilan Pappe; and Derek Penslar, *Israel in History: The Jewish State in Comparative Perspective* (New York: Routledge, 2007).

34. Much of this dissatisfaction with history came from within the profession itself. Historians, especially those interested in visual culture, began to explore the movement between history and memory, an intellectual process that enabled the emergence of space as a productive analytical category.

35. Jean-François Lyotard, *The Postmodern Condition: A Report on Knowledge* (Minneapolis: University of Minnesota Press, 1984).

36. Pierre Nora, "Between Memory and History: Les Lieux de Memoire," *Representations* (Spring 1989): 7–24.

37. Ibid., 8–9.

38. The use of the term metaphorical here is meant to suggest the degree to which these less than physical "sites" (holidays, books, etc.) are always a kind of substitute, an imitation or copy that seeks to represent the imagined fullness of some originary space. Their failure to fully do so—the slippages between the plethora of extant memorial practices and the singular set of events they purport to commemorate—suggests nothing less than the very condition of memory itself, structured, as is Lacan's conception of the unconscious, like a language.

39. Chris Philo, "Foucault's Geography," in *Thinking Space*, ed. Mike Crang and Nigel Thrift (New York: Routledge, 2000), 207–208.

40. Maurice Halbwachs, "The Legendary Topography of the Gospels in the Holy Land," *On Collective Memory* (Chicago: University of Chicago Press, 1992), 196.

41. Nora, "Between Memory and History," 19.

CHAPTER 2 — THE GARDEN

1. We encounter the distinguishing features of *midbar* in chapter 5, *"Bayit."*

2. The idea of the garden as an allegory is one example of how nature more broadly construed has been instrumentalized for human purposes. A recognition of this exploitation of nature for other means, perhaps the very heart of contemporary environmentalism, is discussed in relation to Jewish culture in the concluding chapter.

3. *Kedem* also appears in the location describing exile from Eden, "east of Eden" [*kidmat eden*] (Gen. 4:13), and Jacob travels to the land of the easterners [*Bnei Kedem*, the sons of east] (Gen. 29:1). See another discussion of *kedem* in chapter 4, "The Land."

4. The power sharing implied in this relation is subject to interpretation. See chapter 9, "Environment."

5. Robert Alter, *Genesis: Translation and Commentary* (New York: W. W. Norton, 1997), 9.

6. See Paul Morris, "Exiled from Eden: Jewish Interpretations of Genesis," *A Walk in the Garden: Exegetical, Iconographical and Literary Interpretations of the Garden of Eden* (London: Sheffield, 1992), 117–166.

7. Evan Eisenberg, "The Ecology of Eden," in *Judaism and Ecology: Created World and Revealed Word*, ed. Hava Tirosh-Samuelson (Cambridge, Mass.: Harvard University Press, 2002), 49.

8. Francis Landy, "The Song of Songs and the Garden of Eden," *Journal of Biblical Literature* 98:4 (December 1979): 524.

9. Peter Cole, ed. and trans., *The Dream of the Poem: Hebrew Poetry from Muslim and Christian Spain, 950–1492* (Princeton, N.J.: Princeton University Press, 2007), 123.

10. This is essentially the argument of Jonathan Decter's *Iberian Jewish Literature: Between al-Andalus and Christian Europe* (Bloomington: Indiana University Press, 2007), on which I draw below.

11. Gil Anidjar, *"Our Place in Al-Andalus": Kabbalah, Philosophy, Literature in Arab Jewish Letters* (Stanford, Calif.: Stanford University Press, 2002), 68.

12. See Raymond P. Scheindlin, *Wine, Women & Death: Medieval Hebrew Poems on the Good Life* (Philadelphia: Jewish Publication Society, 1986), 7.

13. *Ketonet passim*—the youthful and seductive garb common to both at least two biblical figures—Joseph and King David's daughter Tamar.

14. In Scheindlin, *Wine, Women & Death*, 34–35, and Carmi, *The Penguin Book of Hebrew Verse* (London: Penguin, 2006), 323.

15. Decter, *Iberian Jewish Literature*, 180.

16. Ibid., 81–86, on various garden poems.

17. Carmi, *The Penguin Book of Hebrew Verse*, 280.

18. Scheindlin, *Wine, Women & Death*, 44.

19. Ammiel Alcalay, "A Garden Enclosed: The Geography of Time," *After Jews and Arabs: Remaking Levantine Culture* (Minneapolis: University of Minnesota Press, 1993), 163.

20. Decter, *Iberian Jewish Literature*, 20.

21. Ibid., 25.

22. For a discussion of how the idea of exile permeates Jewish thought, see chapter 6, "Diasporas."

23. Decter, *Iberian Jewish Literature*, 182–187.

24. See ibid., 87–95.

25. Cole, *The Dream of the Poem*, 133.

26. Epistles and poems by Yehuda Halevi, another important voice of this period, written during his late-in-life pilgrimage to Jerusalem, also contain images referencing the Garden of Eden, whose River Pishon was believed to be the Nile. See Raymond P. Scheindlin, *The Song of the Distant Dove: Judah Halevi's Pilgrimage* (Oxford: Oxford University Press, 2008), 115.

27. Tova Rosen, "Medieval Hebrew Literature: Portrayal of Women," http://jwa.org/encyclopedia/article/medieval-hebrew-literature-portrayal-of-women. Also see Shirley Kaufman, Galit Hasan-Rokem, and Tamar S. Hess, eds., *The Defiant Muse: Hebrew Feminist Poems from Antiquity to the Present: A Bilingual Anthology* (New York: The Feminist Press at CUNY, 1999); and Joel L. Kraemer, "Women's Letters from the Cairo Geniza" (Hebrew), in *A View into the Lives of Women in Jewish Societies*, ed. Yael Azmon (Jerusalem: Zalman Shazar Center, 1995), 161–182.

28. Cited in Tova Rosen, *Unveiling Eve: Reading Gender in Medieval Hebrew Literature* (Philadelphia: University of Pennsylvania Press, 2003), 9.

29. The one notable exception being the remaining fragment attributed to "The Wife of Dunash." See Cole, *The Dream of the Poem*, 27, and the brief but suggestive discussion "Missing Pages: Women's Poetry in the Levant," in Alcalay, *After Jews and Arabs*, 191–194.

30. Rosen, *Unveiling Eve*, 33.

31. Carmi, *The Penguin Book of Hebrew Verse*, 360–361.

32. Yosef Yerushalmi, "Exile and Expulsion in Jewish History," in *Crisis and Creativity in the Sephardic World, 1391–1648*, ed. Benjamin R. Gampel (New York: Columbia University Press, 1998), 11.

33. Ibid.

34. Ibid., 14.

35. Cole, *The Dream of the Poem*, 181.

36. Carmi, *The Penguin Book of Hebrew Verse*, 407.

37. Yerushalmi, "Exile and Expulsion in Jewish History," 14.

38. *Selected Poems of Moses Ibn Ezra*, trans. Solomon Solis-Cohen, ed. and annotated by Heinrich Brody (Philadelphia: Jewish Publication Society, 1945), 2.

39. Ibid., 5.

40. Stanley Tigerman, *The Architecture of Exile* (New York: Rizzoli, 1988), 25.

CHAPTER 3 — JERUSALEM

1. Al-Kuds Al-Sharif: "Holy Jerusalem," especially the area known as the Dome of the Rock.

2. Eli Amir, *Yasmin* (Tel Aviv: Am Oved, 2005), 12–13.

3. Ibid.

4. See Adriana Kemp, "Borders, Space, and National Identity in Israel" [Hebrew], *Theory & Criticism* 16 (Spring 2000): 13–44.

5. Though biographically a member of the Palmach Generation of 1948, Amichai's poetic sensibility belonged to that of a slightly younger generation, known as the Likrat group (for the name of their journal) or State Generation. He was part of a group of poets whose work rejected the grandiose imagery and more overtly collective ethos of earlier poets, and instead spoke of colloquial, everyday experience. Amichai first came to public attention with poems written after 1948, which described a self attempting to remain in control vis-à-vis external circumstances, and presented a view of the war that was both personal and more universal. His private world is shot through with metaphors of the public world.

6. Yehuda Amichai, *Poems of Jerusalem and Love Poems* (New York: The Sheep Meadow Press, 1992), 43.

7. Ibid., 52–54.

8. Ibid., 63.

9. Ibid., 51.

10. Ibid., 57.

11. Ibid., 39.

12. Italo Calvino, *Invisible Cities* (New York: Harcourt Brace Jovanovich, 1974), 10.

13. As W. D. Davies wryly notes, "Few peoples have failed to discover some geographic sign of grace." *The Territorial Dimension of Judaism* (Berkeley: University of California Press, 1982), 4.

14. Philip S. Alexander, "Jerusalem as the Omphalos of the World: On the History of a Geographical Concept," in *Jerusalem: Its Sanctity and Centrality to Judaism, Christianity, and Islam* (New York: Continuum Publishing, 1999), 104.

15. Cited in ibid., 114.

16. "Ten *kav* of beauty came down to the world—Jerusalem took nine, and all the rest of the world one. . . . / Ten portions of suffering are in the world—nine in Jerusalem, and one in the rest of the world. . . . Ten portions of wisdom are in the world—nine in Jerusalem, and one in the rest of the world. Ten portions of hypocrisy are in the world—nine in Jerusalem, and one in the rest of the world." Cited in *The Book of Legends: Sefer Ha-agada, Legends from the Talmud and Midrash*, ed. H. N. Bialik and Y. Ravinitzky, trans. William G. Braude (New York: Schocken, 1992), 372. Originally published in Hebrew in Odessa, 1908–1911.

17. This idea of a heavenly city originates in the prophet Isaiah's vision of a heavenly temple in which "the Lord sits upon his throne, high and lifted up," surrounded by angels (*seraphim*) (Isa. 6). It is elaborated upon thus: "Jerusalem is directly above, opposite earthly Jerusalem. It was because of the great love [God] had for earthly Jerusalem that He created another in heaven, as it is said, 'See, I have engraved you upon the palms of My hands, your walls are ever before Me'" (Isa. 49:16). Why then was it destroyed? Because "swiftly your children are coming; those who ravaged and ruined you shall leave you" (Isa. 49:17). Because of that it was destroyed. Thus David said: "Jerusalem built up, a city knit together [Ps. 122:3]—that is, a city which God built. The Jerusalem constructed in heaven is joined together as one with the one that is on earth. God has sworn that His presence will not enter heavenly Jerusalem until earthly Jerusalem is rebuilt" (*Tanchuma Pekudei* 1). Quoted in Reuven Hammer, *The Jerusalem Anthology: A Literary Guide* (Philadelphia: Jewish Publication Society, 1995), 139–140.

18. This is essentially the argument promoted in W. D. Davies, *The Territorial Dimension in Judaism* and also by contemporary theorists of the diaspora. See the related discussions in chapters 4 and 6.

19. Calvino, *Invisible Cities*, 30.

20. Oleg Grabar, "Space and Holiness in Medieval Jerusalem," in *Jerusalem: Its Sanctity and Centrality in Judaism, Christianity, and Islam*, ed. Lee I. Levine (New York: Continuum, 1999), 275.

21. Milka Levy-Rubin and Rehav Rubin, "The Image of the Holy City in Maps and Mapping," in *City of the Great King: Jerusalem from David to the Present*, ed. Nitza Rosovsky (Cambridge, Mass.: Harvard University Press, 1996), 352.

22. Grabar, "Space and Holiness," 276.

23. Ibid., 277.

24. Ibid., 285.

25. Calvino, *Invisible Cities*, 19.

26. Sidra Ezrahi, "'To what shall I compare you?': Jerusalem as Ground Zero of the Hebrew Imagination," *PMLA* 122:1 (2007): 223–224.

27. "The more exalted the metaphoric status of Jerusalem, the more dwarfed its geopolitical dimensions; the more expansive the metaphysical boundaries of the Holy City, the less negotiable its municipal borders." Ibid., 226.

28. Jacob Neusner, "Map without Territory: Mishnah's System of Sacrifice and Sanctuary," *History of Religions* 19:2 (November 1979): 103–127, here 121. Neusner brings a statement by Jonathan Z. Smith to support this tongue-in-cheek proposition: "I should want to go so far as to argue that if the Temple had not been destroyed, it would have to be neglected. For it represented a locative type of religious activity no longer perceived as effective in a new, utopian religious situation with a concomitant shift from a cosmological to an anthropological viewpoint."

29. Ibid.

30. *The Complete Art Scroll Siddur* (Brooklyn: Mesorah Publications, 2006), 109.

31. *The Complete Art Scroll Machzor: Yom Kippur* (Brooklyn: Mesorah Publications, 2007), 554.

32. Ibid., 562–563.

33. From Heinrich Heine, "ein portatives Vaterland."

34. Baruch Bokser, *The Origins of the Seder: The Passover Rite and Early Rabbinic Judaism* (Berkeley: University of California Press, 1984).

35. Raymond P. Scheindlin, *The Song of the Distant Dove: Judah Halevi's Pilgrimage* (Oxford: Oxford University Press, 2008), 168–169.

36. Ibid., 170.

37. In another related poem, Halevi actually uses the phrase *"mi-pa'atey ma'arav,"* a phrase that may be echoed in the Israeli national anthem's *"mi-pa'atey mizrach."*

38. Scheindlin, *The Song of the Distant Dove*, 173. See also the discussion in Ezrahi, "'To what shall I compare you?'" 224–225.

39. Tikva Frymer-Kensky, "Zion, the Beloved Woman," in *In the Wake of the Goddesses: Women, Culture, and the Biblical Transformation of Pagan Myth* (New York: Free Press, 1992), 168.

40. Translation from the Jewish Publication Society.

41. See the examples alluded to in Ammiel Alcalay, *After Jews and Arabs: Remaking Levantine Culture* (Minneapolis: University of Minnesota Press, 1993), 136–143, themselves shaped by the wealth of material in S. D. Goitein, *A Mediterranean Society* (Berkeley: University of California Press, 2003).

42. Elkan Nathan Adler, ed., *Jewish Travellers in the Middle Ages: 19 Firsthand Accounts* (1930; reprint, New York: Dover, 1987), 64–91.

43. Fantasy also played a part in early Jewish voyaging. A midrashic text mentions a river that flows only six days a week and then ceases on the Sabbath (Genesis Rabbah 73:6). Across the mythical river Sambatyon, there supposedly existed an independent Israelite entity; this kingdom, also "discovered" by Eldad the Danite in the ninth century, was said to have been founded by the ten lost tribes sent into exile in 722 B.C.E. by the Assyrian conquerers of Israel. See Shalva Vail, *Beyond the Sambatyon: The Myth of the*

Tens Lost Tribes (Tel Aviv: Beth Hatefutsoth, The Museum of the Jewish Diaspora, 1991), and Adler, *Jewish Travellers in the Middle Ages*, 4–21.

44. Adler, *Jewish Travellers*, 131.

45. Goitein, *A Mediterranean Society*, 124. See also Margalit Shilo, *Princess or Prisoner?: Jewish Women in Jerusalem: 1840–1914* (Waltham, Mass.: Brandeis University/University Press of New England, 2005), xxiii; and Yisrael Bartal, *Galut ba-aretz* (Jerusalem: Ha-sifriyah ha-tsionit, 1994).

46. Goitein, *A Mediterranean Society*, 206.

47. Theodor Herzl, *Old-New Land*, trans. Lotta Levensohn (1960; reprint, Princeton, N.J.: Markus Wiener Publishers, 1997), 42. Originally published in German in 1902.

48. Ibid., 44.

49. From October 31, 1898. Cited in Shlomo Avineri, "Theodor Herzl's Diaries as Bildungsroman," *Jewish Social Studies* 5:3 (1999): 40.

50. Dan Miron, "Depictions in Modern Hebrew Literature," *City of the Great King: Jerusalem from David to the Present* (Cambridge, Mass.: Harvard University Press, 1996).

51. S. Y. Agnon, *Only Yesterday* (1946; reprint, Princeton, N.J.: Princeton University Press, 2002), 485, 595.

52. Amos Oz, *The Hill of Evil Counsel* (New York: Harvest, 1976), 11.

53. Ibid., 17–18.

54. David Grossman, *Someone to Run With* (New York: Farrar, Straus and Giroux, 2004), 16.

55. Doreen Massey, "A Place Called Home?" in *Space, Place and Gender* (Minneapolis: University of Minnesota Press, 1994), 169.

56. From Philipp Misselwitz and Tim Rieniets, *Cities of Collision: Jerusalem and the Principles of Conflict Urbanism* (2006), excerpted in *Blok 4: Occasional Cities* (Spring 2007): 37–40.

57. Michael Sorkin, "Introduction: Thinking about Jerusalem," in *The Next Jerusalem: Sharing the Divided City*, ed. Michael Sorkin (New York: Monacelli Press, 2002), 12.

58. Moshe Safdie, "Jerusalem: United City, Two Sovereignties," in Sorkin, *The Next Jerusalem*, 277.

59. Alona Nitzan-Shiftan, "Capital City or Spiritual Center? The Politics of Architecture in Post-1967 Jerusalem," *Cities* 22:3 (2005): 229.

60. Eran Tamir-Tawil, "To Start a City from Scratch: An Interview with Architect Thomas M. Leitersdorf," in *A Civilian Occupation: The Politics of Israeli Architecture*, ed. Rafi Segal and Eyal Weizman (New York: Verso, 2003), 153.

61. Safdie, "Jerusalem: United City, Two Sovereignties," 278.

62. Ibid., 280.

63. Further discussion of the "new Jewish global architecture" is found in chapter 7, "The City."

64. See the recent article by Saree Makdisi, "The Architecture of Erasure," *Critical Inquiry* 36:3 (Spring 2010): 519–559, and responses by Gehry and others.

65. Philip Nobel, "Art/Architecture: What Design for a Synagogue Spells Jewish?," *New York Times*, December 2, 2001.

CHAPTER 4 — THE LAND

1. Arnold Eisen, *Galut: Modern Jewish Reflection on Homelessness and Homecoming* (Bloomington: Indiana University Press, 1986), xiv–xv and all of part 1.

2. It is beyond the scope of this study to survey the vast history of traditional Jewish attitudes toward the land of Israel and their expression in Jewish culture. See W. D. Davies, *The Territorial Dimension in Judaism* (Berkeley: University of California Press, 1982), for a comprehensive account of how relatively little territory has mattered, and Jean-Christophe Attias and Esther Benbassa, *Israel, the Impossible Land* (Stanford, Calif.: Stanford University Press, 2003), for an opposite view.

3. Judges 11:19 is but one of many other examples.

4. According to Isaiah Gafni, "Sensitivity to the plight of the Land—and ensuing calls for commitment—appear precisely at a watershed in the history of the Land of Israel, when Jews slowly ceased to be the dominant ethnic factor in the Land, or at least came to fear this possibility for the first time." See Gafni, *Land, Center and Diaspora: Jewish Constructs in Late Antiquity* (Sheffield: Sheffield Academic Press, 1997), 78.

5. Thus in Zali Gurevitch's reading, settlement in the Land is always ambivalent. See the discussion below.

6. For a cogent summary see Gafni, "Between Activism and Passivity: Rabbinic Attitudes Towards 'The Land,'" in *Land, Center and Diaspora*, 58–78. For more discussion of rabbinic writing and space, see the discussion in chapter 5, "*Bayit*."

7. Attias and Benbassa, *Israel, the Impossible Land*, 86.

8. Gurevitch, "The Double Site of Israel," in *Grasping Land: Space and Place in Contemporary Israeli Discourse and Experience,* ed. Eyal Ben-Ari and Yoram Bilu (Albany: State University of New York Press, 1997), 206.

9. See Benedict Anderson, *Imagined Communities: Reflections on the Origin and Spread of Nationalism* (London: Verso, 1983).

10. Though it has been commonly read as a Zionist vision of the intimate bond between Jews and *Eretz Yisrael*, his long poem "Man Is Nothing But the Image of His 'Homelandscape'" (1925) actually celebrates the rich and storied world of the Ukrainian steppes in which the poet was born.

11. Literally, "months or moons of old."

12. "Before a Statue of Apollo," *Shaul Tchernichovski: Shirim* [Poems], vol. 1 (Tel Aviv: Dvir, 1966), 86.

13. This valorization of an earlier, pre-diasporic setting as the necessary model for Israeli's cultural development reaches its fullest expression in the Canaanite movement of arts and letters in Israel in the 1950s and afterward.

14. For example, Richard Wagner's "Jewry in Music" (1850).

15. Ivan Davidson Kalmar and Derek J. Penslar, "Orientalism and the Jews: An Introduction," *Orientalism and the Jews* (Waltham, Mass.: Brandeis University Press, 2005), xiii.

16. Yaron Peleg, *Orientalism and the Hebrew Imagination* (Ithaca, N.Y.: Cornell University Press, 2005), 8–9.

17. Yigal Tsalmona, "To the East?" in *Kadima: Orientalism in Israeli Art* (Jerusalem: Israel Museum, 1998), ix.

18. Ammiel Alcalay, *After Jews and Arabs: Remaking Levantine Culture* (Minneapolis: University of Minnesota Press, 1993), 27.

19. See Alexandra Nocke, *The Place of the Mediterranean in Modern Israeli Identity* (Leiden: Brill, 2009).

20. For a recent reevaluation, see Lital Levy, "Reorienting Hebrew Literary History," *Prooftexts* 29:2 (2009): 127–172.

21. From *The Song of the Architect* [Hebrew] (Jerusalem: Zmora, Bitan, 1987), 37.

22. See the discussion of Yehuda Halevi's famous medieval ode in chapter 3.

23. Quoted in Boaz Neumann, *Land and Desire in Early Zionism* [Hebrew] (Tel Aviv: Am Oved, 2009), 56.

24. Brenner, "Nerves," *Eight Great Hebrew Short Novels* (New Haven, Conn.: Toby Press, 2004), 31.

25. Ibid., 32.

26. Avraham Shlonsky, *Shirim,* vol. 1 (Tel Aviv: Hakibbutz hameuchad, 1954), 197.

27. A. D. Gordon, "People and Labor" (1911), in *The Zionist Idea* (Philadelphia: Jewish Publication Society, 1997), 372.

28. Hanan Hever, "Mapping Literary Spaces: Territory and Violence in Israeli Literature," in *Mapping Jewish Identities,* ed. Laurence J. Silberstein (New York: New York University Press, 2000), 203.

29. Shlonsky, *Shirim,* vol. 2., 311–317.

30. See Yochai Oppenheimer, *Barriers: The Representation of the Arab in Hebrew and Israeli Fiction, 1906–2005* [Hebrew] (Tel Aviv: Am Oved, 2008), 102–110.

31. Anita Shapira, *Land and Power: The Zionist Resort to Force, 1881–1948* (Palo Alto, Calif.: Stanford University Press, 2000), 1999.

32. For publication details see Hanan Hever, *Paytanim u'viryonim: Tsemichat hashir hapoliti ha'ivri be'erets yisrael* (Jerusalem: Mosad Bialik, 1994).

33. Italo Calvino, *Invisible Cities* (New York: Harcourt Brace Jovanovich, 1974), 18.

34. For this view see Orit Ben-David, "Tiyul (Hike) as an Act of Consecration of Space," in Ben-Ari and Bilu, *Grasping Land*, 129–146.

35. Rebecca L. Stein, "Travelling Zion: Hiking and Settler-Nationalism in Pre-1948 Palestine," *Interventions* 11:3 (2009): 334–351.

36. See Yael Zerubavel, *Recovered Roots: Collective Memory and the Making of Israeli National Tradition* (Chicago: University of Chicago Press, 1997).

37. See Maoz Azaryahu, "From Remains to Relics: Authentic Monuments in the Israeli Landscape," *History & Memory* 5:2 (1993).

38. Don Handelman and Leah Shamgar-Handelman, "The Presence of Absence: The Memorialisation of National Death in Israel," in Ben-Ari and Bilu, *Grasping Land*, 85–128.

39. S. Yizhar, *Khirbet Khizeh* (1949; reprint, Jerusalem: Ibis Editions, 2008), 73, 77.

40. Ibid., 49, 50.

41. Ibid., 26–27.

42. Ibid., 104.

43. Ibid., 108.

44. Ibid., 88.

45. Ibid., 113.

46. For a persuasive and detailed account of the story's reception, see Anita Shapira, "Hirbat Hizah: Between Remembrance and Forgetting," *Jewish Social Studies* 7:1 (2000): 1–62.

47. Meron Benvenisti, "The Hebrew Map," *Sacred Landscape: The Buried History of the Holy Land Since 1948* (Berkeley: University of California Press, 2000), for an evocative account of this process. For a detailed account of how villages were destroyed in both space and memory, see Noga Kadman, *Erased from Space and Consciousness: Depopulated Palestinian Villages in the Israeli-Zionist Discourse* [Hebrew] (Tel Aviv: November Books, 2008), esp. 50–68.

48. Meron Benvenisti, "Blank Spaces: Talbiyah and Rehavia," *SAIS Review* 20:1 (2000): 215–220, here 217.

49. A. B. Yehoshua, "Facing the Forests," in *Modern Hebrew Literature*, ed. Robert Alter (1963; reprint, New York: Behrman House, 1975), 364.

50. See discussion of Gurevitch in chapter 1, "*Makom*."

51. In addition to their extended dialogue in print, portions of Shammas's novel *Arabesques* (1986) may be read as a critique of the depiction of Arabs in Hebrew fiction, especially in Yehoshua's work. See Gil Hochberg, *In Spite of Partition: Jews, Arabs, and the*

Limits of the Separatist Imagination (Princeton, N.J.: Princeton University Press, 2007), 90–91.

52. See Naama Meishar, "Fragile Guardians: Nature Reserves and Forests Facing Arab Villages," in *Constructing a Sense of Place: Architecture and the Zionist Discourse*, ed. Haim Yacobi (London: Ashgate, 2004), 303–325.

53. See Kadman, *Erased from Space and Consciousness*, 68–97.

54. The term "nakba" is used to describe the events of 1948, with specific reference to the destruction of Palestinian property and the removal of the Palestinian population, whether by expulsion or flight.

55. According to Haim Breyshit, "The Zionist occupation is not merely a military occupation, but also erases the many layers of memory trapped in the spaces of Gebalyia." Haim Breyshit, *"Givat ha-aliya* as an Allegory," *Teoria u'vikoret* 16 (Spring 2000): 238.

56. Susan Slyomovics, *The Object of Memory* (Philadelphia: University of Pennsylvania Press, 1998), xxii.

57. Eitan Bronstein, "Restless Park: On the Latrun Villages and Zochrot" (2008), http://www.zochrot.org/index.php?id=336.

58. Azmi Bashara, "Between Place and Space," *Studio* 37 (October 1992): 6–9.

59. Interview with Thomas Leitersdorf in *A Civilian Occupation: The Politics of Israeli Architecture*, ed. Eyal Weizman (New York: Verso, 2003), 160.

60. See the essays and images in *A Civilian Occupation*. The settlements may be viewed as an extension of the "wall and tower" (*homah u-migdal*) phase of Israeli architecture, responsible for many of the country's collective settlements that were often situated near borders or on perceived lines of defense. See Sharon Rotberd's "Wall and Tower," in *A Civilian Occupation*.

61. For a detailed account see Rene Backmann, *A Wall in Palestine* (New York: Picador, 2010).

62. Michael Feige, *Settling in the Hearts: Jewish Fundamentalism in the Occupied Territories* (Detroit: Wayne State University Press, 2009), 113.

63. Significantly, the Palestinians and Israelis are not the only populations obscured or separated by these roads; many of the same routes effectively isolate some portion of the ultra-Orthodox population, allowing for the passage of vehicular traffic on the Sabbath.

64. See, in this regard, Oren Yiftachel's argument regarding what he terms Israel's "ethnocratic" character, the degree to which the state's democratic apparatus belies its nature as an essentially expansionist enterprise: Yiftachel, *Ethnocracy: Land and Identity Politics in Israel/Palestine* (Philadelphia: University of Pennsylvania Press, 2006).

65. The presence of this vertigo in cultural production in and about Jerusalem is at the heart of Sidra Ezrahi's powerful arguments regarding Jewish creativity in the wake of return.

66. See the discussion about the *eruv* in chapter 5, "*Bayit*," and in part 3.

67. One well-publicized example concerned the Kaadan family, an Arab family that purchased land in the agricultural community of Katzir in northern Israel. The case was in the courts for nearly twelve years and has sparked extensive popular and legal discussion about the state and its constitutional ability to legislate land-use along ethnic lines.

68. For up-to-date accounts and reports, see the website of the Israeli organization *Kav Le-oved*: Worker's Hotline, at http://www.kavlaoved.org.il/section_eng.asp?pid=75.

CHAPTER 5 — *BAYIT*

1. The memory of home abides in different ways within Jewish cultures. According to Joelle Bahloul, "The remembered house is a small-scale cosmology symbolically restoring the integrity of a shattered geography." See *The Architecture of Memory: A Jewish-Muslim Household in Colonial Algeria, 1937–1962* (New York: Cambridge University Press), 28.

2. Vanessa Ochs, "What Makes a Jewish Home Jewish?" *Crosscurrents* 49, http://www.crosscurrents.org/ochsv.htm.

3. For a recent evaluation see Simon J. Bronner, "The Dualities of House and Home," in *Jews at Home: The Domestication of Identity*, ed. Bronner (Oxford: Littman, 2010), 1–42.

4. Yi-Fu Tuan, *Space and Place: The Perspective of Experience* (Minneapolis: University of Minnesota Press, 2001), 164.

5. Hindy Najman, "Towards a Study of the Uses of the Concept of Wilderness," *Dead Sea Discoveries* 13:1 (2006): 99–113, here 107.

6. See Ilana Pardes, *The Biography of Ancient Israel: National Narratives in the Bible* (Berkeley: University of California Press, 2000).

7. "Tabernacle," *Encyclopedia Judaica*, 2nd ed., vol. 19, 418–424.

8. For an account of how Pentateuchal documents diverge in their presentation of the *mishkan*, see Benjamin D. Sommer, "Conflicting Constructions of Divine Presence in the Priestly Tabernacle," *Biblical Interpretation: A Journal of Contemporary Approaches* 9 (2001): 41–63. One view presupposes the idea of a sacred center, the other a more "locative" conception of space. In Sommer's terms, this ambivalence "suggests that God is present even as it intimates that God's presence in the world is inappropriate" (63), a harbinger of those rabbinic texts whose authors wrestled with their own distance from a sacred center.

9. Jean-Christophe Attias and Esther Benbassa, *Israel, the Impossible Land* (Stanford, Calif.: Stanford University Press, 2003), 18.

10. See Marjorie Lehman, "Reimagining Home, Rethinking Sukkah," in Bronner, *Jews at Home*, 107–140.

11. Ranen Omer-Sherman, *Israel in Exile: Jewish Writing in the Desert* (Urbana: University of Illinois Press, 2006), 10.

12. Ibid., 2.

13. My focus on rabbinic culture in this chapter derives from the fact that much of what is today commonly considered "Judaism," and our understanding of what it means to be Jewish in a world of ethnic and national diversity, was first formulated in rabbinic texts, and these ideas have historically shaped the evolution of Jewish life. Moreover, recent scholarship has given us an increasingly complicated sense of what, and how, these texts mean, and some sections of this chapter draw explicitly on this new work.

14. Isaiah Gafni, *Land, Center and Diaspora: Jewish Constructs in Late Antiquity* (Sheffield: Sheffield Academic Press, 1997), 13–14.

15. Shabbat 118b.

16. See Charlotte Fonrobert, "The Woman as House," in *Menstrual Purity* (Stanford, Calif.: Stanford University Press, 2000), 50ff.

17. Bereshit Rabbah 18:3, cited in Fonrobert , "The Woman as House," 56–57.

18. See Martin Jaffe, "Rabbinic Authorship as a Collective Enterprise," in *The Cambridge Companion to the Talmud and Rabbinic Literature* (New York: Cambridge University Press, 2007).

19. Seth Schwartz, *Imperialism and Jewish Society,* 200 B.C.E. to 640 C.E. (Princeton, N.J.: Princeton University Press, 2004), 172.

20. Ibid., 175–176.

21. Ibid., 103–105.

22. Cynthia Baker, *Rebuilding the House of Israel: Architectures of Gender in Jewish Antiquity* (Stanford, Calif.: Stanford University Press, 2002), 7–8. The "rebuilding" in her title refers to her own "rereading" and to the rabbinic project of rebuilding of some sense of home.

23. Ibid., 8.

24. Ibid., 113.

25. Ibid., 56.

26. Adin Steinsaltz, *The Talmud: The Steinsaltz Edition, A Reference Guide* (New York: Random House, 1989), 241.

27. My thanks to Beth Berkowitz for this observation.

28. The notion of the *eruv* is connected with the practice of symbolically renting public space from a non-Jewish neighbor or authority, an action that makes the presence of non-Jews more concrete.

29. Charlotte Fonrobert, "The Political Symbolism of the Eruv," *Jewish Social Studies* 11:3 (2005): 9–35, here 28–29. See also Fonrobert, "From Separatism to Urbanism: The

Dead Sea Scrolls and the Origins of the Rabbinic Eruv," *Dead Sea Discoveries* 11:1 (2004): 43-71.

30. Fonrobert, "The Political Symbolism of the Eruv," 9.

31. Stephen Fine, *Art and Judaism in the Greco-Roman World: Toward a New Jewish Archaeology* (New York: Cambridge University Press, 2005), 39.

32. M. Avodah Zarah 3:4. For discussion and context see Yaron Eliav, "The Roman Bath as a Jewish Institution: Another Look at the Encounter between Judaism and the Greco-Roman Culture," *Journal for the Study of Judaism* 31 (2000): 416-454; Azzan Yadin, "Rabban Gamliel, Aphrodite's Bath and the Question of Pagan Monotheism," *Jewish Quarterly Review* 96:2 (Spring 2006): 149-179.

33. Fonrobert, "The Political Symbolism of the Eruv," 10.

34. See Gil P. Klein, "The Topography of Symbol: Between Late Antique and Modern Jewish Understanding of Cities," *Zeitschrift für Religions und Geistesgeschichte* 58:1 (2006): 16-28.

35. Also called *batei am*, houses of the people.

36. Lee I. Levine, *The Ancient Synagogue: The First Thousand Years* (New Haven, Conn.: Yale University Press, 2000), 165-168.

37. The long-influential ideas of Mircea Eliade held that sacredness in "primitive" societies existed in specific, fixed locations.

38. See my discussion in chapter 1.

39. Steven Fine, *This Holy Place: On the Sanctity of the Synagogue during the Greco-Roman Period* (South Bend, Ind.: University of Notre Dame Press, 1997).

40. Levine, *The Ancient Synagogue*, 180-181.

41. M. Megillah 3:1.

42. Jas Elsner, "Cultural Resistance and the Visual Image: The Case of Dura Europos," *Classical Philology* 26:3 (July 2001): 269-304, here 283.

43. Ibid., 299-301.

44. For a good overview see Lee I. Levine, "The Nature and Origin of the Palestinian Synagogue Reconsidered," *Journal of Biblical Literature* 115:3 (August 1996): 425-448.

45. Jean Amery, "How Much Home Does a Person Need?" in *At the Mind's Limit: Contemplations by a Survivor on Auschwitz and Its Realities* (Bloomington: Indiana University Press, 1980), 57.

46. Yosef Yerushalmi, "Exile and Expulsion in Jewish History," in *Crisis and Creativity in the Sephardic World, 1391-1648*, ed. Benjamin R. Gampel (New York: Columbia University Press, 1998). See the discussion of these terms in relation to Andalusian culture in chapter 2, "The Garden."

47. Erika Meitner, "The Mezuzah: American Judaism and Constructions of Domestic Sacred Space," in *American Sanctuary: Understanding Sacred Spaces*, ed. Louis P. Nelson (Bloomington: Indiana University Press, 2006), 182-202.

48. Barbara Kirshenblatt-Gimblett, "Kitchen Judaism," in *Getting Comfortable in New York: The American Jewish Home, 1880–1950* (New York: Jewish Museum, 1990), 75–105.

49. Kirshenblatt-Gimblett focuses on the physical home and the relation between this space and wider spheres produced by food, its preparation and consumption. I am drawing on the term's spatial quality as an example of how Jewish cultures display a consciousness regarding the specific locations in which they are produced.

50. Samuel Kassow, "Travel and Local History as a National Mission: Polish Jews and the Landkentenish Movement in the 1920s and 1930s," in *Jewish Topographies: Visions of Space, Traditions of Place*, ed. Julia Brauch, Anna Lipphardt, and Alexandra Nocke (Burlington, Vt.: Ashgate, 2008), 243.

51. I. L. Peretz, "Impressions," in *The I. L. Peretz Reader*, ed. Ruth Wisse (New York: Schocken, 1996), 58–59.

52. The passage also recalls the image from *Pirkey Avot*, where disciples are urged to study rather than admire their natural surroundings (see discussion in chapter 9).

CHAPTER 6 — DIASPORAS

1. In a letter from 1921, quoted in Peter Eli Gordon, *Rosenzweig and Heidegger* (Berkeley: University of California Press, 2003), 219.

2. For a compelling survey of paradigmatic attitudes see Arnold Eisen, *Galut: Modern Jewish Reflection on Homelessness and Homecoming* (Bloomington: Indiana University Press, 1986).

3. Ammiel Alcalay, *After Jews and Arabs: Remaking Levantine Culture* (Minneapolis: University of Minnesota Press, 1993), 27.

4. For this observation see Eric Gruen, "Diaspora and Homeland," in *Diasporas and Exiles: Varieties of Jewish Experience*, ed. H. Wettstein (Berkeley: University of California Press, 2002), 18–37.

5. See Israel J. Yuval, "The Myth of the Jewish Exile from the Land of Israel," *Common Knowledge* 12:1 (2006): 16–33.

6. See Isaiah Gafni's mention of this tension in relation to both Italian Jewry and Jews of late antiquity in "At Home While Abroad: Expressions of Local Patriotism in the Jewish Diaspora of Late Antiquity," in his *Land, Center and Diaspora: Jewish Constructs in Late Antiquity* (Sheffield: Sheffield Academic Press, 1997), 41.

7. James Clifford, "Diasporas," *Cultural Anthropology* 9:3 (August 1994): 302–338, here 322.

8. See the discussion of this in the next chapter, "The City."

9. America and Israel persist as the defining poles of postwar Jewish experience. For a view from Europe, upon which many Jews had largely, in the wake of the Shoah, turned their backs, see Diana Pinto, "The Third Pillar: Toward a European Jewish Identity," http://web.ceu.hu/jewishstudies/yearbook01.htm.

10. For a good overview, see Richard Cohen, "The 'Wandering Jew' from Medieval Legend to Modern Metaphor," in *The Art of Being Jewish in Modern Times*, ed. Barbara Kirshenblatt-Gimblett and Jonathan Karp (Philadelphia: University of Pennsylvania Press, 2008), 147–175. According to David Meyers, "In response to this perception, Jews have attempted over the past two centuries to uproot the Wanderer within, either by asserting indigeneity in their diaspora countries of residence or by reclaiming Palestine as their own." David N. Myers, "The Condition of Travel," *Jewish Quarterly Review* 99:4 (Fall 2009): 438.

11. Yi-Fu Tuan, *Space and Place: The Perspective of Experience* (Minneapolis: University of Minnesota Press, 2001), 6.

12. Ken Friedan, "Neglected Origins of Modern Hebrew Prose: Hasidic and Maskilic Travel Narratives," *AJS Review* 33:1 (April 2009): 3–43, here 5.

13. For this suggestion see Nancy Sinkoff, "Strategy and Ruse in the Haskalah of Mendel Lefin of Satanow," in *New Perspectives on the Haskalah*, ed. Shmuel Finer and David Sorkin (London: Littman, 2001), 86–102, here 93–94.

14. Friedan, "Neglected Origins of Modern Hebrew Prose," 29.

15. I. L. Peretz, "My Memoirs," in *The I. L. Peretz Reader*, ed. Ruth Wisse (New York: Schocken, 1996), 288.

16. See Leah Garret, *Journeys Beyond the Pale: Yiddish Travel Writing in the Modern World* (Madison: University of Wisconsin Press, 2003).

17. S. Y. Abramovitch, "Shem and Japheth on the Train," in *The Literature of Destruction: Jewish Responses to Catastrophe* (Philadelphia: Jewish Publication Society, 1989).

18. Despite its deep connection to the Zionist project, Modern Hebrew writing also had its share of "wandering Jews," displaying a deep ambivalence regarding the notion of homecoming. Witness the grudging travel to Palestine in fiction by Y. Ch. Brenner, whose "Nerves" tracks the protagonist's restlessness from Russia to New York, London, and finally through Berlin, Trieste, Alexandria, Cairo, and Port Said before arriving, via Haifa, in Palestine. After his arrival he wonders about the degree to which the Jew will be comfortable outside the ghetto. And within Palestine, the wandering continues, in this story and in others by S. Y. Agnon ("From Lodging to Lodging" [1938]) and by Devora Baron ("The Exiles" [1919?], set in Cairo during World War I within a community of Jewish émigrés from Tel Aviv).

19. Kadya Molodowsky, "In My Hand Two Feathers from a Peasant," in *Paper Bridges: Selected Poems of Kadya Molodowsky* (Detroit: Wayne State University Press, 1999), 345. The poem references Birobidzhan, a town at the center of the Soviet Union's "Jewish Autonomous District," established as a Jewish homeland by Stalin in 1934.

20. Dan Miron, "Sh. Y. Abramovitsh and His 'Mendele,'" in *The Image of the Shtetl and Other Studies of Modern Jewish Literary Imagination* (Syracuse: Syracuse University Press, 2001), 110.

21. Sholem Aleichem, *The Letters of Menakhem-Mendel and Sheyne-Sheyndl and Motl, the Cantor's Son*, trans. Hillel Halkin (New Haven, Conn.: Yale University Press, 2002), 6.

22. Simon Dubnow, "The Affirmation of the Diaspora," in *Nationalism and History: Essays on Old and New Judaism*, ed. and trans. Koppel S. Pinson (Cleveland: Meridian Books, 1961).

23. See Ezra Mendelsohn, *On Modern Jewish Politics* (New York: Oxford University Press, 1993), 10.

24. Jeffrey Shandler, *Adventures in Yiddishland: Postvernacular Language and Culture* (Berkeley: University of California Press, 2006), 33.

25. Ibid., 37.

26. Ibid., 49.

27. Ibid., 39.

28. Ibid., 45.

29. See Eisen, *Galut*, 104–109.

30. See Gordon, *Rosenzweig and Heidegger*, 219.

31. See Noam Pianko, *Zionism and the Roads Not Taken: Rawidowicz, Kaplan, Kohn* (Bloomington: Indiana University Press, 2010).

32. William Safran, "The Jewish Diaspora in a Comparative and Theoretical Perspective," *Israel Studies* 10:1 (2005): 36–41, here 37. See also William Safran, "Diasporas in Modern Societies: Myths of Homeland and Return," *Diaspora* (Spring 1991): 83–99.

33. See Sidra Ezrahi, *Booking Passage: Exile and Homecoming in the Modern Jewish Imagination* (Berkeley: University of California Press, 2000), 219–220.

34. Clifford, "Diasporas," 306.

35. Ibid., 307.

36. Barbara Kirshenblatt-Gimblett, "Spaces of Dispersal," *Cultural Anthropology* 9:3 (August 1994): 340.

37. Rebecca Kobrin, *Jewish Bialystok and Its Diaspora* (Bloomington: Indiana University Press, 2010), 180.

38. Arjun Appadurai, *Modernity at Large: Cultural Dimensions of Globalization* (Minneapolis: University of Minnesota Press, 1996), 6.

39. Philip Roth, *Operation Shylock: A Confession* (New York: Vintage / Random House, 1993), 104.

40. Ibid., 125.

41. A. B. Yehoshua has mounted the argument over the years that moral and ethical action is only possible in a Jewish state, where Jews possess power and bear full responsibility for their actions.

42. Daniel Boyarin and Jonathan Boyarin, "Diaspora: Generation and the Ground of Jewish Identity," *Critical Inquiry* 19:4 (Summer 1993): 714–723, here 711.

43. Ibid., 723.

44. Ibid., 718.

45. Also in this regard see R. B. Kitaj, *First Diasporist Manifesto* (London: Thames & Hudson, 1989).

46. Amnon Raz-Krakotzkin, "Exile within Sovereignty: A Critique of the 'Negation of Exile' in Israeli Culture" [Hebrew], *Teoria u'vikoret* 4 (1993): 23–55, and 5 (1994): 113–132. For a brief discussion in English see Laurence J. Silberstein, *The Postzionism Debates: Knowledge and Power in Israeli Culture* (New York: Routledge, 1999), 177–182.

47. Caryn Aviv and David Shneer, *New Jews: The End of the Jewish Diaspora* (New York: New York University Press, 2005).

48. For the relation between these two modern mass movements (people and information), see Appadurai, "Disjuncture and Difference in the Global Cultural Economy," in *Modernity at Large*, 27–47.

49. Tony Kushner, *Angels in America: A Gay Fantasia on National Themes* (New York: Theatre Communications Group, 2003), 16–17.

50. Stanley Cavell, "Departures," in *Diaspora: Homelands in Exile (Voices)*, ed. Frédéric Brenner (New York: HarperCollins, 2003), 133.

51. For particular qualities of the modern Mediterranean diaspora, see Daniel Schroeter, "A Different Road to Modernity: Jewish Identity in the Arab World," in Wettstein, *Diasporas and Exiles*, 150–163.

52. *The One Facing Us* shares this generic hybridity with another paradigmatic novel of diaspora and wandering, W. G. Sebald's masterpiece *Austerlitz* (2001).

53. Ronit Matalon, *The One Facing Us* (New York: Henry Holt, 1998), 4.

54. This persistent presence of "missing" photographs materializes a theme in Roland Barthes's *Camera Lucida*. Writing after his mother's death, Barthes discusses at length, but will not reproduce, the book's most important photograph, a shot of his mother at the Winter Garden in Paris, a photo that "exists only for [him]." *Camera Lucida* (New York: Hill & Wang, 1981), 73.

55. Matalon, *The One Facing Us*, 7.

56. Barthes, *Camera Lucida*, 53.

57. Matalon, *The One Facing Us*, 30.

58. Daniel Boyarin, "Masada or Yavneh?: Gender and the Arts of Jewish Resistance," in *Jews and Other Differences: The New Jewish Cultural Studies* (Minneapolis: University of Minnesota, 1997), 306–329.

59. Matalon, *The One Facing Us*, 181.

60. Franz Kafka, letter to Max Brod, June 1921, *Letters to Friends and Family* (New York: Schocken, 1990), 289.

61. Matalon, *The One Facing Us*, 180.

62. Ibid., 273.

CHAPTER 7 — THE CITY

1. Shimon Ballas, "Iya," in *Keys to the Garden: New Israeli Writing*, ed. Ammiel Alcalay (San Francisco: City Lights, 1996), 97.

2. Sasson Somekh, *Baghdad, Yesterday* (2003; Jerusalem: Ibis Editions, 2007), 58. See also selections about Baghdad in Ammiel Alcalay, *After Jews and Arabs: Remaking Levantine Culture* (Minneapolis: University of Minnesota Press, 1993).

3. For background and analysis see Ivan Marcus, "A Jewish-Christian Symbiosis: The Culture of Early Ashkenaz," in *Cultures of the Jews: A New History*, ed. David Biale (New York: Schocken, 2002), 449–516.

4. Kenneth R. Stow, "Sanctity and the Construction of Space: The Roman Ghetto as Sacred Space," *Proceedings of the Second Annual Klutznick Chair Conference*, ed. M. Mor (Lanham, Md.: University Press of America, 1991), 54–76, here 57.

5. See the brief but suggestive section "The Jew as Townsman," in Mark R. Cohen, *Under Crescent and Cross: The Jews in the Middle Ages* (Princeton, N.J.: Princeton University Press, 1994), 121–128, here 125.

6. Susan Slyomovics distinguishes the Jewish quarter in Tlemcen, Algiers, from the Moroccan mellahs by virtue of it being a product of Jewish initiative, not enforced (like the mellah); see her article "Geographies of Jewish Tlemcen," *Journal of North African Studies* 5:4 (Winter 2000): 81–96.

7. Emily Gottreich, "Rethinking the 'Islamic City' from the Perspective of Jewish Space," *Jewish Social Studies* 11:4 (Fall 2004): 118–146, here 139.

8. S. D. Goitein, *A Mediterranean Society* (Berkeley: University of California Press, 2003). 49.

9. Ibid., 51.

10. Ibid., 52.

11. Max Weinreich, "The Reality of Jewishness versus the Ghetto Myth: The Sociolinguistic Roots of Yiddish," in *Never Say Die! A Thousand Years of Yiddish in Jewish Life and Letters*, ed. Joshua A. Fishman (The Hague: Mouton, 1981), 103–118, here 109.

12. Susan Gilson Miller, "The Mellah of Fez: Reflections on the Spatial Turn in Moroccan Jewish History," in *Jewish Topographies: Visions of Space, Traditions of Place*, ed. Julia Brauch, Anna Lipphardt, and Alexandra Nocke (Burlington, Vt.: Ashgate, 2008), 102.

13. Susan Gilson Miller, Attilio Petruccioli, and Mauro Bertagnan, "Inscribing Minority Space in the Islamic City: The Jewish Quarter of Fez," *Journal of the Society of Architectural Historians* 60:3 (September 2001): 323.

14. Gottreich, "Rethinking the 'Islamic City' from the Perspective of Jewish Space," 122.

15. Ibid., 139.

16. Dean Philip Bell, *Jews in the Early Modern World* (Lanham, Md.: Rowman & Littlefield, 2008), 36.

17. Ibid., 23.

18. Benjamin C. I. Ravid, "From Geographical Realia to Historiographical Symbol: The Odyssey of the Word *Ghetto*," in *Essential Papers on Jewish Culture in Renaissance and Baroque Italy*, ed. David Ruderman (New York: New York University Press, 1992), 373–385, here 378.

19. Bell, *Jews in the Early Modern World*, 23.

20. Stow, "Sanctity and the Construction of Space," 60.

21. Ibid., 65.

22. Stow adds that "it is thus no wonder that Jewish reactions to the ghetto's establishment betray no anxiety. . . . The earliest Jewish references to Paul IV's actions were limited to the matter of fact: 'The Pope has ordered that all the Jews live together.'" Ibid., 68.

23. Weinreich, "Ghetto Myth," 106. Weinreich argues for an "anti-lachrymose" version of Jewish history, concluding that "it is the positive factor of striving for meaningful survival, and not the negative one of exclusion or rejection, that is paramount in Jewish cultural history" (111).

24. Thomas C. Hubka, "The Shtetl in Context: The Spatial and Social Organization of Jewish Communities from the Small Towns of 18th Century Poland," University of Wisconsin-Milwaukee, accessed on October 14, 2009, http://www.earlymodern.org/citation.php?citKey=18&docKey=i.

25. Ibid.

26. Restrictions on Jewish settlement in Russian and Polish lands, for example, to the Pale of Settlement were primarily semi-rural, and never as strictly imposed as in the Italian case. In the United States, urban Jewish settlement patterns may be more constructively compared with those of other ethnic groups.

27. Weinreich, "Ghetto Myth," 104.

28. See Lois Dobin, *The Port Jews of Habsburg Trieste* (Stanford, Calif.: Stanford University Press, 1999), and David Sorkin, "The Port Jew: Notes Towards a Social Type," *Journal of Jewish Studies* 50:1 (1999): 87–97, and two recent collections edited by David Cesarini.

29. A further instructive example here is the body known as the Council of Four Lands, which constituted a form of Jewish autonomy in Poland from 1580 to 1764. The council was a space produced by interactions between Jewish populations and their relation to local Polish authorities, and as such exemplifies how space may be constituted by non-territorial practices: though space was defined in some sense physically,

it did not presuppose political control over territory. The *kahal* is a term for both the community itself as well as its juridical authority.

30. I. Aksenfeld, "The Headband," in *The Shtetl: A Creative Anthology of Jewish Life in Eastern Europe*, ed. and trans. J. Neugroschel (Woodstock, N.Y.: Overlook Press, 1989), 49–50.

31. From a 1911 review by the writer, cited in Ken Frieden, *Classic Yiddish Fiction: Abramovitsh, Sholem Aleichem, and Peretz* (Albany: State University of New York Press, 1995), 94.

32. See Dan Miron, "Introduction," in *Tales of Mendele the Book Peddler: Fishke the Lame and Benjamin the Third* (New York: Schocken, 1996).

33. Israel Bartal, "Imagined Geography: The Shtetl, Myth and Reality," in *The Shtetl: New Evaluations*, ed. Stephen Katz (New York: New York University Press, 2007), 179–192, here 189.

34. Moshe Leyb Halpern, *In New York*, trans. Kathryn Hellerstein (Philadelphia: Jewish Publication Society, 1989), 1.

35. James Joyce, *A Portrait of the Artist as Young Man* (New York: B. W. Huebsch, 1916), 291.

36. Henry Roth, *Call It Sleep* (1934; reprint, New York: Farrar, Straus and Giroux, 1991), 14.

37. Ibid., 101.

38. Hana Wirth-Nesher, *Call It English: The Languages of Jewish American Literature* (Princeton, N.J.: Princeton University Press, 2008).

39. Roth, *Call It Sleep*, 143.

40. Ibid., 426.

41. Hasia R. Diner, *Lower East Side Memories: A Jewish Place in America* (Princeton, N.J.: Princeton University Press, 2000).

42. Deborah Dash Moore, *At Home in America: Second Generation New York Jews* (New York: Columbia University Press, 1981), 58.

43. Ibid., 52.

44. See Richard I. Cohen, "Urban Visibility and Biblical Visions: Jewish Culture in Western and Central Europe in the Modern Age," in *Cultures of the Jews: A New History*, vol. 3, *Modern Encounters*, ed. David Biale (New York: Schocken, 2006), 9–74.

45. See Gavriel D. Rosenfeld, "Postwar Jewish Architecture and the Memory of the Holocaust," in *Jewish Dimensions in Modern Visual Culture: Antisemitism, Assimilation, Affirmation*, ed. Rose-Carol Washton Long, Matthew Baigell, and Milly Heyd (Waltham, Mass.: Brandeis University Press, 2010), 285–302, and his *Building after Auschwitz: Jewish Architecture and Jewish Memory since the Holocaust* (New Haven, Conn.: Yale University Press, forthcoming).

CHAPTER 8 — *ERUV*

1. Michael Chabon, *The Yiddish Policemen's Union* (New York: HarperCollins, 2007), 110.

2. The *eruv* is almost always located in some sort of urban or semi-urban setting. In this, it provides a conceptual opposition to the trends reviewed in chapter 9, which are expressly pastoral or "back-to-nature" in tone.

3. Cf. Richard I. Cohen, "Urban Visibility and Biblical Visions: Jewish Culture in Western and Central Europe in the Modern Age," in *Cultures of the Jews: A New History*, vol. 3, *Modern Encounters*, ed. David Biale (New York: Schocken, 2006), 9–74.

4. See for example, http://flatbusheruv.org/front_page.htm.

5. Yosef Gavriel Bechofer, *The Contemporary Eruv: Eruvin in Modern Metropolitan Areas* (New York: Feldheim, 1998), 43.

6. From Rashi's comment on Eruvin 6a, cited in ibid., 44.

7. Jennifer Cousineau, "The Urban Practice of Jewish Space," in *American Sanctuary: Understanding Sacred Spaces*, ed. Louis P. Nelson (Bloomington: Indiana University Press, 2006), 65–85, here 75.

8. See Bechofer, *The Contemporary Eruv,* for a good overview, and the website Eruv Online for current updates, http://eruvonline.blogspot.com/.

9. Jennifer Cousineau, "Rabbinic Urbanism in London: Rituals and the Material Culture of the Sabbath," *Jewish Social Studies* 11:3 (Spring/Summer 2005): 36–57.

10. For a study of the effects of the London *eruv*, specifically on women, see Jennifer Cousineau, "The Domestication of Urban Jewish Space in the North-West London Eruv," in *Jews at Home: The Domestication of Identity*, ed. Simon J. Bronner (Oxford: Littman, 2010), 43–74.

11. Blu Greenberg, *How to Run a Traditional Jewish Household* (New York: Simon and Schuster, 1989), 49.

12. On the Barnet *eruv* see Davina Cooper, "Talmudic Territory: Space, Law, and Modernist Discourse," *Journal of Law and Society* 23:4 (December 1996): 529–548.

13. Davina Cooper, "Promoting Injury or Freedom: Radical Pluralism and Orthodox Jewish Symbolism," *Ethnic & Racial Studies* 23:6 (November 2000): 1062–1085; Peter Vincent, "Eruvim: Talmudic Places in a Postmodern World," *Transactions of the Institute of British Geographers* 27:1 (2002): 30–51; Olivier Valins, "Institutionalised Religion: Sacred Texts and Jewish Spatial Practice," *Geoforum* 31 (2000): 575–586.

14. Sophie Calle, *Eruv* (Jerusalem: Jerusalem Center for the Visual Arts, 1996), n.p.

15. Daniel Belasco, ed., *Reinventing Ritual: Contemporary Art and Design for Jewish Life* (New Haven, Conn.: Jewish Museum, Yale University Press, 2009), 49.

16. Ibid., 3–4.

17. At http://www.benschachter.com/Eruvim.html.

18. Blogs and other web-generated virtual Jewish communities such as Second Life may provide a unique opportunity for "cultural dialogue within various streams of Judaism, within various Diasporas and Israel, and between Jews and non-Jews." See Julian Voloj, "Virtual Jewish Topography: The Genesis of Jewish (Second) Life," in *Jewish Topographies: Visions of Space, Traditions of Place*, ed. Julia Brauch, Anna Lipphardt, and Alexandra Nocke (Burlington, Vt.: Ashgate, 2008), 355.

19. At http://www.cabinetmagazine.org/issues/23/.

20. See http://berlinseruv.com/about.html.

21. See http://www.dziga.com/eruv/index.php.

22. Sandback's string art at DIA in Beacon, N.Y., http://www.diaart.org/exhibitions/introduction/95. Sandbank was not Jewish and it is unlikely, though not impossible, that those Jewish artists he knew told him about the *eruv*. Yet Sandbank's work moves against the monumental in ways that resemble the non-institutional practice represented by the *eruv*. I am grateful to Daniel Belasco for his insights into Sandbank's work and the possible relation between *eruv* art and post-minimalism more broadly.

23. Yve-Alain Bois, "World and a String: Yve-Alain Bois on Fred Sandback—Passages," *ArtForum* (October 2003), available at http://findarticles.com/p/articles/mi_m0268/is_2_42/ai_109023328/, accessed January 2010.

24. Ibid.

25. Charlotte Fonrobert notes the gap between actual *eruv*s and critical thought when she concludes that a potentially fruitful theoretical agenda may be undermined by a lack of precision regarding the *eruv*'s original meaning. See her review essay "The New Spatial Turn in Jewish Studies," *AJS Review* 33:1 (April 2009): 155–164, here 163.

26. See Fonrobert, "Political Symbolism of the Eruv," *Jewish Social Studies* 11:3 (Spring/Summer 2005): 29.

27. "'Eruv' Urbanism: Toward an Alternative 'Jewish Architecture' in Germany," in Brauch et al., *Jewish Topographies,* 48. Similar material also found in related articles by Manuel Herz and Eyal Weizman, "Between City and Desert," *AA Files* 34 (Spring 1998), and Eyal Weizman, "The Subversion of Jerusalem's Sacred Vernaculars: Four New Planning Tools for a Holy Environment," in *The Next Jerusalem: Sharing the Divided City*, ed. Michael Sorkin (New York: Monacelli Press, 2002), especially 121–125.

28. "'Eruv' Urbanism: Toward an Alternative 'Jewish Architecture' in Germany," in Brauch et al., *Jewish Topographies*, 48. Granted, we may want to quibble with the sweep of his statement (maybe better "Talmuds" than "Talmud"); for some suggestions on how *eruv* takes on various dimensions in the Babylonian and Jerusalem Talmuds, see Fonrobert, "Political Symbolism of the Eruv."

29. Arjun Appadurai, *Modernity at Large: Cultural Dimensions of Globalization* (Minneapolis: University of Minnesota Press, 1996), 183.

30. Ibid., 182–183.

31. Ibid., 183.

32. Fonrobert, "From Separatism to Urbanism: The Dead Sea Scrolls and the Origin of the Rabbinic Eruv," *Dead Sea Discoveries* 11:1 (2004): 43–71.

CHAPTER 9 — ENVIRONMENT

1. See Vered Shemtov, "Between Perspectives of Space: A Reading in Yehuda Amichai's 'Jewish Travel' and 'Israeli Travel,'" *Jewish Social Studies* 11:3 (Spring/Summer 2005): 141–161.

2. For an extensive discussion, see Shaul Kelner, *Tours That Bind: Diaspora, Pilgrimage, and Israeli Birthright Tourism* (New York: New York University Press, 2010).

3. Chaim Noy and Erik Cohen, "Backpacking as a Rite of Passage in Israel," in *Israeli Backpackers: From Tourism to Rite of Passage*, ed. Noy and Cohen (Albany: State University of New York Press, 2005), 17.

4. Ibid., 27–28, and Darya Maoz, "Young Adult Israeli Backpackers in India," in Noy and Cohen, *Israeli Backpackers*, 176–181.

5. Lisa Anteby-Yemini, Keren Bazini, Irit Gerstein, and Gali Kling, "'Traveling Cultures': Israeli Backpackers, Deterritorialization, and Reconstruction of Home," in Noy and Cohen, *Israeli Backpackers*, 94–95.

6. Arjun Appadurai, "Global Ethnoscapes: Notes and Queries for a Transnational Anthropology," *Modernity at Large: Cultural Dimensions of Globalization* (Minneapolis: University of Minnesota Press, 1996).

7. Lynn White Jr., "The Historic Roots of Our Ecologic Crisis," *Science* 155 (1967): 1203–1207.

8. *Pirkey Avot* 3:7. See the discussion of this verse and various interpretations in Jeremy Benstein, "'One, Walking and Studying . . . ': Nature vs. Torah," in *Judaism and Environmental Ethics*, ed. Martin D. Yaffe (New York: Lexington Books, 2001), 206–224.

9. Micah Joseph Berdichevski, "In Two Directions" (1900–1903), in *The Zionist Idea*, ed. Arthur Hertzberg (New York: Atheneum, 1973), 297.

10. Jeanne Kay, "Concepts of Nature in the Hebrew Bible," in Yaffe, *Judaism and Environmental Ethics*, 90.

11. See the cogent discussion in Eilon Schwartz, "Judaism and Nature: Theological and Moral Issues to Consider While Renegotiating a Jewish Relationship to the Natural World," in Yaffe, *Judaism and Environmental Ethics*, 297–308.

12. See Eilon Schwartz, "Mastery and Stewardship, Wonder and Connectedness: A Typology of Relations to Nature in Jewish Text and Tradition," in *Judaism and Ecology: Created World and Revealed Word*, ed. Hava Tirosh-Samuelson (Cambridge, Mass.: Harvard University Press, 2002), 96.

13. See Michael Fishbane, "Toward a Jewish Theology of Nature," in Tirosh-Samuelson, *Judaism and Ecology*, 17–26.

14. For a recent history see Mark X. Jacobs, "Jewish Environmentalism: Past Accomplishments and Future Challenges," in Tirosh-Samuelson, *Judaism and Ecology*, 449–480.

15. See the Coalition on the Environment and Jewish Life (http://www.coejl.org/) and Hazon (http://www.hazon.org/) for a sense of the diversity of strategies and issues addressed.

16. Isaac Deutscher, "The Non-Jewish Jew" (1958), in *The Jew in the Modern World: A Documentary History*, 2nd ed., ed. Paul Mendes-Flohr and Jehudah Reinarz (New York: Oxford University Press, 1995), 266.

17. Yuri Slezkine, *The Jewish Century* (Princeton, N.J.: Princeton University Press, 2004).

18. For an analysis of why Israeli environmental movements have largely failed to engage with political issues relating to the Palestinians and the territories, see Shachar Sadeh, "The 'Green' Line: Environmental Organizations and the Separation Barrier," *Teoria u'vikoret* 27 (Fall 2010): 184–211.

19. Alon Tal, *Pollution in a Promised Land: An Environmental History of Israel* (Berkeley: University of California Press, 2002), 332.

20. Schwartz, "Mastery and Stewardship," 94.

21. Tal, *Pollution in a Promised Land*, 339.

22. Ibid., 332.

23. For a list and mission statement see http://www.sviva.net/.

24. Tal, *Pollution in a Promised Land*, 403.

Index

183

About the Author

BARBARA E. MANN is an associate professor of Hebrew literature at the Jewish Theological Seminary in New York. She is the author of *A Place in History: Modernism, Tel Aviv, and the Creation of Jewish Urban Space* and co-editor-in-chief of *Prooftexts: A Journal of Jewish Literary History.*